M000316412

*change your*

# MIND

*change your*

# LIFE

THE 7 PILLARS OF THE MODEL FOR DAILY LIVING

# *change your* MIND

# *change your* LIFE

THE 7 PILLARS OF THE MODEL FOR DAILY LIVING

## DAVID E. JAMES

## AMBASSADOR INTERNATIONAL

GREENVILLE, SOUTH CAROLINA & BELFAST, NORTHERN IRELAND

www.ambassador-international.com

# Change your Mind, Change your Life

*the 7 pillars of the model for daily living*

© 2010 David E. James

All rights reserved

Printed in the United States of America

ISBN 978-1-935507-30-7

Cover Design & Page Layout by David Siglin of A&E Media

AMBASSADOR INTERNATIONAL
Emerald House
427 Wade Hampton Blvd.
Greenville, SC 29609, USA
www.ambassador-international.com

AMBASSADOR BOOKS
The Mount
2 Woodstock Link
Belfast, BT6 8DD, Northern Ireland, UK
www.ambassador-international.com

*The colophon is a trademark of Ambassador*

# TABLE OF CONTENTS

# Preface

Many people live their respective lives in a state of constant searching, wanting, needing, looking, striving, seeking, yearning, and hoping. Ironically, and far too often, a significant portion of these same people dually categorize themselves as never finding, never fulfilling, never attaining, never quenching, never clinching, never prospering, or never winning. Admittedly, the complexity of the human experience, due to wide-ranging and unique circumstances, beliefs, and values that vary from continent to continent as surely as they vary from house to house within a single neighborhood, merits that broad sweeping generalizations are rarely 100% accurate. On the whole, however, human beings want to be happy and fulfilled.

We, as human beings, despite our historical and cultural differences, are very much the same the world over. Aside from wanting to be recognized as a winner in life, whether through our own eyes or through the eyes of others, we also must contend with a finite gamut of emotions. Two of the most powerful of emotions that, once manifested, become the root of all kinds of anguish and anxiety, are fear and hurt. I defy you to name one person who has ever walked the Earth who did not at some time in their life experience fear and/or hurt. If you're hard-pressed to do so, most likely it's because there are none. Would you agree?

So, let's think about this carefully. For the most part, human beings, on a global scale, value and seek happiness and fulfillment. If this is true, and assuming that no person, *at birth*, is exempt from the capacity to experience the human emotions that are so common to mankind (*e.g.* happiness, sadness, hurt, fear), then it reasonably follows that one particular person's discovered pathway to happiness and fulfillment in life could also serve as a model to achieve the same for someone else. Accordingly, I assure you that the "7 Pillars of the Model for Daily Living," revealed in-depth in this book, if used correctly, will result in a newfound happiness and peace that is more profitable than silver and offers better returns than gold.

The message and methods found in this book will serve as a source of inner-strength to you. They will help you make the right choices in your everyday life that will set you on a higher road than the road on which you may be currently traveling. To make it plain for you, I ask that you consider the following questions below. Be forthright and honest with yourself as you answer.

- Is there anything in your life that you want to change, but for whatever reason, have not done so?
- Have you ever been hurt by someone and found it difficult to forgive them?
- Is there something in your past, or present, that was (or is) so traumatic, painful, or hurtful, that you haven't told anyone and carry on as if it never happened at all?

- Do you ask yourself, "What is my true purpose in life?" and then wonder why you continue to go to the same job everyday even though you are not passionate about what you do for a living?

- Do you have a talent, skill, or ability that you are *not* using to either make a profit for yourself or to simply help someone else?

- If you are female, do you hope to meet a man who is honest, hard-working, ambitious, strong, respectful, kind, a good listener, a good communicator, funny, compassionate, gentle, good-looking, available, and who will love you and treat you like the jewel that you are?

- If you are male, do you want to find a woman who has all the qualities you desire in a best friend, yet is caring, passionate, intelligent, adventurous, beautiful, and supportive?

- Have you ever told yourself, "I'm not going out to party this weekend, but went out anyways?"

- Have you ever told yourself, "I'm not going to smoke or drink anymore, but did it anyways?"

- Do you tend to attract, or be attracted to, men or women that are no good for you?

- Do you tend to get angry frequently? Would someone else who knows you well agree with your answer? If you answered affirmatively, have you always been that way or can you pinpoint a certain period or a specific relationship where "getting angry" became the norm? Did someone or something hurt you before the anger began?

- Have you ever gotten depressed because of your weight?

- Do you struggle with the motivation to exercise and lose excess weight?

- Have you ever been raped or sexually abused? If so, have you ever spoken about it to someone? Were you confused? Or did you feel it was in some way your fault?

- Have you ever been a victim of domestic violence (*i.e.* has your boyfriend, husband, or significant other ever intentionally hit you, bruised you, shoved you, or pushed you in anger)? If so, did you tell anyone?

- Have you ever wanted to learn a new language or travel to a foreign country, and never accomplished either one?

- In your daily routine, do you always, seldom, or never take note of a person on the street that is homeless, hungry, crippled or lame? How often do you give to that person, if ever?

- Are you depressed about something, or over someone, in your life?

- Do you look at women and wonder what it would be like to have sex with them?

- Whenever an attractive woman passes by, do you habitually turn your head, stare, or undress her with your eyes?

- Do you hope to be a better parent than your parent(s) were to you by spending more time with your child(ren) and/or talking to them more?

- Do you spend time on Facebook, MySpace, Twitter, Match. com, QQ, MSN, (or any other cyberspace means of chatting or meeting people)? Did you post your picture? For every quality person that you've met via cyberspace, were there twice as many people that were merely a waste of time?

- Do you get offended easily?
- Do you wish your "world" was bigger?
- Do you wish you had more money?
- Do you worry about a lack of finances to pay the rent or mortgage, buy clothes, eat food, have fun, or retire?

How did you do? Were you honest with yourself? If you answered "no" to all of the abovementioned questions, then let me save you some time. This book is not for you. On the other hand, if, indeed, you were honest, and you answered "yes" to at least one of the abovementioned questions, then there is one universal conclusion that you should deduce from your varied responses. Life is difficult and there is a premium value attached to peace and genuine prosperity for those who find it.

The question becomes how do *you* define prosperity? How is it measured? Does prosperity mean financial success? Are they the same thing? Does money equate to happiness? What about peace? Does a larger income bring peace? Is peace related to happiness? Of course, these age-old questions will always warrant debate; however, this book was not written in the abstract for the purpose of scholarly debate, but rather provides something much more profound, practical, and concrete. I have written this book on the notion that people who have been hurt are the ones best suited to help people who are hurting. If you are *truly* in a place of wanting to improve your life on the whole – and by that, I mean if you are sick and tired of being sick and tired – then you have taken the first step to what will ultimately be the best decision of your life. It doesn't matter whether you are 19, 26, 34, 47, 52, 68, or 99; if you need empowerment and encouragement, this book is for you. It's irrelevant if you are from America, China, Chile, Spain, Italy or Brazil, this book is for you. Whether you are single, married, divorced, separated, or just stressed out because you can't even classify your social status, this book is for you. If you are a young, a middle-aged, or an elderly man or woman, this book is for you. Although the discussion herein may be new, complex, or foreign to you at first, I will show you exactly where true and lasting happiness and prosperity come from and how to attain them. This book does not talk *at* or *above* you, it talks *to* you. More importantly, the tone of this book is not one of preaching, but teaching. Preaching invokes listening, whereas teaching invokes learning. No person elevates his or her status, improves their current situation, or reaches a higher goal without the process of learning.

If you are at the point of being broken, then here is your opportunity to heal. If you have tried everything else, and it hasn't worked, then it's time for you to wake up. As you read, you will realize that this book was not written for political correctness or monetary gain. It is direct and cuts straight to the heart and core of you. Above all else, it is truth. Among you will be pundits and naysayers who will fall away quickly, which was predestined to occur. But, if this book reaches one – one person in the United States, one in China; one in Chile, one in Spain, one in Italy, one in Brazil – then my ultimate objective will be satisfied.

Finally, as you embark on a potentially life-changing journey through the pages of this book, I merely ask that you do the following three things:

1. Humble yourself
   - Humble: not proud or arrogant; to make meek; modest; subservient; to lower in condition, importance, or dignity.
2. Take notes (whatever comes to mind)
   - Notes: a brief record of something written down to assist the memory or for future reference.
3. Read in a quiet place (preferably alone)
   - Quiet: free from disturbance, noise, or sound

You will find that if you adhere to these three requests, the return on your most pertinent investment (*i.e.* your time) will be much greater. In fact, if you only adhere to Request #2, you will be pleasantly surprised at the amount of notes you have amassed by the time you have completed the material. If done diligently and in an organized fashion, your notes will serve as a constant source of priceless knowledge on which you may reflect *daily*, or consult as needed, to get you through, over, and beyond all of life's challenges in the future. By the end of your journey, you will have a blueprint that will illustrate exactly how to be victorious in any situation. The 7-Pillar Model for Daily Living is derived from my own breadth of experience. It will explain to you, in depth, the various emotional pitfalls that so commonly ensnare us all. More importantly, it will show you how to fight back and win. Additionally, the 7-Pillar Model for Daily Living will give you a level of *confidence* that you never knew existed. (And, by the way, if you ask anyone who has known me personally for any substantial amount of time, they will tell you in no uncertain terms that David E. James has *never* suffered from a lack of confidence at *any* point in his life. In other words, be careful in thinking that the principles of the Model for Daily Living are inapposite to you because *you* don't suffer from a lack of confidence. Remember Request #1: Humble Yourself).

Indeed, the Model has something for everyone, but it is the truly down-trodden and the faint of heart who will find solace here. They are the ones who have already been humbled by their own life's circumstances.  But, no matter who you are, if you are a breathing, feeling, worrying, loving, dreaming, living human being, the Model can take you to new heights personal to your situation, emotionally and financially, but most important of all, spiritually. If it worked (and continues to work) for me, then it can work for you.

America, China, Chile, Spain, Italy, and Brazil, all have a special place in my heart. I have lived, worked or traveled in each of these countries, extensively. In my experience, there is an unwavering commonality amongst the people of each place. A smile brings a smile. A friendly gesture is returned by an act of kindness. If not for this equation of human nature, where would we be? To the people of these countries in particular, and around the world alike, this book will help you and guide you in your daily lives as a source of strength. You, the reader, are a wonderful person and you are about to discover the power that lies within you. Life is a battle. To win, there are two things you must fully understand. First, you must understand what it means **to** *fight the right fight.* Second, you must understand that going through battles without *being equipped with the right weapons,* spells defeat. The 7 Pillars of the Model for Daily Living will explain the value of grasping these two important concepts and why you *must* put them into practice *daily* if you are to realize your goal of becoming victorious in all of life's situations. By the end of the book, you will have acquired the absolute imperative for happiness, fulfillment, peace, and prosperity through knowledge, understanding, discernment, sound judgment, and most of all, wisdom.

### LIFE IS DIFFICULT FOR *EVERYBODY!*

Many of you are facing difficult, if not dire, circumstances right now. If you are even the least bit observant, and sensitive, towards other people and their respective struggles, then you know that people go through *all kinds* of trouble in life. The sheer variety of problems that people face never ceases to amaze me. To assign a face or name for every individual one of life's "curveballs" would be virtually impossible. Take a moment to reflect on the less-than-desirable things you've faced in your own life. Then, imagine how many people you literally walk past in a day and multiply the number of difficult decisions or events in your own life, times the number of people you pass in one day. Next, imagine that with every person you pass during the course of any given day, each person's problems become increasingly more serious, more challenging, and potentially more detrimental and destructive to their emotional, physical, psychological, and spiritual well-being. Here is my point. *Never take for granted what someone else might be going through or has already been through in life.* Just because an acquaintance, a co-worker, a classmate, a fellow church member, a neighbor, a business associate, a friend, or even a family member, may be smiling or seemingly in an "ok" state of mind, you never really know what issues lie beneath the surface or the pain that is buried down deep.

### RAPE / SEXUAL ABUSE

One in every three women are raped in their lifetime, and according to the U.S. Department of Justice, an American is raped or sexually assaulted every two minutes. I want to say that again. One in three women has experienced some form of sexual abuse during their lifetime. This includes the act of rape. The issue is not whether the statistic is completely accurate. The issue is that among some, if not many, parts of the world, a fundamental indifference exists, on the part of men, towards sexual abuse against women, perpetrated *by* men. Rape and sexual abuse against women carry such a heavy stigma and negative connation to them that this topic tends to fall within a realm of dark and depressing conversation which often times, people, in general, don't want or care to discuss openly. Rape and sexual abuse are occurrences that are common in the world in which we live. Chances are, whether you are a woman or a man, you have met, or will meet someone in your lifetime who has been victimized by rape or sexual abuse in its many forms. Unfortunately, knowing the person is not tantamount to being aware of what has transpired in their life. In other words, you may eat lunch with "Maria" every day, and have done so for years, and still have no idea that "Maria" had been raped or sexually abused. By the age of 33, I had already met far too many women who had experienced either rape or sexual abuse. What do I mean by "far too many?" A simple question deserves a simple answer. One is far too many.

I want to be clear. Rape is an absolute abomination. It is an act rooted in selfishness and driven by pure evil. It is often facilitated where there is some measure of deceit, manipulation, anger, and/or a need to exercise, prove, or display control that is based in cowardice, arrogance, insensitivity, and a total lack of compassion or love. And let's be honest with ourselves. If men were not physically stronger than women, on balance, the physical dynamic that is an undeniable component in many acts of rape and sexual abuse would not exist. Without that component, statistics may be different. For even if the male does not actually employ his superior physical strength against a woman, the threat of doing so in many cases still exists, which in turn creates an atmosphere of duress. In other words, in this instance, force and the *threat* of force, are viewed as one and the same.

Similarly, if an adult male perpetrator was not physically stronger, amongst other things, than a younger and weaker child, then the imbalance of physical strength that is pivotal in the act of molestation or rape would not exist (not taking into account the obvious imbalance of emotional maturity that often results in coercion). Here is my point. Aside from the reason I stated above (*i.e.* control), the males who have committed acts of atrocity of this kind have done so simply because, physically, they could.

I have witnessed firsthand the sheer evil that surrounds rape, sexual abuse, and child molestation. In my adult life, I have encountered kind-hearted women, smart women, professional women, good-humored women, (in other words, just really great people) who have endured unspeakable acts of sexual violence at some point in their respective lives. And these are just a handful of women that I happened to meet. Unquestionably, there are *scores* of women around the world, some of whom are reading this book, who have had to endure similar or same situations. As a human being, I hate it. As a person who was raised, in large part, by women, I detest it. As a God-fearing man, I abhor it. As a man to whom God has entrusted the gift of strong voice, written word, and the ability to encourage others, *I speak up and speak out for those who cannot speak for themselves.* More importantly, I will share with you *the way* to confront it, get through it, and to emerge stronger and better than you ever thought you could be.

### Why Is The Subject of Rape / Sexual Abuse Relevant?

Contextual learning is learning at its finest. Think about it. Whenever a person hears a story, a situation, or a problem to which they can relate due to a past or present personal experience of their own, the person immediately has a context to which the moral of the story, situation, or problem may be applied. This is how a connection is established amongst those seeking help and those offering it. Often times, the connection is a similar experience, event, or occurrence communicated between two people, or a group of people, that fosters trust and potentially can lead to self-improvement. For example, take Alcoholics Anonymous. In that instance, you have people who share a common problem, vocalizing their thoughts and feelings amongst one another in order to gain support. Usually, a person who has gained some measure of success with sobriety will offer his or her advice or support to a newer member. It is within the context of alcoholism that one individual may relate to another, express their experiences, learn from one another, and hopefully conquer their problem.

Here, and in the previous section, I set forth the context of this abomination called rape and sexual abuse because of my own experiences with physically, emotionally, spiritually, and legally confronting males who have raped women. Note my choice of wording. Members of my gender classification who commit sexual acts of violence against women are, indeed, male, but they are not *men*. My experiences and willingness to publicly speak and write about certain issues surrounding rape and sexual abuse will hopefully affect those of you who can in some way relate regardless of your gender classification. Again, if this isn't you, then I'm not talking to you. If it is you, then I have your ear and your attention, and that is the place where healing, progress, and learning begin.

### IDENTIFY YOUR ISSUE *AND* EXPRESS IT CORRECTLY

Faith, as defined in the Bible, "is the substance of things hoped for, the evidence of things not seen." (Hebrews 11:1, KJV). Depending on which version of the Bible you reference, the same scripture is written as, faith, "is being sure of what we hope for and certain of what we do not see." (Hebrews 11:1, NIV)

Now, that's all well and fine, but what does that really mean? It's one of those definitions that use simple words in an attempt to convey a much deeper meaning. For anyone who works, or has worked, in the American legal system, the ambiguity of the definition of "faith," as stated above, reminds me of how the American legal system defines the evidentiary principle of "hearsay." In other words, after reading the definition of faith in Hebrews, you really are left not knowing exactly what it means. Let's face it. Sometimes, when people talk about their "faith," they are merely referring to their belief system or religion. For our purposes, "religion" is a word that we will avoid altogether. Discussing "religion" invites controversy and understandably so since there are countless views and opinions surrounding "religion" on just about everything under the sun. Instead, I want you to pay close attention to this initial discussion of faith and the methodology that I employ in explaining it to you. Rather than associate the word "faith" with some former or existing notion of what it means, we will begin to build a foundation of understanding, through the impartation of knowledge, of what faith really is and how it may be utilized in your daily life to empower you and guide you. At this juncture, we will start to build a vocabulary of key terms and definitions that you should record in your notebook. Writing key issues (e.g., faith) on paper and their corresponding definition is a huge part of this process. It will enable you to later *identify and express* issues that you are facing in your everyday life, but using *spiritual language rather than natural language*. To elucidate, here are some basic "issue-spotting" examples that describe a situation using natural language, but cite the real issue using spiritual understanding:

### Example #1:

Life situations expressed using natural language: A husband is sitting at a sidewalk café having lunch with his wife. As attractive women pass by their table in various directions, the husband's eyes follow each woman who strolls by, *during* conversation with his wife, who is sitting directly opposite of him.

What is the real issue? *Hint*: The answer is not "he's just a dog."

Real issue expressed using spiritual language: **Honor**

### Example #2:

Life situations expressed using natural language: A rich man is walking down the street and is approaching a homeless man, who is also crippled, hungry, and lame, sitting on the sidewalk in front of him. The rich man is carrying $10,000 total - $5,000 in each pocket. As he walks past the homeless man, the rich man reaches into his left pocket and pulls out $5,000, gives it to the homeless man, and continues on his way.

Five minutes later, a woman of very modest means is walking down the same street and approaching the same homeless, crippled, hungry and lame man sitting on the sidewalk. The woman of modest means is down to her last $10 – carrying $5 in each pocket. As she walks past the homeless man, she reaches into both of her pockets and pulls out a total of $10 (the sum total of her monetary possessions), gives it to the homeless man, and continues on her way.

What is the real issue? *Hint*: Who gave more (the rich man or the woman of modest means)?

Real issue expressed using spiritual language: **Greed**

### Example #3:

Life situations expressed using natural language: After class at a local university, a professor finds a student's purse that was accidentally left behind. Upon ascertaining that the bag belonged to a member of her class, the Professor promptly sends an email to the student informing the student that her purse will remain in the Professor's possession until a convenient time can be agreed upon for the student to retrieve her personal belonging. The student replies via email, "Thanks, Professor. Now that I know my purse is with you, I'm not worried. I can get it sometime next week."

What is the real issue? What is the student really saying? *Hint*: The answer is not that she's at ease because there is no money in the purse.

Real issue expressed using spiritual language: **Trust**

In the next three examples below, each life situation is similarly expressed using natural language, but they are taken from three ancient Chinese proverbs. The point is that you, the reader, begin to develop an understanding of how to *identify and express* the *real issues* in your daily life, which are *always* extractable from a larger situational context expressed in everyday language (*i.e.* natural language). Unfortunately, *my* written words cannot begin to do justice to conveying the importance of understanding how to discern what the real issues are in each and every one of life's situational problems. Arguably, lawyers, and other analytical thinkers by trade, have an advantage in issue-spotting because they are trained to do so. Remember, earlier in this book, I enumerated two key principles that underscore the 7-Pillar Model for Daily Living:

1. You *must* learn to *fight the right fight,* and
2. You *must* equip yourself with the *right spiritual weapons*


In order to "fight the *right* fight" concerning all of the many challenges that you face every single day, it will benefit you ten-fold if you master the ability to *identify and express* the true underlying issue using spiritual terminology, rather than natural terminology. As you progress further through the book and deeper into the Model, you will gain greater insight as to why the "spiritual" almost always precedes the "natural." This concept, is the root of "understanding," and once properly engaged, will empower you beyond measure to change any circumstance in your life. Consider the next 3 examples:

**EXAMPLE #4:**
Ancient Chinese Proverb expressed using natural language: *"Even the tallest tower started from the ground."*
What is the real issue?
Real issue expressed using spiritual language: *Patience*

### EXAMPLE #5:

Ancient Chinese Proverb expressed using natural language: *"The old horse will know the way."*

What is the real issue?

Real issue expressed using spiritual language: *Wisdom*

### EXAMPLE #6:

Ancient Chinese Proverb expressed using natural language: *"Wisdom is attained by learning when to hold one's tongue."*

What is the real issue?

Real issue expressed using spiritual language: *Self-Control*


Words are important! *Your* words are all that you have to express your thoughts and feelings that arise out of any and all issues in life. People often take for granted the art of vocal expression by trying to convey a certain message using the wrong words. Then, they assume that a listener will comprehend their intended meaning, although, in reality, their lackadaisical efforts to communicate effectively have "shortchanged" the listener. However, if *you* can learn to (1) identify the real issues *(i.e.* fight the *right* fight), that so commonly manifest themselves in our daily lives, albeit in a myriad of ways, and (2) gain the ability to express these issues using set definitions that don't change, then you begin to develop an arsenal of verbal weapons, based in spiritual understanding, that will help you to view your natural problems in a clearer light. Remember, what I am now giving to you, piece by piece, are foundational prerequisites to the 7-Pillar Model for Daily Living.

This process requires that I first provide you with the "trees," so that you may eventually see the forest.

### PRETEXT TO THE FIRST PILLAR:  FAITH

Every word that is written in this book has come out of my own faith. What is faith and where does it come from? In response to the first question, the Word of God says that faith is [defined as] "the substance of things hoped for and the evidence of things not seen." (Hebrews 11:1, KJV). As to the second inquiry, the Word of God says that "…faith comes from hearing the message, and the message is heard through the Word of Christ." (Romans 10:17, NIV)

Now, let's get some housecleaning out of the way. From this point on, whenever I refer to "the Word," I am simply referring to the Bible. More specifically, I am referencing God's words concerning, in relation to, and toward us. Remember what I said in the previous section about words. Words are so important! As human beings, our words are our primary form of expression: what we want, what we must have, and how we feel. Well, God's words are no different. God's words express what He wants, what he demands, and what his will is for our lives. When I say God's "will," this means God's "purpose" for our lives.

So, we know two things thus far:

1. *"Faith is the substance of things hoped for and the evidence of things not seen."* (Hebrews 11:1, KJV)

2. *Faith comes by hearing the message, and the message is heard through the word of Christ.* (Romans 10:17, NIV)

This is where the 7 Pillar Model for Daily Living really begins. But, before we dive into the *first pillar* of the model for daily living (*i.e. faith* - what it is and where it comes from), I want you to first understand the deeper implication attached to the phrase, the "Word of God." I hope you have your pens, pencils, and paper ready. Here we go.

## THE WORD OF GOD

How many of you have ever picked up the Bible and started reading it as you would any other novel, magazine, newspaper, or book, from start to finish? Maybe I should back up. Do you own or have immediate access to a Bible? If not, figure out how to get one. I am going to assume that you read several, if not tons of email messages, daily. In this day in age, I'll also assume that you read your share of text messages during the course of any given week. Similarly, I am going to assume that many of you enjoy browsing various online articles that may catch your eye, or simply enjoy reading a copy of the newspaper of your choice. Some of you may even find pleasure in reading novels of various genres in your spare time. The point is that reading is something that we do on a daily basis. It may be for work, for mere pleasure, or solely for information.

Generally, when we begin to read something (*e.g.* articles, magazines, books), from where do we start reading? I'm fairly certain that the majority of you will answer that question, "from the beginning." Yes, we generally begin reading *anything* from the beginning, with the exception of a dictionary, encyclopedia, or any factual reference book of some kind. Whenever a piece of reading material encompasses a storyline, common sense dictates that the reader *should* start at the beginning of the story, that is, if the reader is to gain the author's intended meaning or message. Now, some of you may never have picked up a Bible in your life, and that's ok. Others of you may classify yourself as being familiar with the Word because you go to church on a regular or irregular basis. A handful of you may be daily readers of God's Word and that is wonderful too. Remember, this book is not meant to assess, or judge, anyone's spirituality. This book *is* meant to show you how to find lasting prosperity in life.

I strongly suggest that as you take inventory of your own life, your trouble spots, and your areas where you want to improve, pick up a Bible and start reading *from the beginning*. I can hear it now:

"But I don't have time..."

"I'm too busy."

"The *whole* Bible...are you crazy?!

"I'll try..."

You have to understand that *real change comes from within.* There is no gain or improvement in any area of life until a person decides from within that he or she is willing to do something different than that which they have done in the past. A wise person once said, "*To get something that you've never had, you've got to do something that you've never done.*" As stated above, those people who have already been humbled by whatever difficult situation that they are facing in their respective lives, are the ones who tend to be most receptive to instruction. *Their breaking point is their turning point; and often times, their misery becomes their ministry.* That is why Chapter 1 speaks so candidly to any person who has been affected by sexual acts of violence. because, it is that person who may be facing utter despair and who, consequently, is ready to go in a new direction - and God's Word is direction, literally.

Understand that your hearing the Word of God is imperative to this process. Do not become immediately overwhelmed by the daunting notion of having to read the entire Bible in order to capitalize on the principles found in the 7-Pillar Model for Daily Living. That is not the case. However, you *cannot* get anything from this book without also reading and referencing the Word of God constantly and consistently. Throughout the book, I will provide scriptural references that you should write down, read, re-read, and meditate on, repeatedly. As your exposure to the Word increases, your faith will also begin to increase.

## As Your "Word" Level Increases, Your "Faith" Level Increases

Faith is simply a level of *confidence*. When we speak of faith, we are talking about having *confidence* in God's Word. When you read the Word of God, you begin to extract notions of who he is and what he expects from you in your everyday life. Understandably, your concept of who God is was likely shaped by your individual experiences in life. If you were never exposed to God, then there is a good chance you won't think very much of him. That's reasonable. However, just like anything else in life, whenever you are exposed to something or someone in an increasing amount, then your understanding of that thing or person begins to change, to grow, to deepen. Put another way, you only get to know someone if you spend time with them. That's "Basic Reasoning 101." So, as you expose your eyes, mind, and heart increasingly to what God commands, demands, and wants for your life, your *confidence* in Him correspondingly increases. This *confidence* is simply another word for faith. Now, let's leave the abstract thinking alone for a second and add some context for the sake of effective learning.

Do you ever worry about *anything*? Paying bills, relationships, loneliness, illness, unemployment, etc., etc., etc. Everybody worries about something. When we worry, that translates into our confidence level being low about that specific thing. Well, what if God told you that you don't ever have to worry because He promised you that he would *always* be with you. Really think about that for a moment. In your life, doesn't it make you feel better whenever a loved one, a friend, or a family member tells you, "don't worry, you know I'll be with you?" Or, "things will be ok, I'm here for you." Isn't that what drives some people into an abyss of depression – the fact that they feel alone and don't have another person to lean on, love, or look to for help? Of course, you don't have to admit it out loud to anyone within earshot whether you've ever felt this way, but at least admit it to yourself. By our very nature, knowing that we are not alone, especially during times of difficulty, is comforting.

Proceeding on that truth, how comforting would it be to know that God, himself, promised you that he would never leave you? To answer that question, you *first* have to know that God, indeed, made that promise to you!

Read it for yourself! Open your bible and go to Hebrews 13:5-6. (For those readers that are not yet familiar with how the scriptures are written, go to the book of Hebrews, Chapter 13, verses 5 through 6). In pertinent part, it reads:

…"Never will I leave you; never will I forsake you." So we say with confidence, "The Lord is my helper; I will not be afraid. What can man do to me?" (Hebrews 13:5-6, NIV)

Think about that for a moment. Take two moments. Even if your knowledge of God is limited, I want you to consider how comforting it would be to know that somebody promised you that they would *never* leave you. Imagine that. Who in your life has ever said those words to you? Perhaps, if you've been blessed with a devoted husband or wife, a committed friend, a loving family member, or my personal favorite, a happy-go-lucky pooch that seems to always want to lick your face *no matter what* you had for lunch - then perhaps, these various people (or dogs) have uttered something similar to God's promise. Of course, we then must consider the source of that promise. People, as we all know when we look in the mirror, are fallible. God knows that human beings are not perfect, which is one reason why it gives great peace to know that *he* has promised us that He would *never* leave us, nor forsake us.

But wait a minute. If you don't ever open and read the Bible, how would you know this? How would you ever *hear* God's Word concerning you? Moreover, if you don't know God's Word and how it relates to you, then you will also never know what incredibly comforting promises He has made to you. In other words my friend, if you don't know all of God's wonderful and comforting promises that he has made to you concerning your life, you don't know what you're missing. And isn't that a possible issue – that there may be something missing in your life that can propel you over that emotional hump, get you past that hurtful relationship, or empower you to confront that thing that you're afraid of? What you are missing is the Word of God and knowing that you are *never* on your own because He said that He would never leave you, nor forsake you. Take that scripture and *memorize it*. Write it down! Say it out loud. Think about it during the day and at night. Start believing that God is *always* with you.

# FIRST PILLAR:
## *Faith*

This is where the Model begins. I congratulate you in advance for having made it to the first pillar because the role that *faith* must play in your life in order to achieve true prosperity cannot be overstated.

We know from reading the Word that faith is "the *substance* of things hoped for..." From here on, do not confuse *faith* and *hope*. They ar*e not* the same thing. Remember, words are important! And sometimes it's "the little foxes that spoil the vines," which simply means that I cannot afford to become complacent in my effort to communicate my message effectively because that would "short-change" you, the reader, which may result in misunderstanding thus leading to an ineffective model. That's unacceptable. So, write down in your notebook that *faith is the **substance** of things hoped for.* For now, set the word "hope" to the side.

Now, open your Bible and go to the following scripture: Acts 22: 6–9. (Don't be concerned about the nuance differences that appear between different translations and versions of God's Word. That will not hinder your understanding whatsoever). The scripture reads:

(6) "About noon as I came near Damascus, suddenly a bright light from heaven flashed around me. (7) I fell to the ground and heard a voice say to me, 'Saul! Saul! Why do you persecute me?'

(8) "'Who are you, Lord?' I asked.

" 'I am Jesus of Nazareth, whom you are persecuting,' he replied. My companions saw the light, but they did not understand the voice of him who was speaking to me. (Acts 22: 6-9, NIV)

For the sake of those who are not familiar with this passage, let me provide the proper context. In the short passage above, there was a man named Saul who was traveling from Jerusalem to Damascus. Saul was born of Jewish descent and was thoroughly trained in Jewish law and custom, and by his own contention, "was just as zealous for God" as the other Jewish citizens of the town of Jerusalem. (*See,* Acts 22: 3). Here, it is important to understand that at the time of Saul's journey from Jerusalem to Damascus, Jesus of Nazareth had already been crucified (*i.e.* put to death on the cross). Saul, notwithstanding his Jewish descent, was against the teachings of Jesus Christ (as many Jews were at that time, hence the persecution and crucifixion of Jesus). In fact, the reason why Saul was traveling from Jerusalem to Damascus was to persecute (*i.e.* arrest) a select group of people in Damascus who were considered to be "followers" of Jesus Christ and his teachings. It wasn't until the occurrence of this event on the road to Damascus that Saul's transformation took place and his emergence as the Apostle Paul ensued. If you are not familiar with the Apostle Paul due to limited Bible knowledge, don't worry. For now, just understand that this background information (which you can only get from reading the Bible in sequential order) is critically important as we dissect this highlighted text and the key issue of faith.

Now, look at the same passage again, found directly below. But this time, pay careful attention to the words that are in italics.

(6) "About noon as I came near Damascus, suddenly a bright *light* from heaven flashed around me.  (7) I fell to the ground and *heard a voice* say to me, 'Saul! Saul! Why do you persecute me?'

(8) "'Who are you, Lord?' I asked.

"'I am Jesus of Nazareth, whom you are persecuting,' he replied.

(9) *My companion saw the light, but they did not understood the voice* of him who was speaking to me.[1]

If you will recall, I suggested that you write down the word "faith" and to also temporarily set the word "hope" aside. Well, here is where the impartation of knowledge from me to you takes place, and I will check your level of understanding at the end of the section.

The *light* in the passage represents, or is equivalent to, *hope.*

The *voice,* in the passage represents, or is equivalent to, *substance.*

Please allow me to say that again.

The *light,* in the passage represents, or is equivalent to, *hope.*

The *voice,* in the passage represents, or is equivalent to, *substance.*

I'll repeat that one more time solely for the sake of efficiency. Please humor me.

The *light,* in the passage represents, or is equivalent to, *hope.*

The *voice,* in the passage represents, or is equivalent to, *substance.*

If you only see the light of God and never hear His voice, it means your hope has no substance.

1. In the King James Version, verse (9), reads: "And they that were with me saw indeed the light, and were afraid; but they heard not the voice of him that spake to me." (Acts: 22: 9)(KJV).

In practical terms, the *light* is the written Word of God. By "written Word," I am referring *directly to the actual letters and words written* in the pages of the Bible. (Some people refer to this as the "dead letter"). You will recall that God's written Word is full of promises to you concerning your life. The example given to you earlier in this chapter was God's promise that he would never leave you, found in Hebrews 13: 5. Well, that was one promise from God, located in one verse, in one chapter, in one book of the Bible. There are 66 books of the Bible in all, beginning with Genesis and ending with Revelation, full of God's promises concerning you and your life. The written Word of God enumerates His promises throughout the entire Bible and I guarantee that each time you read one of God's many promises (such as the promise that God will never leave you), the promise perpetuates hope. For anyone who hears, understands, and accepts God's promises as truth, the hearer is immediately supplied with hope. Hope that you will obtain the thing or object of your desire, whatever it may be (happiness, peace, love, a new job, etc.). The *light* (or God's written word), equals *hope.*

*But, if you only see the light of God and never hear His voice, it means that your hope has no substance.* Put another way, if you only have the "dead letter," then you have the hope, but no substance.

Remember, *faith* is the *substance* of things *hoped* for. (*See,* Hebrews 11:1, KJV). So, what am I really saying? If you only have the Word of God (*i.e.* the dead letter), but you can't or don't hear His voice, then you are lacking the substance to fill your hope! You see, this is why words are so important. Many of you are probably guilty of thinking that "faith" and "hope" are the same. If you're completely honest with yourself, you're probably thinking, "Yeah, I knew they were different, but I just didn't know how to say it." That's ok. At least you were aware of the difference.

*Faith fills hope.* Imagine that hope is a mold. A mold is defined as "a frame in which something is formed or made[2]." The most common or recognizable example for Americans, or those of you who are familiar with cooking, might be a "Jell-O" mold. "Jell-O" is the bright, flavorful dessert that kids (and a few adults that I know, who shall remain nameless) love to eat. Well, imagine that the "Jell-O" mold represents hope. Faith is the *substance* that fills the mold. To ensure that you understand, I want you to consider the 5-step "comprehension check" directly below.

Hope comes from God's promises, found in his written Word (*i.e.* the "dead letter").

Hope is like a mold, or an empty container.

Faith is "the *substance* of things hoped for", which means that…

Faith is the *substance* that fills the hope. (Or, simply stated, faith fills hope).

But remember, if you only have the *written* word (*i.e.* the "dead letter") and not the *voice*, you only have the hope, not the substance! Therefore, your hope cannot be fulfilled or realized if there is no substance (which is faith). And *true* faith begins when we hear God's voice.

If you quickly refer back to the Bible passage in Acts 22: 6-9, Saul (also known as the Apostle Paul after this event) was the only

---

2. Dictionary.com, LLC.

one of his companions who *heard the voice,* even though they *all* saw the light! Therefore, the real issue to decipher becomes, how do we not just get the Word *of* God, but how do we get a Word *from* God?

I already know what some of you are thinking. Someone is saying, "What does that mean exactly…hearing God's voice?" When God speaks, does it resemble an actual voice as if another person were audibly speaking aloud? Or, is it a soft voice that I can only hear in my head? Is the voice actually just a "feeling" that I get inside like an instinct? And how do I know when God, or *if* God, is really speaking to me? How can I be sure?

These are all legitimate questions. First, however, let's not gloss over the fact that we first *identified the pertinent issue.* I will continue to hammer this point because it is of the utmost importance in learning how to "fight the *right* fight" in life. "Fighting the *right* fight" simply means having the ability to extract the root issue out of any situation. You may be the most intelligent, articulate, and successful person on Earth in your respective profession, but that doesn't mean you know how to spot the *real* issue of a problem or situation. Please understand that the person who knows how to identify *the root* of a problem, or stated otherwise, "spot the real issue," is a person who can directly and more quickly affect change to their circumstance, problem, or situational context.

In so adamantly hammering the point of "fighting the *right* fight" (*i.e.* spotting the real or root issue), I run the risk of someone missing the equally-as-important second part of this principle. The second element to this principle was stated clearly at the beginning of the book. In addition to identifying the root issue of your problem(s) for the purpose of "fighting the *right* fight," you must also learn to fight your life's battles with the *right spiritual weapons*.

Now that you have begun to understand some of the basic tenets of the First Pillar called *faith*, I can state things more eloquently. The two-part principle that underscores the entire 7-Pillar Model for Daily Living," clearly stated, is: "Fight the *right* fight with *fighting faith!*" and "fight life's battles with *spiritual weapons.*" Don't worry, we won't move too fast. We will discuss this fundamental two-part principle in greater detail as we progress through the Model. For now, let's resume with the issue-at-hand. What exactly does it mean to hear God's voice and how do we put ourselves in a position to hear His voice? In other words, now that I understand how to get the Word *of* God, how do I get a Word *from* God?

### HEARING THE VOICE OF GOD

The Word of God says that "…faith comes from hearing the message, and the message is heard through the Word of Christ." (Romans 10:17, NIV). We have already established that the *written* Word is absolutely vital to acquiring faith because the *written* Word is the door. It's the entryway, if you will. Now, here is the key element. If you just meditate on and engage God's *written* Word long enough, you will come to recognize and hear his voice when he speaks to you. But, as a starting point, it is imperative that you are ingesting the Word of God on a consistent basis.

In the example above, we saw how Saul heard the voice of God while his companions, who were in his immediate presence, did not. Hearing God's voice happens differently for different people. For example, a person may be spiritually moved by something they heard someone else say regarding God's spiritual truth. Someone else may have been listening to a certain multimedia outlet and genuinely connected to the message being taught on a spiritually-based television, web, or radio broadcast. Perhaps an acquaintance recently invited you to church or Bible study and you were touched by something the speaker said. A few people may have become inspired to seek more knowledge of the Lord upon hearing a conversation between co-workers, family members, or friends regarding whether they believe in God. My point is simple. There are numerous ways that a person can be introduced to the gospel of Christ, but there is one constant that is always present – the hearing. Somehow, the person *heard* God's message, and that message comes out of the Word of God.

Although this seems to be common sense, it's one of those things that may not really register mentally until it happens. Consider this. Think about a time in your life where you heard a communication of some sort that contained a powerful message which subsequently affected you positively. As elementary as this next statement may be, it is a true statement. Unless you *heard* the message that was communicated, you would not have been affected. For example, if you are a business-minded individual who heard a valuable "stock tip," and purchased stock to your benefit in reliance on the information heard, the change in position would never have occurred had you not heard the relevant information. In this context, it is the element of "hearing" that brings about the opportunity for a positive change.

(Of course it also depends on what you do with the information heard, but we are getting to that later).

Listen to any person who has a success story or a "rags to riches" testimonial. By "rags to riches," I mean there will be a person who was "down on their luck," hurting, stressed out, hungry, poor, depressed, emotionally bankrupt, or just sad and lonely and at some point, things changed, improved, and became better on the whole. Often times, the testifier's breaking point became his turning point where hope was instilled by something he heard. It's not uncommon that such a person ultimately becomes inspired to *do something* different to change their circumstances based on something positive they heard. Well, there is no difference in our scenario concerning the gospel of Christ. You must *hear* God's message in order for real transformation to take place. Once Saul heard God's voice, he was transformed from a man who previously had persecuted the followers of Jesus Christ, to a self-proclaimed "ambassador in chains." (*See*, Ephesians 6:20, NIV).

You must put yourself in a position to hear God's message! If you want to change your posture and change your position in life, then put yourself in a position to succeed. The real issue is what are you hearing? What are you listening to? The Bible says, "How can they believe in the one of whom they have not heard. And how can they hear without someone preaching it to them. And how can they preach unless they are sent." (See, Romans 10:14, NIV). In other words, you must put forth the effort to hear the Word of God. You cannot be a "candidate for change" if you are not hearing God's message.

Although I acknowledge the existence of various widespread religious practices that are dispersed throughout the world, not all religious sects preach the gospel of Jesus Christ. In fact, not all so-called "Christian" churches teach the gospel of Jesus Christ. This is one reason, of many, why religion can be such a hotbed of controversy. As stated earlier, discussing "religion" is not the purpose or objective of this book. However, you should understand that with spiritual knowledge come discernment, sound judgment, and wisdom. It is in your best interest to put yourself in a position to hear the spiritual truth from the right source. The best source is God which is why you need to read the Word for yourself and know God for yourself. As your Word knowledge increases, your understanding of who God is will increase. As your understanding increases, the potential to be able to hear God's voice will increase.

Today, we live in an interconnected world facilitated by and through innovative technological inventions that serve as mediums of instant communication for and between people on a global scale. If I so choose, I can sit in my modest apartment located in Shenzhen, China, in front of my computer and watch (via an internet connection that is either a product of live-streaming or a pre-recorded broadcast) a speech or a sermon that is being transmitted from another country, on a different continent, within a different time zone. I can stay apprised of the latest happenings in world news that have geo-political implications which may affect me in the future by the simple click of a button. I can conduct business with transnational partners. I can watch sporting events from around the world. I can even chat online with a person who may live oceans apart from my current address. In other words, modern information technology affords us the option to connect our vision and our *hearing* with an infinite amount of messages that are being transmitted on a daily basis. The question I pose to you is what kinds of things are you listening to?

Open the Bible and begin to read it. Don't stop there. Study it. Take notes. Meditate on the words. Work with it. Make every effort to understand the gospel contained within. Get familiar with who God is, how much He loves you, and what He wants for your life. Focus and dissect the story of Jesus Christ. Become knowledgeable and seek the understanding that God sent His only Son to this Earth to die for the atonement of our sins and be raised again so that all who confess with their mouth that "Jesus is Lord," and who believe in their heart that God raised Jesus from the dead, will have salvation and everlasting life. (*See,* Romans 10:9, NIV). Go to church. If you don't go, start going. If you don't know where to go, find a church that teaches on the principles in the Bible, and start going every week. Don't make excuses. Begin to put seeking God first in your life. The Word of God says, "Seek first his kingdom and his righteousness" and everything else in life will be given to you as well. (Matthew 6:33, NIV).

You must understand something. You came to me, I didn't come to you. If you want real change, and you are ready for real change, then make the decision and the commitment to bring God's goodness into your life. Too many of you have been partying for too long. In fact, it's a way of life. I don't even need to qualify that statement because I know it's true. How many of you do crazy things on the weekends that you generally don't do during the week…just because it's the weekend?! How many of you have old habits that you haven't been able to break no matter how much *willpower* you try to use? How many of you are lacking something in your life and there is an empty space or void that needs to be occupied or filled? The real issue is how long are you going to do the same things, but expecting a different result? By definition, that is the meaning of insanity. Insanity means to do the same thing over and over again expecting a different result. It just doesn't work like that! I know from personal experience.

Some of you are just plain tired of fighting negative emotions such as hurt, fear, anger, depression, and loneliness. Others of you have been on the losing end of an addiction that has lasted for years (drugs, alcohol, smoking, pornography, sex). The good news is that there is replenishment for those who are humble enough to receive it! Jesus said, *"Come to me, all you who are weary and burdened, and I will give you rest."* (Matthew 11:28, NIV). Trust me. There is a better way of living than the situation you find yourself immersed in right now! There is a better way! Get God's Word! It will become the root of your faith. As your faith grows, you will learn to put your confidence in Him rather than in people, things, or substances. But, the first step is getting God's Word.

If you should happen to find yourself sitting in front of the television one random night with the remote control in your hand, turn to the channels with spiritual-based programming.

Watch and listen to what they have to say. Just like anything else in life, there are some good ones and there are some bad ones. Here are some good ones: T.D. Jakes, Cynthia D. James, Creflo Dollar, Joyce Meyer, Charles Stanley, to name a few. (For obvious reasons, I won't mention the bad ones). To know the difference, you need knowledge, understanding, discernment, sound judgment, and wisdom. What I will *not* do right now is tell you to simply ask God to grant you wisdom if you have never opened a Bible in your life. To borrow from an old American adage, that would be "putting the cart before the horse." Divine wisdom (*i.e.* wisdom that comes from God, as opposed to earthly wisdom) comes from meditating on His Word. Accordingly, what I *will* do is tell you to read Proverbs 2:6, which says, *"For the Lord gives wisdom, and from his mouth come knowledge and understanding."*

The process is important. Whatever you need in life, God will give it to you. Knowledge, understanding, discernment, sound judgment, and wisdom from God are the most valuable gifts a person can ask for and receive. The Bible says, "Blessed is the man who finds wisdom, the man who gains understanding, for she is more profitable than silver and yields better returns than gold." (Proverbs 3:13-14, NIV). However, there is a process! Unless you are *hearing the message in God's Word,* spending time getting to know Him, praying, and making a daily concerted effort to submit your will to God's will (by operating in love rather than in selfishness), then you will not be a candidate to receive the divine knowledge, understanding, discernment, sound judgment, and wisdom that come from God. Of course, someone might say, "Well, why does that matter?" (Or, stated in the form of an issue) "What is the overall objective attached to hearing and understanding the gospel of Jesus Christ, or the spiritual truth?" Well, that's a good question which can be answered in one word: *power.*

In the sections ahead, you will come to understand that there is power tied to God's voice, *if you* (1) can engage the Word *of* God long enough to receive a word *from* God; and (2) if you *obey* what he told YOU to do. For now, focus on the process at work, which begins with *hearing* the message that is found in the Word *of* God. Then, and only then, will you be in a position to hear His voice (*i.e.* get a Word *from* God). Then, and only then, will you be a candidate for the empowerment that his tied to His voice. And in a life full of struggles, hurt, lies, pain, and difficulties, God's empowerment is exactly what we need! But, before you can receive the power that is tied to God's voice, you must first be able to *recognize* His voice. That is important. In the following section, I will give you five (5) key factors to consider when in determining whether God has spoken to you. I hope you're still taking notes!

*How can I recognize God's voice? How will I know it's Him, and not me?*

These are two great questions that universally apply to everyone regardless of your nationality, your religious affiliation, your native language, or the country in which you live. If God speaks to me, how can I recognize His voice? How will I know it's really God speaking, and not me? Consider the five (5) factors below and let them be your guide. You'll know when God speaks to you because…

When God speaks to you, *it will always require faith.*

When God speaks to you, *it will require courage.*

When God speaks to you, *it will line up with His written Word.*

When God speaks to you, *it will go against "the world's" way of doing things.*

When God speaks to you, *peace will rule in your heart.*

Let's take a look at each of the abovementioned factors, individually, for purposes of developing a deeper understanding. Remember, contextual learning is learning at its finest. When a person has a real-life context in which to place a new spiritual principle, there is often a clearer understanding of the message being imparted through personal attachment or relationship by way of similar circumstance. I'll set forth two real-life examples derived from my own life to provide a context to which some of you may relate. The purpose is to view the five (5) factors involved in hearing God's voice through the lens of a real-world situation.

In late 2008, I discovered that an acquaintance of mine had been the victim of multiple unreported rapes in years past by a "family friend." To add insult to injury, the alleged rapist (a "white collar" individual), who had never been reported to the police authorities prior to 2009, had simultaneously assumed a "choke-hold" on the victim's financial well-being by perpetrating an ongoing fraudulent real-estate scheme against the victim and her family, (as well as other similarly-situated, unsuspecting, non-native English-speaking, Hispanic families). After allegedly committing the first rape incident years ago while on a "date" with the young lady (who was 18 years old at the time, while he was approximately 30 years of age), the man succeeded in instilling a level of *fear* in the young lady – a fear so deeply-rooted that it would grip her for several years thereafter.

Now, this is the context I want you to digest. I wish I could tell you that I conjured up this anecdote solely for the purpose of demonstrating how a person can hear God's voice in a time of trouble or distress, but that would be false. As terrible as it is, the context that I just laid out for you is a true account of events that transpired. Not just that, I selected this true factual account on the belief that there will be at least one reader, if not dozens, who will in some way be able to relate to an incident of this magnitude. I told you at the beginning of this book, *never take for granted what someone else might be going through or has already been through in their own life.* Although the context that I laid out could easily be the storyline of a Sunday night dramatic television movie, these kinds of things are happening all around you whether you are aware of them or totally oblivious to their existence.

Here is the central point of the story. After what seemed to be an eternity of swirling emotions on the part of the victim (and me) surrounding this unfortunate reality upon the filing of police reports, interviews with detectives and district attorneys, the retention of lawyers, therapists, and counselors, I was at least able to assist a person who had been suffering in silence for years to disclose to the proper authorities and the appropriate loved ones, exactly what had happened in regard to the past crimes of rape, and what was still ongoing in regard to the fraudulent behavior being perpetrated against the victim, and her family, involving three real estate investment properties. But for any woman who has been the victim of any kind of traumatic sexual encounter, abuse, attack, or rape, there is something much more profound concerning the reasons why a victim may *not* tell anyone or report it for years, decades, or even a lifetime. The reason can be attributed to *fear*. We will discuss the element of "*fear*," and the dangers attached thereto, in greater detail at a later stage in the 7 Pillars of the Model for Daily Living. For now, just be cognizant that *fear* is a major issue that is the polar opposite of *faith*.

Significantly, even though the facts surrounding this ill-fated incident had come to light with the proper authorities and an assertive effort was established to undermine the ongoing fraud being perpetrated against the victim and her family, there was a definite lack of true understanding on my part of what this whole thing was about. Pay close attention and listen intently to what I am about to say. *Many of life's battles that you think are simply waged in the natural sense are actually the product of spiritual warfare.* Recall an earlier exercise that we performed at the start of the book when I directed you to read and consider three (3) mini fact-patterns and three (3) ancient Chinese proverbs written in *natural* language, then to identify and express the "real issue" therein, but using *spiritual* language. Do you remember? Take a moment and return to the section to which I am referring if need be because this is a key principle that you *must* understand. *The spiritual precedes the natural.* The spiritual drives the natural. The spiritual world is the parent. The natural world is the child. What you see, hear, and touch with your natural senses can actually be changed by spiritual forces. Remember, *faith* is a spiritual principle. Your *faith* in God and in God's Word can literally change the circumstances that surround you. Are you still with me?

There I stood, seemingly helpless to help someone who not only had been the victim of a violent crime at such a young age, but who was *still* within the reach of her alleged rapist due to an intricate residential property scheme entangling her, and her family, that involved identity theft, as well as the criminal act of forging signatures on sizeable bank loan modifications for the purpose of keeping the residential properties he had obtained fraudulently from going into foreclosure. It was an absolute nightmare. I had encountered "shady" people in my life, but never had I encountered anyone with a darker soul than this man.

In response to God's direction, and in faith, I took a stand for this woman (and her family) that needed to be taken. With my educational background and relevant past professional experience working for two federal district court judges, law firms, etc., I was no stranger to the legal process. Within two weeks of eliciting key facts from the victim surrounding the rape and fraud, I had moved from Northern California to Southern California in order to help her through this process. She trusted me and I advised her to immediately file a police report even though the initial rape had occurred years prior. I prepared her, one-on-one, to speak to a Sex Crimes Police Detective and Deputy District Attorney, both of whom believed her story without hesitation. Moreover, I strongly suggested to her that she disclose all information regarding the past sexual abuse and ensuing fraud to her parents, who at that point in time, were unknowing of either (even though the fraud directly implicated the parent's financial assets). In short, there were numerous legal maneuvers and actions taken against this individual in several different government agencies and venues in hopes of regaining some sense of security and dignity. Not to be overlooked, I inspired my friend to attend rape counseling and complete a self-defense training course for purposes of building self-esteem. All of these things were positive and necessary, but at that point, I wasn't practicing what I'm preaching to you now. As a result, even after all of that work and worry, I still did not have a concrete understanding of the entire situation. I was simply reacting out of compassion for a friend and fellow human being, but at the same time, becoming depleted, day-by-day, of my own emotional resolve.

Then something happened. After months of reading the Bible everyday (almost without fail), seeking God's counsel, meditating on God's Word early in the morning when I first awoke and late at night before I fell asleep, going to a Christian Bible-based church, and really listening to the spiritual guidance of a few well-established and renowned spiritual speakers that have daily broadcasts on television, something happened. I began to here God's voice. In so many words, this is what He told me.

When God speaks to you, it will always require *faith*.

I began to understand that I had been giving 100% of my emotion, time, and energy to help someone who suffered a grave injustice, but I was not fighting the *right* fight! Yes, the police, the detectives, the lawyers were all a necessary part of the process, but those "players" had nothing to do with the broader question of why a woman could suffer something as traumatic as rape, and not tell anyone about it for years *and* continue to have dealings with the man for years to follow? In fact, it is not uncommon that out of sheer ignorance or insensitivity, bystanders will often times pose questions regarding a woman who has been a victim of rape or sexual abuse asking, "Well, why did she put herself in that position?" "Why didn't she report it immediately after it happened?" The truth of the matter is that in more instances than not, *the victim is simply afraid, confused*, in a state of *disbelief*, and must first contend with whether the events that just took place *actually* took place! In other words, *fear*, in this context, can and will keep a person paralyzed and/or stuck (*i.e.* no forward motion) no matter what the circumstances may be.

But, it was God who told me that the real issue at hand was a spiritual issue, not a natural one.

The police, detectives, lawyers, agents, etc., always wanted to know the "natural" explanation of why certain events unfolded the way that they did. This was their job and their approach was understandable. For our purposes, however, what *you* should pick up on regarding certain problems in your own life is that "the world" will always question you as to why you didn't do *this*, or why you didn't do *that*. For example, "Why didn't you leave your boyfriend the first time he hit you?" Or, "Why didn't you walk away from the marriage the first *10* times your wife failed to tell you the truth?" Often times, in situations such as these, there may not be an answer that is logically comprehensible to the natural ears. (I know that there is at least one reader of this book who knows what I'm talking about). In the world that we live in, the sad fact is that if a woman is abused but doesn't report it until several years have passed, the first question people generally ask her is, "Why didn't you say something immediately after it happened?" But, to the spiritual ears, there is a spiritual understanding and a spiritual discernment that a victim of a sexual crime as traumatic as rape must first contend with the element of *fear*. Second, through no fault of her own, if she has not yet been exposed to the element of *faith* that comes out of hearing God's word, then she will likely be seized and overtaken by that *fear* which tends to manifests itself through the woman remaining silent. Of course, by no means, am I suggesting that a victim of a violent sexual crime, who had already been strongly established in her *faith* prior to that crime, would not also need to confront the element of *fear* that arises from such a devastatingly traumatic event. But, what I am suggesting is this. It is the presence of *faith* that arises out of hearing the message found in the Word of God that brings with it a divine knowledge, understanding, discernment, sound judgment, and wisdom that enables a person to view problems in the natural world through a spiritual lens. This is the divine wisdom that only comes from hearing God's voice. This is the substance beyond the hope.

Now, I don't take the issue of sexual abuse lightly. I don't take any kind of abuse lightly. I have a strong distaste for any man (or woman) that mistreats and/or abuses another human being that is weaker in physical strength or that possesses a lesser emotional maturity. This is my rule and there is no exception. I have the utmost respect for a great number of women mainly because of the inner strength that these women necessarily exude in having to deal with certain abuses carried out by men. Not all men, but some men.

In the context that I described above concerning my own life, it was my *faith* that placed me in a position to hear, discern, and understand God's voice. My *faith* is what brought about my level of understanding of how to view and approach life's problems from a spiritual perspective rather than a natural one. My *faith* came out of an earnest effort to read God's Word diligently. Likewise, it also came from a tremendously humbling experience in which I seemingly reached a breaking point under the weight of the circumstance that was on top of me. (I have chosen not to go into detail regarding a host of other difficult things that were happening during this time, but there were others, including the death of a grandparent. We all know that "when it rains, it pours.") It was my *faith* that steadily grew into what became my core mental and emotional source of strength, and which brought me to the realization of what life is *really* about.

Like I said before, there is *power* tied to God's voice, *if* you (1) can engage God's written Word long enough to hear His voice, and (2) *obey* what He told *you* to do. And to hear His voice, you must be in a place of *faith*. As you move on to the next factor, take with you the following two Bible scriptures that embody the faith of two well-known biblical patriarchs. Read the scriptures. Think about them. Write them down in the section of your notes entitled "Faith" so that you may refer back to them daily. The first scripture references Noah, the man of God who built an ark to preserve human and animal life notwithstanding the flood that destroyed every living creature except the inhabitants of Noah's ark. The scripture reads:

"By faith Noah, when warned about things not yet seen, in holy fear built an ark to save his family. By his faith he condemned the world and became heir of the righteousness that comes by faith." (Hebrews 11:7, NIV)

It is the first sentence of this passage that I emphasize to you. Take note that the sentence is grammatically separated into three parts, by two commas. (1) *By faith Noah,* (2) *when warned about things not yet seen,* (3) *in holy fear built an ark to save his family.* This is important because as you may have noticed thus far in your reading of this book, my intent is to train you to use your spiritual eyes and spiritual ears whenever you are presented with a situation in the natural sense to identify and express the real issue(s) using spiritual language. Remember, in this particular section of the book, we are discussing faith and the ability to hear God's voice; or, put another way, the faith attached to receiving a word *from* God. So, looking at the three parts of the scripture using your spiritual eyes and spiritual ears, and setting the three parts against the backdrop of what we are discussing (*i.e.* faith and hearing God's voice), what do you see? How can you analyze the scripture, which is expressed in natural language, using your spiritual senses? Your answer should, in some way, resemble the following:

*The facts expressed in natural language:*

Noah built a boat to save his family from the flood.

*Real issue(s) extracted from natural context, expressed in spiritual language:*

Faith

Hearing God's Voice (or, put another way, getting a Word *from* God)

Obedience

Power

Now, if you got the first two (*i.e.* faith and hearing God's voice), then you are on the right track. To this point in the 7-Pillar Model for Daily Living, we have not yet covered the last two, so put "obedience" and "power" on the back burner for now. But, as for the two issues of "faith" and "hearing God's voice," let's take a moment and look at the three parts again.

By faith Noah, (2) *when warned about things not yet seen,* (3) in holy fear built an ark to save his family.

What do your spiritual eyes and spiritual ears see and hear when you read the second sentence fragment, which says, "... *when warned about things not yet seen.*" The correct answer is that Noah *heard* a warning (with his spiritual ears, perhaps) concerning something that he had not yet seen with his natural eyes. In other words, Noah heard God's voice.

Let's look again. Looking at the third sentence fragment, which states, *"in holy fear built an ark to save his family,"* what issue jumps off of the page? The correct response is *obedience.* An even more comprehensive answer would be, "obedience to God's voice." In this scenario, Noah *obeyed* what God told *him* to do! Understand that anyone looking at the third sentence fragment only using his or her natural senses rather than their spiritual eyes and spiritual ears would likely give the simple response, "Noah built the ark." This answer, although correct on a natural level, is spiritually deficient of what we should be seeing and hearing as followers of Jesus Christ. The reason why this is so important is because the person that understands the *root* of a problem can address it more efficiently and effectively. Another way of saying "the root of a problem" is "the real issue." By developing your ability to identify and express the real issues that are commonplace concerning your daily struggles as men and women and boys and girls on this Earth, and that are also common themes in God's Word, then you become a much better equipped soldier on the battlefield of life through the attainment of spiritual knowledge, understanding, discernment, sound judgment, and above all else, wisdom. Write this down!

"We have not received the spirit of the world but *the Spirit* who is from God, that we may *understand* what God has freely given us. *This is what we speak, not in words taught us by human wisdom, but in words taught by the Spirit, expressing spiritual truths in spiritual words.* The man without the Spirit does not accept the things that come from the Spirit of God, for they are foolishness to him, and he cannot understand them, because they are *spiritually discerned.*" (I Corinthians 2:12-14, NIV) Emphasis added.

I ask you to recall this statement, "there is *power* tied to God's voice, *if you* (1) can engage God's word long enough to hear His voice, and (2) *obey* what God told *you* to do. Well, if you are a believer of God's Word, then there is very little room for argument that Noah's obedience in building the ark (to God's exact specifications[3])

---

3. For the exact specifications of Noah's ark, as given from God to Noah, read Genesis, chapter 6. In regard to the issue of "obedience to God's voice," note verse 22, which reads, "Noah did everything just as God commanded him."

empowered him to save his own life, the lives of his family, and various species of animal life as well. In short, Noah heard and obeyed God's voice. The result was life and peace. Going a little further, we can reasonably deduce that any inability to hear God's voice on the part of Noah *or* merely disobeying what he heard would have had a much less desired result.

Finally, let's look at the first sentence fragment.

(1) *By faith Noah,* (2) when warned about things not yet seen, (3) in holy fear built an ark to save his family.

Prior to hearing God's instruction to build the ark, had Noah not already been in a place of faith, then how would he have known God was speaking to him?[4] If Noah had not already been favorable in God's sight (*i.e.* blameless in the eyes of the Lord), then how would he have been in a position to recognize God's voice? Let me save you some time. He wouldn't have. The Bible affirms that, "Noah found favor in the eyes of the Lord." (Genesis 6:8, NIV). The next verse states that, "Noah was a righteous man, blameless among the people of his time, and he walked with God." (Genesis 6:9, NIV). This is a pertinent point not to be overlooked. Remember the rule.

There is *power* tied to God's voice, *if you* (1) can engage the Word of God long enough to get a word *from* God, and (2) *obey* what He told *you* to do.

Here, Noah was deemed to be a righteous man amongst a great many people whom God considered full of "wickedness." (See,

---

4. Read I Samuel 3:1-9 [A young Samuel heard the voice of the Lord, but did not recognize God's voice because "the word of the Lord had not yet been revealed to him."]

Genesis, 6:5, NIV). Your *spiritual discernment* should be working for you to enable you to realize that Noah had been in a place of faith long enough to be able to hear God's voice. This is easily extracted from the last five words of Genesis 6:9, which say, in pertinent part, *"...and he walked with God."* Noah had a relationship with God that was pleasing in God's sight. Consequently, Noah was established in his faith which placed him in a position to hear and obey God's voice. For Noah, it was "by faith" that he heard God's voice and "by faith" that he obeyed God's warning and built the ark. His hearing and obedience were both by faith.

Now, I ask you. Are you beginning to see the power and importance of *faith*? Follow this point. Noah's lifestyle, prior to hearing God's voice, was pleasing to God. In other words, it was Noah's existing daily lifestyle (*i.e.* his decision to walk with God *prior to* any knowledge that there would be a flood) which placed him in a position to hear God's voice. Accordingly, God deemed Noah righteous and warned him of the ensuing flood that would surely destroy everyone else. So, there seems to be a sliding scale of faith in the life of Noah. Stay with me as I explain what is meant by "sliding scale." Noah had already possessed a certain measure of faith *before* God warned him of the flood. We know this because God ascribed righteousness and blamelessness to Noah based on Noah's walk with God. Once Noah heard God's voice (*i.e.* received a word *from* God), *and obeyed* what God told *him* to do, Noah's measure of faith increased! You see, it is the point at which a person begins to hear God's voice with his spiritual ears where the potential for decipherable change takes place. *Hearing ears are the key!* As Jesus said, *"He who has ears to hear, let him hear."* (Mark 4:9, NIV).

Hearing and obeying God's voice makes you a candidate for change. In the third to last sentence of the previous paragraph, the reason why I used the words "potential" and "candidate" is because the 7 Pillars of the Model for Daily Living are not mutually exclusive. They work together. For now, you have made great strides in your spiritual growth by understanding that your goal should be to put yourself in a position to hear and obey God's voice. In other words, don't just stop at getting the Word *of* God. Get a word *from* God! And be sure to write down one of my favorite scriptures in the section of your notes entitled "*faith*." It says, "And without faith it is impossible to please God, because anyone who comes to him must believe that he exists and that he rewards those who earnestly seek him." (Hebrews 11:6, NIV).

When God speaks to you, it will require *courage.*

Anytime the topic of discussion revolves around faith and deeds, courage must be included in the conversation. We have established that faith is the evidence of things that you cannot perceive through any of your physical senses (*i.e.* eyes, ears, taste, smell, touch). For example, the overwhelming majority of Christians believe in the existence of an eternal dwelling place in the afterlife for those who receive salvation through Jesus Christ. On what basis do they derive this belief? The Word of God clearly states: "No eye has seen, no ear has heard, no mind has conceived what God has prepared for those who love him – but God has revealed it to us by his Spirit." (I Corinthians 2:9-10, NIV). Given this scripture, consider the question again and tell me on what basis do many people set their belief that, indeed, there is a heaven? If you take the Word as literal, no person has perceived through his or her *natural senses* the actual existence of a heaven. Do you see where I'm going with this? By now, you know that the answer, of course, is *faith*. Your faith causes you to believe in God and all of the promises that are found in his Word.

But the root issue for this section can be expressed using spiritual language in a very specific way. What happens when you have righteously put yourself in the position to hear God's voice, and then He actually tells you to *do* something?! You were already made aware that there is power tied to God's voice. To receive the power, you must *obey* what He told *you* to do. Often times, if God tells you to *do* something, obedience to his instruction will require *courage* on your part. Said in a simpler way, following God's word requires courage, period. Contextual learning is learning at its finest, so let's proceed with two contextual examples, one biblical, and one contemporary.

In the Bible, Abram (later, known as Abraham) is a figure to whom God attributed the moniker, "father of many nations," and consequently whom many Christians consider to be the spiritual father of Christian faith. (*See*, Genesis 17: 4; *See also*, Galations 3:29). It was through Abraham's line of offspring that Isaac, Jacob, and the twelve tribes of Israel were created. It's a fascinating account of events set in the Old Testament that you will read as you embark upon, or continue with, your daily Bible study. For our purposes, however, we will simply focus on the courage it must have taken on Abraham's part in obeying what God told *him* to do. The Lord told Abram (later, known as Abraham):

"Leave your country, your people and your father's household and go to the land I will show you. I will make you into a great nation and I will bless you; I will make your name great, and you will be a blessing. I will bless those who bless you, and whoever curses you I will curse; and all peoples on earth will be blessed through you. *So Abram left, as the Lord had told him* and Lot went with him. Abram was seventy-five years old when he set out from Haran." (Genesis 12:1-4 NIV)  Emphasis added.

Here, Abram (later, known as Abraham) began his journey in obedience to God's instruction. The journey encompassed leaving the land of "Haran," and traveling to his intended destination of "Canaan.[5]" (Genesis 12:4-5). Let me say that again. God told Abram, "Leave your country, your people and your father's household and go to the land I will show you." I'm going to repeat that one more time using modern terminology, for those of you who didn't quite catch it. God told Abram to get up, gather together everything that you own…

Leave your country

Leave your people

Leave your father's house, and

Go to a new land that I *will* show you!

---

5. A comprehensive reading of this portion of Genesis provides that Abram's father, Terah, took Abram, his grandson Lot, and Abram's wife, Sarai (later known as Sarah) and they set out from "Ur" (land of the Chaldeans) to go to Canaan. But when they came to Haran, they settled there. Terah died in Haran. (Genesis 11:31-32). Afterwards, Abram received and obeyed God's instruction to leave Haran and set out for the land of Canaan. (Genesis 12:1-5).

(I place special emphasis on the word "will," as in, "I won't tell you where you're going until you actually get up and go!").

Now, I don't mean to be facetious, but how many of *you*, upon hearing a Word *from* God instructing you to leave your house, leave your family, and leave your country to go to a foreign place (which God won't disclose until a later date) - how many of *you* would have enough courage, confidence, and faith in God to carry out the Word *from* God that you had received? Perhaps, right now, you should just sit quietly and keep your answer to yourself because I don't want to be responsible for making somebody tell a lie knowing that God sees everything. I jest, of course. But seriously, really ponder the question for a moment and consider the courage that it took for Abram to follow God's Word. Now let's bring it closer to home.

Many of *you* are likely in a position in your life where you could benefit greatly from picking up and leaving the familiarities of your surroundings behind in order to better position yourself to be in line with God's Word. Sure, you may cite, with some legitimacy, opposition to such a notion pointing to job restraints, family commitments, and all sorts of personal and professional reasons why you are locked into your current routine. To be candid, I have no interest in judging you. Everyone has their own set of unique responsibilities to fulfill. However, often times, God can do the most with us when we are not inundated with distractions. Distractions include, but are not limited to, friends, family, jobs, relationships, recreational fun, business, personal goals, and much more.

At the start of the book, I requested that you (1) humble yourself, (2) read in a quiet place with no distractions, and (3) take notes.

There is something about having a personal relationship with God that is in and of itself, very humbling. It is a one-on-one connection that you establish through your willingness to expose your eyes, ears, and heart to his Word, obey it, and sacrifice your own natural human desires for His glorification. Unfortunately, when we are so caught up in our daily routine and the daily politics that surround our lives, there is rarely a scarce moment of solitude or quiet to focus on developing your *faith* in God.

Let's be frank. Some of you are surrounded by people who are not exactly furthering your chances of getting into heaven. It's not a personal attack on them, but rather it's a wake-up call to you! If you truly want to stop smoking cigarettes or marijuana, or drinking alcoholic beverages, then stop hanging around so-called "friends" who smoke and drink socially all the time! You'll recall that I told you at the start of this book that I have no interest in being politically correct. I told you that my message would cut straight to the heart of you and that the naysayers and pundits were predestined to quickly fall away. It's because sometimes, hearing the truth hurts. If someone else is causing you to sin, drop them. Do it definitively and quickly. Now, of course, that is easier said than done. Often times, whenever you try to distance yourself from a specific person, that person seems to press even harder to be near to you. But consider a relevant word from Jesus Christ:

"If your hand causes you to sin, cut it off. It is better for you to enter life maimed than with two hands to go into hell, where the fire never goes out. And if your foot causes you to sin, cut it off. It is better for you to enter life crippled than to have two feet and be thrown into hell. And if your eye causes you to sin, pluck it out. It is better for you to enter the kingdom of God with one eye than to have two eyes and be thrown into hell, where the worm does not die, and the fire is not quenched." (Mark 9:43-48, NIV)

Now, I respectfully urge those of you who find yourself getting offended or put off by these words to make every effort to *humble yourself!* Jesus loves us so much that he gave us the *truth!* And you know as well as I do, even as human beings, only people who genuinely love you will tell you the truth, even if it stings a little. What Jesus is saying in the above mentioned passage is subject to interpretation, but you must use your spiritual eyes and spiritual ears to *discern* His spiritual meaning. It is better to lose something that you consider vital or valuable in this life on Earth if that thing is causing you to miss the mark and sin, and enter eternal life in heaven, rather than to hold on to that thing that is leading you to commit sinful acts, and go to hell. (Now, that's what I call, "laying it down." In other words, I can't make it any plainer for you than that.)

Depending on the stage that you are in (with respect to life's various stages), the element of removing ungodly distractions will undoubtedly manifest itself in different forms. It might be that in order to hear God's voice, you need to distance yourself from the same group of friends that you go out and party with on the weekend. Or perhaps, it's putting some distance between you and your partner in a relationship that has every element attached to it *except* your edification in spirituality. It could be a nagging wife or an overbearing husband. It could be a job that has beat you down emotionally and spiritually to the point of negatively affecting your health. It could be a number of things. But, the point is that sometimes God has to get you alone, away from the nonsense and the distractions in order for you to actually *hear* what it is that He has to say to you.

The point is fundamental. Just look at the word "*h**ear***" God put the word "*ear*" in the center of your "*h**ear***" so you could "*hear*" him. Your heart condition determines your hearing condition. A cluttered heart results in clogged ears. Consider a few short scriptures. All are set in the time period of Jesus Christ and illustrate an act of Jesus speaking (or teaching something of great importance) and His followers listening. The key focal point is on the common element of solitude (*i.e.* physical removal) that is present in each of the following examples.

"…As a result, *Jesus* could no longer enter a town openly but *stayed* outside *in lonely places. Yet the people still came to him* from everywhere." (Mark 1:45, NIV).

*"Jesus went up on a mountainside and called to him those he wanted, and they came to him.* He appointed twelve – designating them apostles – that they might be with him and that he might send them out to preach and to have authority to drive out demons." (Mark 3:14-15, NIV).

"With many similar parables Jesus spoke the word to them, as much as they understand. He did not say anything to them without using a parable. *But when he was alone with his own disciples, he explained everything.*" (Mark 4:33-34, NIV).

"The apostles gathered around Jesus and reported to him all they had done and taught. Then, *because so many people were coming and going* that they did not even have a chance to eat, *he said to them,*

*"Come with me by yourselves to a quiet place* and get some rest." *So they went away by themselves in a boat to a solitary place."* (Mark 6:30-32).

"After six days *Jesus took Peter, James and John with him and led them up a high mountain, where they were all alone.* There he was transfigured before them...Then a cloud appeared and enveloped them, and *a voice came* from the cloud: 'This is my Son, whom I love. *Listen* to him!'" (Mark 9:2; 9:7).

"Once when Jesus was praying *in private* and his disciples were with him, *he asked* them, 'Who do the crowds say I am?'" (Luke 9:18).

This concept will not be completely foreign to a lot of you. It is no secret that one's ability to concentrate on something greatly increases in the absence of distractions. Well, it is no different with your walk with God. For many of us, there needs to be a physical displacement from our current environment in order for God to really get our attention. Now here is the caveat.

This period of isolation may result in a time of loneliness and hardship for some people. In other words, there may be a price to pay for seeking God with all you heart that comes in the form of solitary moments. However, it is important to realize that when you feel that you have hit "rock bottom" in any given situation, this moment in time doesn't merely mark the end of a downward spiraling painful situation in your life. The difficult trial or tribulation concurrently represents an opportunity for God to get your undivided attention through the pain and suffering that was caused by the humbling, trying experience. The Bible so poignantly tells us to:

"Endure hardship as discipline; God is treating you as sons. For what son is not disciplined by his father? No discipline seems pleasant at the time, but painful. Later on, however, it produces a harvest of righteousness and peace for those who have been trained by it." (*See,* Hebrews 12:7-11, NIV)

When God speaks, his instructions will require that you take heart and have courage! Remind yourself daily that God doesn't leave us stranded or alone, but rather he offers to us his promise, "Never will I leave you, nor forsake you." (Hebrews 13:5, NIV). As a result of trusting and depending on His promise that He will never leave us nor forsake us, our *faith* in His word undergirds our *courage* to obey His voice. Conversely, we can obey His voice with *courage* as a result of our *faith* in His word.

In regard to *your* life, only you are an authority on the things, and people, that are influencing you to either sin, and miss the mark that God has set for you, or miss the mark that you have set for yourself! I am telling you these things from a place of love. You cannot live your life in "people-bondage." It takes a measure of courage to take a stand for yourself concerning the boundaries you need to set on friendships, acquaintances, and activities in your life. It takes courage! It's not always easy. But one way of knowing that God has spoken to you (perhaps regarding certain people in your life) is that His instruction will often require courage *on your part.*

To provide a personal example that may illustrate my own willingness to be courageous in following God's plan for my life, I left family and friends behind in the United States, and came to work, live, create and run a business, and write a book in Shenzhen, China[6].

---

6. Shenzhen is a city of sub-provincial administrative status in southern China's Guangdong province, situated immediately north of Hong Kong. *See,*

Before you become too alarmed, I should mention that I am no stranger to international travel and have lived and worked in several countries around the world. The difference, however, is that I did so previously prior to giving my life to the Lord. My experience in coming to Christ happened while I was in the United States, and I received a Word *from* God that, in so many words, gave me a clear set of instructions. God spoke to me in a dream. And you know as well as I do, dreams can be absolutely crazy all by themselves! But, after developing my faith over an extended period of time, I learned to do exactly what I have been telling you to do throughout this book. I learned to take the happenings of a particular dream, view them through a spiritual lens using my spiritual mind, and discern what it is that God is telling me to do. *All dreams are not spiritual dreams,* but some of them are.

Again, many of you may be skeptical of what I am saying and that's ok. But, chances are that if you have read this far, you have given some credence to the things I am telling you. *God speaks to us in dreams.* Instead of the word "dream," the Bible uses the word, "visions." On many occasions throughout the Bible, there were several notable Biblical figures that had "visions" come to them while they were asleep including, but not limited to, Abraham, Jacob, and Joseph. We can reasonably infer that these "visions" are synonymous with, what is modernly and commonly referred to as, dreams.

I strongly urge that you don't be so quick to merely dismiss and discard your dreams as some "crazy" string of images that pop into your head while you are asleep. Many of you wake up in the

*Wikipedia: Shenzhen, China.*

morning and remember that you definitely dreamt *something* the night before, but you can't remember what it is that you dreamt! Well, I'm here to tell you to make the effort to *remember your dreams*. Don't simply dismiss them as unimportant. Don't always attribute them to some horror movie that you saw the night before (although I admit, that could be the source if you are into watching scary movies). Write your dreams down. Work with them. As you read God's Word and develop a relationship with him, your faith grows. As your faith grows, you are able to decipher the difference between a spiritual dream and a "common" dream. There *is* a difference. And because you have immersed yourself in God's Word, you become familiar with how he speaks. This gives you a familiarity with his voice. Once your faith reaches a certain level, there are instances where you can spiritually discern, or interpret, the meaning of certain spiritual dreams, by faith.

In my case, as my Word level increased, my faith level increased. In regard to dreams, I began to discipline myself to remember the dream the next morning. Since I was already in the habit of taking notes during Bible study, it was not a far stretch for me to also write down the factual circumstances of certain dreams where I felt God may have been trying to tell me something. Now think about it. At that point, what would I have had sitting in front of me on a piece of paper that uncannily resembled exactly what you and I have already discussed in this book? Essentially, after the recording of each dream (on a piece of paper) that I deemed to be spiritual, I had a short paragraph or two filled with factual happenings (*i.e.* natural context) that I could look at and *identify*, *extract*, and *express*

the *real issue(s)* underlying the dream, but using *spiritual language.*
Sound familiar? It should be familiar to you because that is one
of the key foundational principles to the 7-Pillar Model for Daily
Living expressed throughout this book. Identify and express the
real issue (or, root issue) concealed in any factual context, or
problem, and express it using spiritual language. This is the process
you must engage if you are ever going to escalate in your faith to
the point of discerning God's message for you through dreams. As
you practice it more and more, and continue to get closer to God,
your confidence in what God is telling you to do will increase.
(But I digress back to my own personal experience whereby God's
instruction to me required courage, on my part.)

In the midst of seeking God diligently and earnestly through the
tumultuous situation in which I found myself involving supporting
a loved one through the crime of rape, and the additional ongoing
criminal fraud being committed against her and her family, and
after approximately two years of dealing with the deeply-rooted
psychological effects that had manifested themselves *in her* in some
way, shape, or form, I had a life-altering dream. At this juncture,
the description of the actual images and events in the dream, in
the natural sense, is unimportant[7]. What is of importance is that
through my increasing faith, I was able to spiritually discern what
God was telling me to do. There were three simple instructions:

Get up and go. Leave the country. For I will be with you.

When you get there, an angel of the Lord will tell you where
to go, and what to do.

---

7. For specifics of the dream, see Section 3 entitled, "When God speaks to
you, it will line up with his written Word."

Be *blameless* in my sight

Remember, this is what the Lord told *me* to do. I ask you to recall the following principle. There is *power* tied to God's voice, *if you* (1) can engage God's word long enough to hear His voice, and (2) *obey* what He told *you* to do! That is a detail that is not minor and that I must take time to acknowledge. For example, an attempt by "John" to carry out what God told "Peter" to do will not produce the same end result for "John" as it will for "Peter." You must obey what God told *you* to do. That is why it is imperative to build and maintain your own personal relationship with the Lord. There are no shortcuts.

Continuing with my example, it was during this time period (in which I had the spiritual dream) that I had been entertaining the idea of leaving the country and working abroad anyways. In years past, I had already worked in Rome, Italy in the field of international law for Italy's Alternative Dispute Resolution Center, and also in the Patagonia region of Chile in the realm of education for the Government of Chile's Ministry of Education. These two examples are representative of a myriad of experiences that I've been blessed with living and working outside of the United States of America. The reason why I am providing this background information is to remind you that *God knows who we are.* He knows what talents, gifts, and interests, he has equipped you with from birth. For me, at this exact point in my life, the spiritual dream to which I am referring was directly in line with who I am, who I have always been, and where God was about to take me.

Don't forget. We are talking about *courage in relation to hearing God's voice*. How many of you know that *one idea from God can change your life*? It may be an idea for a new business or simply a revelation concerning the use of a talent or skill that you already possess. For me, I have always been a writer. But I had never written anything that directly (or indirectly) glorified God. Maybe some of you can relate to this. I had written poems for at least ten years prior to the date this book was published - poems that were, in my humble opinion, heartfelt and unique and which were inspired by travel, love, a lost love, friendship, or a simple wistful state of mind. I have written poems in English, Spanish, and Italian, in Spain, Italy, Bermuda, and New York (to name a few), and just kept them in a beat-up, raggedy, old travel journal. Professionally, I had written numerous judicial case orders for criminal court and civil court matters which have reflected complex legal analysis and have served as the foundation for various case dispositions in federal district court. Similarly, I had written almost every kind of legal brief (or motion) inherent to class action / complex litigation in the field of employment law. But never before had a written *anything* that glorified God, and as a by-product, that also profited me spiritually, emotionally, mentally and financially, along the way. You see, this book is not the product of my own vision. This book is not the realization of an idea that I can claim as my own. Not in the slightest did it happen that way. This book is nothing more than a by-product of my time spent learning about God and serving him. Please listen carefully.

When I reached a low point emotionally under the weight of all that was happening in my life, I had nowhere else to turn but to God. I had already been humbled through events that required physically leaving my family and friends by moving from one city to another, voluntarily resigning from a *good* job *during* an economic downturn, and leaving a brand-new condominium apartment less than sixty days from the inception of the contractual lease obligation. I made these life-changing decisions with an eye towards enduring the next indefinite number of months serving as the emotional backbone for a loved one who had been the victim of multiple rapes in years past, but who was just facing it now. Not to mention, the loved one and I were also facing an uphill legal battle against an intricate scheme of fraudulent real estate transactions, all perpetrated by the *same individual* that committed the rape! Can you imagine? It wasn't until I began to develop spiritually that I could discern God's voice and everything became clear from that point on. Toward the end, we succeeded in revitalizing much of my friend's emotional well-being and also made monumental strides concerning the legal process. But, while still in the midst of it all, it was God who rewarded me with something much more - something that I had never dreamed of. He gave me *an idea.*

*One idea from God can change your life.* At the heart of this book is the message that I received directly from the Lord. Interestingly, writing the book became just the tip of the iceberg. He gave me an idea for a lucrative business that entailed using the natural talents that he instilled in me from birth. As the newly-formed concept began to take shape in my head and in my heart, I questioned it and whether I could actually make it happen. In response to my *lack* of faith, (and that's exactly what it was), God answered me in a way that only He could. How many of you know that God is a God of simplicity when He speaks to you? He speaks softly and simply. There is no confusion, but his words are always straightforward, yet powerful. I recall to this day sitting in my southern California apartment thinking to myself, "How can I do the things that God has put into my head?" Then, God responded to me in the softest and simplest way and said,

"*Be you, for Me.*"

To some people, that may not mean much. But to me, it meant everything. Rather than allowing a seed of *fear* to incubate in my mind, God's words gave me confidence to proceed. In other words, I went forward in *courage*. Do you remember that I told you that I had been writing practically my entire life, for various reasons whether personal or professional? Well, think about it. Now, in writing this book for the purpose of growing the kingdom of God and helping others who may find themselves in a place of despair, I'm simply doing what I've always done, except I'm doing it for him!

"*Be you, for Me.*"

Instead of using my law school education and business savvy to merely bring home a paycheck that would frequently be squandered away on excessive "fun" in the past, I have now utilized those same talents and skills to create and run an international language company entitled, Team Spirit International Ltd. (www.tsienglish.com) which specializes in offering cutting-edge English language services via interactive multimedia software solutions to international businesses, companies, and hotels around the world; and as a result, exemplifies to the people of China, Chile, Spain, Brazil, and Italy, the goodness of the Lord.

*"Be you, for Me."*

Rather than employing what many acquaintances have labeled throughout my life as a "magnetic personality" to go out carousing on the weekends in an attempt to satisfy an unquenchable desire for extracurricular activities, I display those same personality traits within the confines of being an example of how a man of God interacts and reacts in any given social setting.

This, for me, marked a significant growth in my spiritual understanding. For all of the males out there who consider themselves a "casanova" by trade, consider this small tidbit of wisdom. Who you are *for the moment*, is attributed to being *charming*. Who you are *all the time* is a reflection of your *character*. In regard to most men, being charming is often tantamount to being a "con man." It's the men of character, of love and faithfulness, who win favor and a good name in the sight of God and man.[8]

*"Be you, for Me."*

Instead of using my passion for speaking foreign languages to enact superficial displays of "cool" – such as, ordering a five course meal in Italian while dining at a quaint little restaurant on the Isle of Capri in the south of Italy, or impressing a few curious Brazilian onlookers at a local piano bar somewhere in the heart of Copacabana, Rio de Janeiro, by singing a shaky

---

8. *See*, Proverbs 3:3-4

rendition of "The Girl from Ipanema" in Portuguese – I have employed that same passion for languages to write and publish books in English, Portuguese, Spanish, Italian, and Chinese, for the purpose of trying to spread the gospel of Jesus Christ across international borders.

In short, hearing God's voice is what we should all be seeking. But it is incumbent upon us that we take heart and be courageous in obediently fulfilling the words, instructions, or message that God gives us to carry out. Before we move on to the next factor, consider the word of the Lord as it was heard by the Apostle Paul the night after he testified to his hope in the resurrection of Jesus Christ in front of the Sanhedrin[9] in Jerusalem:

"The following night the Lord stood near Paul and said, *'Take courage! As you have testified about me in Jerusalem, so you must also testify in Rome.'*" (Acts 23:11, NIV)

If we do employ that necessary courage, the *super-power* of God couples with our natural ability for a *super*-natural result that can then be perceived by the natural senses and is evident to all. If you don't believe me, just hold this book in both of your hands and squeeze it to see if it's real. It is the product of my *faith* and my *courage* in carrying out what God told me to do. And the beautiful thing is that my obedience in following his instruction will ultimately have a life-changing effect on *someone else's* life! That's how God works. He brings *you* through the fire so that you can bring somebody else through the fire. Often times, those who

---

9. In Jewish history, the Sanhedrin was the highest council of the ancient Jews, consisting of 71 members, exercising authority from the 2nd century B.C. *Dictionary.com.*

have been hurt are best situated to help somebody who is hurting, if they are willing to be an instrument for God's use. Praise God!

Now, let's move on to factor #3 regarding how you can be sure that God has spoken to you. The next factor is a good one!

## When God speaks to you, it will line up with His written Word

In my life, I have encountered many people who operate in *fear* more so than in *faith*. I must be careful not to get ahead of myself because God has given me a divine order to teaching the 7-Pillar Model for Daily Living and I must make every effort to obey that order. Everything begins with the Word of God. We engage the Word *of* God until we get a Word *from* God. We obey God's voice which engages God's power. To engage God's power in our lives, we must be able to recognize His voice. To this point, you have learned that when God speaks to you, it will require *faith*. You have also learned that when God speaks to you, it will require *courage*. Here, is where I must exercise a great measure of self-discipline and be cognizant to proceed to the third way of knowing God has spoken to you (*i.e. it will line up with His written Word*), rather than tangentially dipping into my lesson on the dangers of *fear* and allowing *fear* to resonate in our lives. *Fear* will be discussed shortly and is a lesson that you cannot afford to miss *if* you are seeking answers to the pain and/or problems in your life. I implore you, set "*fear*" aside for the moment, and remain with me in "*faith*," so that I may faithfully execute God's divine order for teaching the 7-Pillar Model for Daily Living.

As we discuss how *God's voice lines up with His written Word,* it will require your spiritual eyes and spiritual ears to be fully operational, guiding you, by faith. This will be fun and interesting. I say that because every reader of this book is their own individual person. Every reader has their own set of issues, problems, situations, responsibilities, thoughts, feelings, obstacles, and challenges in life. Additionally, different people process information differently. To our credit as human beings, we can be different in so many ways, yet so similar at the same time. For example, many of you already had an established belief in God prior to being introduced to the 7-Pillar Model for Daily Living. Many of you may talk to God and hear from God on a regular basis, read the Bible, go to church, or just consider yourselves to be spiritual by nature. These are all possible similarities. On the other hand, based on the fact that this book was published in English, Spanish, Chinese, Portuguese, and Italian (and sold in various countries throughout the world), the exact same group of people that I just mentioned may claim diverse differences in regard to their country of origin, native language, or personality traits. Here is the point. *Humble yourself* to focus on the similarities that exist between you and me. Like it or not, they exist because God created us all.

Join me in a creative exercise that will display my intended message to you regarding God's voice and His *written* Word. I am going to share with you some specific instances that I believe, by faith, God has spoken to me. Contextual learning is learning at its finest and this exercise will provide plenty of context to which you may, or may not, relate. Remember, when you are given any factual circumstances in the natural sense, always use your spiritual eyes and spiritual ears to identify, extract, and express the real underlying issue using spiritual language. If you do this, I guarantee that you will find more similarities than differences as you engage the following exercise. Here we go.

Ever since I made the commitment to follow the Lord and live my life according to His Word, I have had a new outlook on the interpretation of dreams. As I explained in previous sections, God speaks to us in dreams. Often we dismiss them as "crazy" images that have no further meaning or implication other than we shouldn't have watched that scary movie the night before. (I don't know why but the very thought of someone having a nightmare because they went against their better judgment and watched a horror movie that they *knew* would probably give them a nightmare is a bit humorous). As we have seen on several biblical occasions, however, dreams are often God's way of speaking to us. Essentially, dreams are no different than the parables that Jesus told to his followers which are found throughout the gospels of Matthew, Mark, Luke, and John. Dreams are stories with characters, places, and occurrences that most people would agree have a deeper and more profound meaning attached. Unfortunately, dreams sometimes appear to us to have no apparent logic or reason. They may be sporadic, jumping from scene to scene. Sometimes our dreams include people from our distant past that have somehow remained in our subconscious mind. Other times, dreams include powerful, yet frightening events that cause you to question whether you should have, indeed, eaten that steak sandwich at

1:30 in the morning before going to bed. Admittedly, dreams are difficult to rationalize completely. But, I am convinced of one thing. God speaks to some people through dreams.

I don't know about you, but I dream rather frequently. It was during my period of difficulty (which I have talked about at length in previous pages regarding providing emotional support for a loved one who was the victim of sexual abuse), that I began to have certain dreams that were indubitably distinct from the norm. At this point, I was submerging myself in reading God's Word. To be clear, over an approximate four-month period, I read the Bible from start to finish, (Genesis to Revelation) excluding a few pages. Three months into my reading, I began to have dream sequences which, by faith, I deemed to be God trying to tell me something specific. Significantly, I recall that I had turned to reading the Bible because I was in agony emotionally and seeking solace from a higher power. In hindsight, it was the best decision I ever made.

After three months into reading the Bible and watching a few Christian television shows regularly, I had developed the habit of recording scriptures and related notes on paper. (I cannot overemphasize the importance of writing things down! Imagine if the Apostle Paul decided that he didn't feel like recording by hand his thoughts and experiences concerning the gospel of Jesus Christ. We wouldn't have 70% of the New Testament and 40% of the Bible! (If I were you, I wouldn't quote those statistics publicly as my math skills may be a bit "fuzzy," but you get the point). If it's in your head, or especially in your heart, write it down.

After each dream, I did the following two things systematically:

I recorded the dream sequence on a piece of paper, to the best of my memory

I wrote down what I *heard in my heart* in regard to the dream's meaning

As I continued growing spiritually in God's Word and receiving the knowledge and understanding that comes as a result thereof, I was able to reconcile the dreams with the actual Word of God. In other words, as I continued to meditate on God's Word and focused on the wisdom-filled messages that are found throughout the Bible, I could compare my *spiritual interpretation* of each dream with God's *written* Word. Don't forget the title of factor #3:

"When God speaks to you, it will *line up with His written Word.*"

First, I want you to read through the facts of the dream sequences below. Remember, dreams are simply images in your mind that involve people, places, and things that our *natural* senses can perceive. For example, a man, a woman, a tree, a house, etc. We have all seen a man, a woman, a tree, or a house. It's a story, a parable, involving images that are familiar to your natural senses. Also, remember that often times dreams are not logical to your natural senses. So, don't be alarmed if my dreams sound a little "left of center."

Second, read my *interpretation* of each dream. Remember, each interpretation is a product of using my spiritual eyes and spiritual ears. Each interpretation is a result of identifying and expressing the real (or, root) issue using spiritual language. In the end, I will demonstrate to you just what I have been telling you from the beginning of this book. There is *power* tied to God's voice *if* you

(1) can engage the Word *of* God long enough to hear His voice, and (2) *obey* what He told *you* to do.

### DREAM SEQUENCE # 1
(there were *three* separate parts)

**Part 1**: I was sleeping peacefully in what appeared to be an army barracks-type facility. Although I was sleeping, I was anticipating the army Sergeant calling my name loudly (along with the other soldiers) as a wake-up call. In specific, I was expecting this commanding officer to give me my "orders" concerning the destination of my next tour of duty. Every name called prior to mine had resulted in soldiers going to the same place. I felt content with the status quo knowing that I would likely be following suit.

When the Sergeant finally called my name, the words that followed were not what I expected. She told me, *"You've been deported. You've been ordered to leave the country."* At that moment, *I felt a sense of peace.*

**Part 2:** I was in a completely different surrounding located outdoors, walking along what appeared to be the edge of a huge grassy park-like area on a calm and peaceful day. Separating the pathway that I was walking along and the actual park was a fence approximately 6 feet in height.

Suddenly, I noticed that my grandfather (who had recently passed away four months earlier) was walking towards my direction, but on the other side of the fence. When the fence came to an end, I hugged him and talked to him for awhile and it was a peaceful meeting. Then he motioned with his arm pointing in a certain direction and accompanied his pointing with these words…

"*Go to the other side. When you get there, ask for my brother* (name omitted). *Once you find him, walk north with him and ask him about his son.*"

**Part 3:** I arrived at the location to which my grandfather directed me to go. Once I was inside the building, I noticed that there were four people sitting on a couch. After determining which person I was supposed to talk to, I helped him stand and began to walk with him.

Immediately, I noticed that the man I was walking next to was from a previous dream (*i.e.* I knew him and he knew me). This is what he said to me as we walked.

"*I remember you. You came and asked me for advice before, but I couldn't help you then because I wasn't in a place in my life where I could give advice to help someone else.*"

*End of Dream Sequence # 1*

### Spiritual Interpretation of Dream Sequence # 1

(*exactly* as I recorded it the next morning)

Part I. Get up, and go – God will be with you.

Part II. An angel of the Lord will tell you where to go, and what to do.

Part III. You can't help anybody if you're not living righteously. Be sure you are living as God wants you to live, so you'll have the confidence – when the moment presents itself – to help others who come to you in need. Be blameless.

*End of Spiritual Interpretation, Dream # 1*

Right now, I want you to understand something that I deem noteworthy. Draw an imaginary timeline in your head. First, I began reading the Bible. After three months, I had this three-part dream sequence and subsequently wrote the spiritual interpretation, but *I hadn't yet finished* reading the Bible. Now, pay close attention.

### WHEN GOD SPEAKS TO YOU, IT WILL LINE UP WITH HIS *WRITTEN* WORD

Open your Bible to the Book of Acts in the New Testament. Specifically, turn to Acts 22:10-11, 14-16. The scripture reflects the moment that Saul (later known as the Apostle Paul) first heard God's voice while he was traveling on the road to Damascus. Note that the first verse is Saul speaking, responding to God's voice with a question of his own. (Interestingly, earlier in the book we talked about Acts 22:6-9 where the *light* seen by Saul and his companions represented *"hope,"* but God's voice, heard only by Saul, represented *"substance"*). Take a second to quickly glance at my spiritual interpretation of Dream #1 to refresh your memory. Then, see for yourself if *it lines up* in any way *with God's written Word* in Acts 22:10-16, found directly below:

(10) " 'What shall I do, Lord?' I asked.

" *'Get up,'* the Lord said, *'and go into Damascus. There you will be told all that you have been assigned to do.'*

(11) My companions led me by the hand into Damascus, because the brilliance of the light had blinded me.

(14) "Then he said: 'The God of our fathers has chosen you to know his will and to see the Righteous One and to hear words

from his mouth. (15) You will be his witness to all men of what you have seen and heard. (16) And now what are you waiting for? Get up, be baptized and wash your sins away, calling on his name.'

Let's be clear. I do not mean to suggest that I am in any way on par with the Apostle Paul. That is not my intent. That would violate the first rule that I posed to you when you started this journey. *Humble yourself.* However, what I am suggesting to you is that as surely as God spoke to Saul, God spoke to me (and he can speak to you). The Bible says, "Jesus Christ is the same yesterday and today and forever." (Hebrews 13:8, NIV). It also says that, "God does not show favoritism." (*See,* Acts 10:34, NIV).

*Stay with me! You can't miss this!* I want you to follow the process, step-by-step:

At the time of the dream, I had been engaging the Word of God diligently and consistently for an extended period of time, meditating on many of God's promises and amazing works found throughout His Word.

By faith, I heard His voice in a dream that I ascertained to be a spiritual dream.

I wrote down the facts of the dream (using natural language). By faith, I then interpreted God's message to me using my spiritual knowledge and understanding of His Word, identifying and expressing the real issues (*i.e.* faith, obedience, power) using spiritual language.

In confidence (remember: "faith" is simply a level of confidence), I *confirmed* that, indeed, it was God speaking to me through a spiritual dream. The confirmation was that my interpretation of the dream (which consisted of God's instructions for my life), was directly in line with his *written* Word. (Interestingly enough, it wasn't until months *after* I had written my interpretation of the dream on paper that I one day took note of the key scripture in the book of Acts!)

Now, take a closer look with your spiritual eyes and ears and see for yourself!

### SPIRITUAL INTERPRETATION *(IN LINE WITH)* GOD'S WRITTEN WORD

*Get up, and go – God will be with you.*
" 'Get up,' the Lord said, 'and go… (Acts 22:10, NIV)

*An angel of the Lord will tell you where to go, and what to do.*
"There you will be told all that you have been assigned to do.'" (Acts 22:10, NIV)

"See, I am sending an angel ahead of you to guard you along the way and to bring you to the place I have prepared. Pay attention to him and listen to what he says." (Exodus 23:20-21, NIV)

*You can't help anybody if you're not living righteously. Be sure you are living as God wants you to live, so you'll have the confidence – when the moment presents itself – to help others who come to you in need. Be blameless.*

"The God of our fathers has chosen you to know his will and to see the Righteous One and to hear words from his mouth. You will be his witness to all men of what you have seen and heard. And now what are you waiting for? Get up, be baptized and wash your sins away, calling on his name.'" (Acts 22:14-16, NIV)

Some of you may be surprised, or at the very least, intrigued. I'm not surprised if you are intrigued, but I am intrigued if you are surprised. God is real and He has given us his Spirit. That's right.

You have God's Spirit inside of you! Here is another scripture that is a powerful scripture to recite daily.

*"God has not given us a spirit of fear, but of power, and of love, and of a sound mind"* (2 Timothy 1:7, NIV) Emphasis added.

Again, I remind you not to stumble over insignificant minutia such as which version of the Bible you may have in your possession. The message is the same. God's Holy Spirit will lead you through the most difficult of times. What did you think I was referring to each and every time I have instructed you to "use your spiritual eyes and spiritual ears" when assessing and addressing a "natural" problem? Translation: *Allow your Spirit,* God's Holy Spirit which is also in you, *to guide you."* You have a Spirit of power, love, and of sound thinking! "Sound thinking" simply means that your thoughts line up with God's written Word.

People don't realize the God-given power that lies within them just beneath the surface! Consider this. If you took a random survey of 100 people (in any one of several countries around the world) and asked them the simple, but thought-provoking, question, "do you believe in God," it wouldn't be surprising if 50% answered affirmatively. Many people do believe in God, even if they don't outwardly express it in an obvious manner. Yet, when we, as human beings, face times of sadness, despair, loneliness, and heartache, often times we don't realize the strength that we have inside of us. Read it for yourself and write it down.

*"We have not received the spirit of the world but the Spirit who is from God, that we may understand what God has freely given us."* (1 Corinthians 2:12, NIV) Emphasis added.

*"Don't you know that you yourselves are God's temple and that God's Spirit lives in you?"* (1 Corinthians 3:16, NIV) Emphasis added.

*"We know that we live in him and he in us, because he has given us his Spirit."* (1 John 4:16, NIV) Emphasis added.

You see, you can't realize God's power in your life, if you don't know who you are *in him*, and who *he* is *in you!* This is why everything begins with reading and meditating on the Word of God. For those of you who may be facing something difficult in your life that tends to bring *fear* upon you, I want you to pay close attention to this next point that I am going to share with you.

You now know, or are reminded, that God's Spirit lives in you because God gave it to you the day you accepted Christ as the Lord of your life. Well, *"God has not given us a spirit of fear, but of power, and of love, and of a sound mind."* (2 Timothy 1:7, KJV). You now know, or are reminded, that God's Spirit (inside of you) is of (1) power, (2) love, and (3) sound thinking. The Bible also tells us that:

*"God is love."* (1 John 4:16, NIV).

*"There is no fear in love. But perfect love drives out all fear."* (1 John 4:18, NIV).

So, what is it that I'm saying to all of you (my dear readers) who allow stress to come in and rule your life to the point of reaching depression or anger or extreme hurt? What I'm telling you is that because of God's Spirit, which he has freely given to you and which is inside of you, you have the *power* to conquer *any* situation and go forward in life. Like I said, any random survey in many countries around the world would likely reveal that at least 50% of the population believes in God. In other words, they have FAITH that God exists. Believing in God is equivalent to believing in his Word. The Bible says that, "In the beginning was the Word, and the Word was with God, *and the Word was God*" (John 1:1, NIV). If you believe in his Word, then you have faith that God's Spirit of "power, *love*, and sound thinking" is inside of you. Still standing in that same faith, you meditate on God's Word that says, "*...perfect love drives out all fear.*" And where does that leave you? What does all of this mean? It means the following:

You have the Spirit of God inside of you.

God's Spirit is of power, love, and sound thinking.

Your "sound thinking" means that you believe God's word.

If you have God's Word, you have God (remember, they are one and the same)

If you have God, you have "love" (remember, "God is love.")

If your love is perfected, then it drives out all fear

With no fear, you are em*power*ed to make it through *any* difficult situation.

This is who you are! A powerful, loving, sound thinking son or daughter of God! That's it. But, if you don't *know* who you are, you are susceptible to defeat by the infinite number of challenges that we deal with on a daily basis as human beings.

Now, that was a prelude to our later discussion on *fear*. For now, I want you to proceed onward to "Dream Sequence #2" and the subsequent *spiritual interpretation* thereof. By now, you should understand that *spiritual interpretation* is made possible through allowing God's Spirit (which is in you) to lead you and guide you to understanding and wisdom. As you move through the following pages, you will continue to see the process of taking scenarios, problems, dreams, or situations (that are perceivable by our natural senses), and identifying and expressing the real (or root issue(s)) using spiritual language. In doing so, your faith will help you determine when God is speaking to you, through spiritual dreams, or otherwise, because the spiritual interpretation will line up with his *written* Word. Please remember in humility, that dreams, in the natural sense, are often illogical and perhaps even, unreasonable. But, just like many parables, stories, or even ancient proverbs, there is a deeper underlying message for those who can decipher it.

## DREAM SEQUENCE # 2

(there were *two* separate parts)

**Part 1:** This dream did not take place in any specific indoor or outdoor location. The mainstay of the dream was that I was fighting against an enemy. The enemy, however, had a supernatural power to appear and disappear whereas I did *not* possess this power.

Both the enemy and I were equipped with weapons. To my recollection, the weapons resembled swords of a notable length and weight. There were no other people in the dream besides me and the enemy I was fighting.

When the enemy exercised his power to disappear, he could reappear either in front of me, or behind me. In other words, there were times that I could see him and other times when I could not. However, at all times, one thing was constant. The enemy was literally trying to take my head off with his sword. He meant not only to harm me, but to destroy me.

**Part 2:** As I fought the enemy, I fought boldly and fared well every time he was standing directly in front of me. Then, he would simply disappear and usually remain invisible from my sight for a few moments and reappear behind me. Every time the enemy reappeared behind me, I did not perceive he was there with my physical sight. I did not see him. But, someone or something would tell me that he was there, and I would "duck" or "stoop" just in time to avoid a swing of his sword that would have decapitated me.

By the end of the dream, I came to depend on the voice or feeling that told me when the enemy was behind me, and when to "duck" or "stoop" to avoid the swinging of his destructive sword.

*End of Dream Sequence # 2*

## SPIRITUAL INTERPRETATION OF DREAM SEQUENCE # 2

(*exactly* as I recorded it the next morning)

*Faith*: (Fight Your Fight with Faith)

Use a Visible Faith Against An Invisible Enemy

*Have faith in God!*

You must *display* a *fighting faith* in God. He will enable you.

He will empower you to fight an enemy that is seen and unseen.

The most powerful forces are unseen. But *fighting faith* is the key.

Do not be afraid, nor ashamed, to *show* your faith; to act *in* faith; to act *on* faith.

Your faith can help others. Your faith can lead others. Your faith is your best and only weapon to fight the enemy who you cannot always see (or never see).

The enemy is trying to destroy you; to hurt you; to kill you. Make no mistake. But you have authority, strength, and *faith* in God – a weapon that will allow you to evade the enemy's tactics and win; defeat him.

There are levels of danger. There are different battles. Fight the Right Fight.

Fight a fight of faith

Fight your fight with faith

Faith is your weapon. Trust in the Lord to lead you, to tell you how to move, when to move, what is coming at you to harm you.

Have faith in God

Display your faith in God openly and outwardly

Listen to his voice

Fight the fight of faith; fight your fight with faith

God speaks to me in dreams. You know it's him because it lines up with his written Word. But, if you don't know his Word, by meditating on it day and night, you can't recognize his Voice. (Without his voice ⇨ no power).

*End of Spiritual Interpretation, Dream # 2*


Again, what is our focus?

When God speaks to you, it will line up with his *written* Word!

This is going to be good. Stay with me, please. You're going to love this. I'm going to lay it out step–by–step so that you may follow without confusion. Open your Bible and turn to the book of Ephesians in the New Testament. Specifically, turn to Ephesians 6:11-12, and read the following scripture from the Word of God, which states:

"Put on the full armor of God so that you can take your stand against the devil's schemes. *For our struggle is not against flesh and blood, but against the rulers, against the authorities, against the powers of this dark world and against the spiritual forces of evil in the heavenly realms.*" (Ephesians 6:11-12, NIV) Emphasis added.

As stated earlier, whichever version of the Bible you may have in your possession is unimportant because God's message is the same. But, for this particular point, I want to include a different version of the same scripture you just read. Take a look below.

"Put on the whole armor of God so that you may be able to stand firm against the devil's strategies. *For our struggle is not against human opponents, but against rulers, authorities, cosmic powers in the darkness around us, and evil spiritual forces in the heavenly realm.*" (Ephesians 6:11-12, ISV) Emphasis added.

Inevitably, there will be a diverse cross-section of people reading this book. Some of you are well-establish in your faith and belief in the Lord and some of you may never have given your spirituality a second thought. Others of you fall somewhere in the middle. Whichever category you fall into is irrelevant. What is important is that you are being exposed to the hard and fast spiritual truth. That is what matters. There is nothing better in this life than knowing that you have heard the truth.

When I referred to "the enemy" in Dream Sequence # 2, I was referring to Satan. Whether you choose to label him "the enemy," "the evil one," "Satan," or "the devil," the labels are interchangeable and reference the dark force(s) that are unseen, but that are real, which battle us in our everyday existence. Figuratively speaking, some of you who are reading this book have been to hell and back in your respective lives. Maybe it was a situation of being sexually abused in the same manner as my loved one that I have referenced throughout this book. Perhaps you (or someone you know) are facing a life-threatening illness that has turned your life upside down. Or, maybe some of you have spent *years* (we won't say how many) with a relationship partner who has treated you terribly, but you've stayed out of complacency, habit, or an inability to find the inner-strength and courage to move on and go forward. It could be a number of things. Well, I am here to tell you something that is pivotal to your spiritual understanding and future. These negative forces do not simply come into your life by happenstance. It's not a fluke. It's not by chance. Neither is it a mere coincidence that certain "bad" things happen. There is a devil, an evil one, an enemy, Satan, and his sole purpose is to wreak as much havoc in your life as he possibly can in an effort to deter you from knowing and following God's truth, and to ultimately destroy you.

Whether you choose to listen to wisdom is not my responsibility. My obedience comes in the form of spreading God's gospel truth with as much fervor as I can muster. But, as I have been telling you from the beginning, there is a spiritual world, and there is a natural world. There are spiritual senses, and there are natural senses. There is spiritual language, and there is natural language. The spiritual world is the parent. The natural world is the child. The spiritual drives the natural. The natural is subject to the spiritual.

(If you need to take a break, get a drink of water, go to restroom, make a phone call, now is the time because I am going to stay on this subject until *you* can recite it in your sleep! That's how important it is.)

The natural world is subject to the spiritual world. This is the precise reason why I am teaching you that no true believer in Jesus Christ is ever stranded or stuck in a heartbreaking situation that has depleted your very health, confidence, will to live, or positive outlook on life. You see, every difficult, hurtful situation that happens to you in life is not something that you have to put up with, accept, or live with as the norm. If you hate your job because the work is meaningless or because you are treated unfairly, that is a "natural" problem that can be changed with spiritual weapons.

### Women: listen carefully!

If you are a woman who, at any point in your life, has been raped, abused, molested, mistreated, or subjected to violence, sexual or otherwise, *you can do something about it.* The actual event that transpired in your life surrounding the abuse that happened in the natural sense is nothing more than Satan trying to break you. *fight the right fight!* Remember, the Word of God!

*"For our struggle is not against flesh and blood, but against the rulers, against the authorities, against the powers of this dark world and against*

*the spiritual forces of evil in the heavenly realms."* (Ephesians 6:11-12, NIV) Emphasis added.

On a daily basis, Satan tries to knock you down, discourage you, depress you, taunt you, hinder you, distract you, block you, mislead you, and above all, put *fear* in you. The fight that you are in, *daily*, is not against some man or woman with whom you are physically wrestling in the natural sense. Many of you may have the worst day ever by simply waking up, going to work, and coming home without any *physical* confrontation whatsoever, as our natural eyes and ears would perceive a physical fight. Truth be told, it is your mental, emotional, and psychological state of being that gets "worn out" by simply waking up, going to work, and returning home.

So, if you are not fighting with your actual arms and fists, then what exactly is the struggle? Who is the fight against? The answer is a spiritual one. As the Bible so clearly warns us:

*"...our struggle is not against flesh and blood, but against the rulers, against the authorities, against the powers of this dark world and against the spiritual forces of evil in the heavenly realms."* (Ephesians 6:11-12, NIV) Emphasis added.

If you are in a *spiritual* battle, you need *spiritual weapons!* If you would humor me for one moment and think back to the early pages of this book, I gave you the principle upon which the 7-Pillar Model for Daily Living is built. You must learn to:

Fight the *right* fight (with Fighting Faith)

Fight your fight with Spiritual Weapons

Satan knows God's Word. But, Satan will test you to see if *you* know God's Word. He wants to see if you know who *you* are in

Christ Jesus. This is why you have to read the Bible for yourself and learn that you have a heavenly Father who has already defeated Satan! That's right. *Satan has already been defeated.* See for yourself! Open your Bible to the New Testament and read Luke 10:18-19 (NIV), and listen to what Jesus said:

(18) He replied, *"I saw Satan fall like lightening from heaven.*

(19) *I have given you authority to trample on snakes and scorpions and to overcome all the power of the enemy; nothing will harm you."*

Praise God. Jesus said, "I have given you *authority* to trample on snakes and scorpions and *to overcome all the power* of the enemy." How many of you know some snakes and scorpions in your life? (If it's your boss, and you're still at work, don't say his name out loud…wait until you get home. I don't want you blaming me because you got fired for calling your boss a snake or scorpion. That's not our focus. I'm only kidding.). What I am saying to you is that *Jesus gave you the authority over all the power of the enemy!*

At this point, I turn your attention to two very important details:

Number 1: The *authority* that Jesus has given to you.

Number 2: What *powers does the enemy have?*

### YOUR *AUTHORITY* IN JESUS CHRIST:

After Jesus arose from his crucifixion, he appeared to eleven disciples on the mountain in the town of Galilee, where Jesus had told them to go. There, Jesus came to them and said, *"All authority in heaven and on earth has been given to me."* (*See*, Matthew 28:18, NIV). You see, Jesus, God's only begotten Son, was sent by God, the Father. When Adam sinned in the Garden of Eden, Adam's *dis*obedience to God brought sin into the world. But, Jesus, through his obedience, brought righteousness to the world. The Bible tells us in the following scriptures:

(18) "Consequently, just as the result of one trespass was condemnation for all men, so also the result of one act of righteousness was justification that brings life for all men.

(19) For just as through the disobedience of the one man the many were made sinners, so also through the obedience of the one man the many will be made righteous." (Romans 5:18-19, NIV)

(31) "But the world must learn that I love the Father and that I do *exactly* what my Father has commanded me." (John 14:31, NIV)

Here is the point. Adam, the first man, was flesh and blood, like you and me. Adam (and Eve) faced temptation, just like you and me. Adam believed the contradiction that Satan proposed and consequently disobeyed God's instruction in the Garden of Eden, thus giving the devil a foothold in the minds of mankind from that point on. Through God's eternal love, he sent his only begotten son as the messiah, Jesus Christ (our Savior). Jesus, the man, was also flesh and blood, like you and me. Jesus faced temptation, just like you and me[10]. However, the difference between Jesus and Adam is that Jesus, in the face of temptation by the devil, was without sin. In other words, Jesus didn't buy the devil's contradiction. Jesus didn't fall for the devil's lies and schemes. Jesus was obedient to God's Word and to the purpose for which he was sent. Thus, when he died on the cross, he fulfilled the very purpose for which God sent him. Three days later, after his burial, Jesus rose to life! He defeated death! No

---

10. To read about the temptation of Jesus, see Matthew 4:1-11.

power on Earth or in the spiritual realm was over Him. This is why he said the following:

*"All authority in heaven and on earth has been given to me." (See,* Matthew 28:18).

"I will not speak with you much longer, for the prince of this world is coming. *He has no hold on Me." (See,* John 14:30).

But, here's the jewel that people fail to realize as they struggle with their addictions, their hurt, their pains, their depression, their anger, their sadness.

*Jesus gave His authority to us!*

Within you lies a Spirit of *power* that is unmatched by any force in existence! It's the authority that is in Jesus Christ that he gave to you. You see, the devil knows this! And the first thing the devil wants to see is if *you* know who you are in Jesus Christ. Take the following example. In Genesis, chapter 3, the devil (in the form of a serpent) cunningly deceived Eve to partake of the fruit that God had forbidden Adam and Eve to eat. But, focus for a moment on what the devil told Eve as a rationalization for why she *should* eat from the forbidden tree. After Eve tells the devil that God instructed them not to eat from the tree "in the middle of the garden," lest they die, take note of the devil's contradictory reply (or in other words, his lying response):

"You will not surely die," the serpent said to the woman.

For God knows that when you eat of it your eyes will be opened, *and you will be like God,* knowing good and evil. (*See,* Genesis 3:2-5, NIV) Emphasis added.

Note that Satan told Eve that the reason God didn't want for her or Adam to eat the fruit was because God knew that upon doing so, she (and Adam) would then "*be like God,*" knowing good and evil. But, wait just one minute! The Bible says in Genesis 1: 27:

"So God created man *in His own image,* in the image of God He created him; male and female he created them."

In other words, when Satan told Eve that God didn't want them to partake of the fruit on the reasoning that their eyes would be opened and that they would "be like God," the truth of the matter was that *they were already like God,* because God created Adam and Eve *in His own image!* This is how the devil works. He first wants to know if *you* know who you are in Jesus Christ and the fact that you have authority over all the power of the enemy!

*What powers does the enemy have?*

First of all, understand that Satan is "the father of lies." Read how Jesus describes the devil in the New Testament, John 8:44. It reads, it pertinent part:

"He was a *murderer* from the beginning, not holding to the truth, for there is no truth in him. *When he lies he speaks his native language, for he is a liar and the father of lies.*" (*See,* John 8:44, NIV) Emphasis added.

Now, I don't know about you, but I'm not too keen on murderers and liars. This is who Jesus refers to as, "the prince of this world." Just turn on your television or pick up the latest newspaper. Death, in this world, is an everyday occurrence no matter what country you reside in. Rape, is an everyday occurrence no matter what nation you belong to. The most heinous of crimes that are committed by mankind day in and day out, on a global scale, against each other, is a mirror reflection of Satan's work in the lives of many lost souls. So, even if you have not directly been affected by the most dramatic of negative events, here is how the enemy does try to bring destruction, hurt, pain, sadness, fear, and difficulty into your life.

Always remembering that Satan is "the father of lies," these are three major ways that he tries to get to you:

- Satan has the ability to make *suggestions* to you
- seduce your *emotions* or your *feelings*
- *whisper* things to you by putting *thoughts* in your mind

Satan is limited in what he can do because he has no physical body! Therefore, he is *always trying to get some body*! His evil spirit can only do harm in the natural sense if he is able to enter a natural body. That is why he is constantly trying to attack us through thoughts, suggestions, and emotions. We will discuss *fear* and *emotions* in later chapters. For now, understand the enemy's powers and how he uses them against you.

### To the women of the world!

Remember when I told you: *"listen carefully* especially, if you are a woman who, at any point in your life, has been raped, abused, molested, mistreated, or subjected to violence, sexual or otherwise, *you can do something about it.*" I told you before that the actual event that transpired in your life surrounding the abuse that happened in the natural sense was nothing more than Satan trying to break you. But now, you understand what it means to *fight the right fight!* It's a *spiritual* fight, not a natural fight. The aftermath of the natural event that transpired involves fighting against the suggestions, thoughts, and whispers in your ear, by

Satan, that has kept you in *fear*. The enemy *lies* to you, telling you that you can't speak up; that you can't tell anyone what has happened to you; that *no one will believe you* (that's a big one). As a man who has full understanding that I have God's Spirit of love inside of me, I'm telling you the truth!

You have *authority* over *all* the power of the enemy! Authority to…

*Speak up and speak out!*

*Tell somebody!*

*Report it!* (It doesn't matter how long ago the abusive event occurred!)

*Heal!*

Get counseling

Take a self-defense / self-empowerment class!

Chase your dreams!

And do all of this in full knowledge that God has not given you a spirit of fear, but of *power*, and of *love*, and of a *sound mind*.

If you don't like the situation that you are in right now, *change it!* Take whatever problem or negative event that has happened to you in your life, and do the following:

Know that you have God's Spirit of power, love, and sound thinking inside of you.

Know that every *natural* problem has a *spiritual* root.

Know that the *spiritual realm* precedes the *natural realm*. The *spiritual realm* is the parent. The *natural realm* is the child. (God is a Spirit. He created the natural world (*i.e.* the Earth) from his spoken words, "Let there be…" the Spirit gave birth to the natural. Know this.

Take your problem (*e.g.* a tyrant boss, lack of finances, broken heart) perceivable by the natural senses, identify and express the *real issue(s)* using your spiritual eyes and spiritual ears. In other words, let the Holy Spirit inside of you, lead you and guide you.

Fight the *right* Fight by addressing the real root spiritual issue rather than focusing on the sensory-perceived natural problem.

Fight the *right* fight, with fighting faith (that means, *using spiritual weapons*)! What is your spiritual weapon? The Word of God.

The Word of God tells you to *put on the full armor of God*!

Read it for yourself and keep this scripture in your head and in your heart.

(13) "Therefore, put on the full armor of God, so that when the day of evil comes, you may be able to stand your ground, and after you have done everything, to stand.

(14) Stand firm then, with the *belt of truth* buckled around your waist, with the *breastplate of righteousness* in place,

(15) and with your feet fitted with the readiness that comes from the *Gospel of peace*

(16) In addition to all this, take up the *shield of faith* with which you can extinguish all the flaming arrows of the evil one.

(17) Take the *helmet of salvation* and the *sword of the Spirit*, which is *the word of God*

(18) And pray in the Spirit on all occasions with all kinds of prayers and requests. (*See*, Ephesians 6:13-18, NIV) Emphasis added.

You will know when God speaks to you, because it will line up with His written word. His spoken Word and His written Word are congruous. Now, if you are still with me (and I have faith that you are), take a brief look at Dream Sequence #2 again to refresh your recollection. Then, view the assessment chart and allow the Spirit to guide you in your determination of whether my *spiritual interpretation "lines up"* with God's written Word.

## DREAM SEQUENCE # 2

(Remember: there were *two* separate parts)

**Part 1:** This dream did not take place in any specific indoor or outdoor location. The mainstay of the dream was that I was fighting against an enemy. The enemy, however, had a supernatural power to appear and disappear whereas I did *not* possess this power.

Both the enemy and I were equipped with weapons. To my recollection, the weapons resembled swords of a notable length and weight. There were no other people in the dream besides me and the enemy that I was fighting.

When the enemy exercised his power to disappear, he could reappear either in front of me, or behind me. In other words, there were times that I could see him and other times when I could not. However, at all times, one thing was constant. The enemy was literally trying to take my head off with this sword. He meant not only to harm me, but to destroy me.

**Part 2:** As I fought the enemy, I fought boldly and fared well every time he was standing directly in front of me. Then, he would simply disappear and usually remain invisible from my sight for a few moments and reappear behind me. Every time the enemy reappeared behind me, I did not perceive he was there with my physical sight. I did not see him. But, someone or something would tell me that he was there, and I would "duck" or "stoop" just in time to avoid a swing of his sword that would have decapitated me.

By the end of the dream, I came to depend on the voice or feeling that told me when the enemy was behind me, and when to "duck" or "stoop" to avoid the swinging of his destructive sword.

*End of Dream Sequence # 2*

| Spiritual Interpretation (in line with) God's Written Word | |
|---|---|
| God will empower you to fight against an enemy that is *seen and unseen.*<br>Your faith is your best and only weapon to fight the enemy who you *cannot always see (or never see).* | "For our struggle is not against human opponents, but against rulers, authorities, cosmic powers in the darkness around us, and evil spiritual forces in the heavenly realm." (Ephesians 6:11-12, NIV) |
| The most powerful forces are unseen. | "Have *faith* in God." Jesus answered. "I tell you the truth, if anyone says to this mountain, 'Go, throw yourself into the sea, and does not doubt in his heart but believes that what he says will happen, it will be done for him. Therefore, I tell you whatever you ask for in prayer, believe that you have received it, and it will be yours." (Mark 11:22-24, NIV)<br><br>"…and if I have faith that can move mountains, but have not *love,* I am nothing." "And now these three remain: faith, hope, and love. But the greatest of these is *love.*" (1 Corinthians 13:2; 13:13, NIV) |

| | |
|---|---|
| The enemy is trying to *destroy* you; to *hurt* you; to **kill** you; to **deceive** you. Make no mistake. | *"He was a <u>murderer</u> from the beginning, not holding to the truth, for there is no truth in him. When he lies he speaks his native language, for <u>he is a liar</u> and the father of lies."* (John 8:44, NIV) |
| But you have **authority**, strength, and FAITH in God – a weapon that will allow you to evade the enemy's tactics and win; defeat him. | "All authority in heaven and on earth has been given to me." (Matthew 28:18, NIV)<br><br>"I have given you authority to trample on snakes and scorpions and to overcome all the power of the enemy; nothing will harm you." (Luke 10:19, NIV)<br><br>"I saw Satan fall like lightening from heaven. (Luke 10:18, NIV) |
| Your faith is your best and only weapon to fight the enemy. Faith is your weapon.<br>Fight the fight of faith;<br>Fight your fight with faith | "Take up the **SHIELD OF FAITH** with which you can extinguish all the flaming arrows of the evil one." (Ephesians 6:16, NIV)<br><br>"…and the **SWORD OF THE SPIRIT**, which is    **THE WORD OF GOD**." (Ephesians 6:17, NIV) |

I have every confidence that you are beginning to understand the profound wisdom and resultant power that is in the 7-Pillar Model for Daily Living. I hope that my clear expression and your willingness to humbly accept the message results in a similar seed planted in you, as it was planted in me. God's Word is that seed of knowledge and understanding which brings forth spiritual discernment, sound judgment, and wisdom.

As we move along to factor #4 in regard to knowing when God speaks to you, keep factors #1 through #3 in the forefront of your memory. You will know when God speaks to you because (1) it will require *faith*, (2) it will require *courage*, (3) his spoken Word *lines up with his written word*, and now number (4), it will *go against the world's way of thinking*.

### 4. WHEN GOD SPEAKS TO YOU, IT WILL *GO AGAINST THE WORLD'S WAY OF THINKING*

In life, there are two systems in operation regarding the human mentality. These two "systems of thinking" are in complete and total opposition to one another. They are contradictory by nature. The first system of thinking is known as "*God's way of thinking*" or "*the Kingdom's way of thinking.*" (For our purposes, I will use both of these monikers interchangeably). The second system of thinking is known as "*the World's way of thinking.*" Let's take a closer look at both "systems" and how each one is either in agreement with, or contradictory to, God's Word, both spoken and written.

If you live on this planet, then you are familiar with the following word: Money. In modern society, most would agree that the possession of money is fundamental to one's ability to obtain many of the basic necessities of life. These fundamental necessities for survival are not in dispute. Monetary currency (usually exchanged for labor or services) enables a person to purchase food, water, medicine and other fungible goods that are considered pertinent to the continued existence of humankind. This principle is not the topic of discussion. Rather, it is the "love of money" and its tendency to underscore the World's way of thinking that is our main focus. But, we won't stop there. We will identify a deeper root issue that escapes any person whose mindset is *not* based in the Kingdom's way of thinking. That issue is referred to as "*love versus selfishness.*"

According to the World's system of thinking, money (regardless of which country you call home), represents power. The World's system equates money with happiness. Now, you, the reader, will have to make a genuine effort as you read through this section to humble yourself. I put that challenge to you at the start of this section because a measure of self-introspection is needed when reflecting on our own mentality, desires, thoughts and feelings concerning money. Be honest. There are many of you who would readily accept a million dollars (or, the equivalent thereto depending on your country's currency) if it were offered to you, without so much as blinking an eye. Let's be *very* honest. The vast majority of you would likely consider doing something, or performing some act or feat, that is out of your normal character, habit, or routine *if* there was a substantial compensation attached to that abnormal task. Arguably, depending on your motivation, such a mentality may or may not be admirable. I do not judge anyone because I, myself, am human. The Bible clearly says, "There is only one Lawgiver and Judge, the one who is able to save and destroy. But you – who are you to judge your neighbor." (James 4:12, NIV).

However, here is the jewel that many people fail to ever realize. The *motivation(s)* for our corresponding gestures, acts, and decisions, is of prime importance to our spiritual health *and* our financial well-being! This is a very profound principle that is rooted in faith and that we will discuss thoroughly. First, you must understand what the Word says about your internal motivation(s):

"All a man's ways seem innocent to him, but *motives* are weighed by the Lord." (Proverbs 16:2, NIV) Emphasis added.

"You do not have, because you do not ask God. When you ask, you do not receive, because you ask with *wrong motives,* that you may spend what you get on your pleasures." (*See,* James 2:3-4, NIV) Emphasis added.

The World's system of thinking is rooted in its reverence of money. Money is the World's power. Money drives the World's ambitions and its motivations. Money shapes the World's plans and schemes. The World builds its dreams, its hopes, and its desires around its love of money. All you have to do is open your spiritual eyes to the World that is all around you. Turn on your television, log on to the internet, listen to the radio, read the newspaper, walk down the street and the influence of money is inescapable to the natural senses. Of course, money, in and of itself, is only a piece of paper that has a currency value attached to it. A piece of paper, by itself, is harmless. A piece of paper is without life. Rather, it is the underlying motivation of selfishness and greed that is so often attached to money that arguably is the root of all kinds of evil. The Bible says, "For money is the root of all kinds of evil." (*See,* 1 Timothy 6:10, NIV). Be aware that *selfishness* is a *key root issue* that we will discuss in greater detail in subsequent chapters. For now, you should focus on the structure. There are two systems in operation, two ways of thinking: The Kingdom of God's way of thinking and the World's way of thinking.

The Kingdom of God's way of thinking is *faith-based* and the Kingdom's power is rooted in *love*.

The World's way of thinking is *fear-based* and the World's power is rooted in *selfishness*. The Kingdom of God's power is love and faith. The World's power is money.

If you utilize your spiritual senses, your understanding of daily current events and affairs will sharpen exponentially. For example, I may not be a trained economist, but I do have knowledge and I can say with confidence on the most basic of levels that the following statement holds universal truth on a global scale: *"the World" fears an economic crisis because the resultant effect is a lack of money.* Pay close attention. Your spiritual eyes will assist you in your understanding. *The World fears* an economic crisis because the resultant effect is *a lack of money.* In many countries spanning the globe, the occurrence of a substantial economic downturn (albeit a recession or a depression) brings notable increases in despair-related deaths (suicides and homicides). Admittedly, the Western-based ideology of "capitalism" is fundamentally different than some of its counterpart ideologies practiced widely throughout the world; but, political views aside, when money becomes sparse, worries begin to rise.

The very thought of people taking their own lives (and in some instances, the lives of their family) because of a drastic impact to their finances is utterly absurd. It's sad. Specifically, I am referring to cases where people, deemed to be successful by most standards, have taken their lives because they may have lost millions of dollars, or hundreds of thousands of dollars as a result of a downturn in the economy. I'll put it into perspective. How many men, women and children in certain parts of Africa are subjected daily to substandard living conditions with scarce supplies of potable water for irrigation purposes or even to drink? If money, or a lack thereof, was the driving motivation behind whether we should harbor suicidal tendencies (let alone carry them to fruition), what would happen to a large part of the African continent? Of course, we needn't look to Africa as an example. People struggle everywhere, everyday, and don't commit suicide, but it's the underlying principle that is of interest to us.

The World's system of thinking is *fear-based*. This system of thinking is rooted in *selfishness*. The World's power is money.

Somewhere, someone will inevitably say, "Well, there are two sides to every argument." This may be true, but, remember what we're talking about here. I wrote this book as a "Model for Daily Living," a guide, (a survival kit, if you will) on how to attain true and lasting happiness and peace. Truth be told, any person who is operating within the World's system of thinking, who ends his or her own life out of the fear of not being able to provide for themselves or their family, is acting in selfishness rather than in love. Life is a gift from God. What gives anyone the right to voluntarily and prematurely end a life for fear that a lack of money will result in a life not worth living? Do you see the dangers attached to operating within the World's way of thinking in regard to its love of money? If you don't take my word for it, then simply turn on your television or log on to the internet and listen to, or read, the latest news. Money (or, "the Economy") accounts for 50% of the news. More importantly, *fear* infiltrates the airwaves traveling into people's homes and into their subconscious minds. *Fear* is the antithesis of *faith*. (For the readers who merely read that last sentence without a moment to ponder, let me say that again with more emphasis):

*Fear is the antithesis of faith*

One Bible verse tells us that,

"*Godliness with contentment is great gain.* For we brought nothing into the world and we can take nothing out of it. But if we have food and clothing, we will be content with that. People who want to get rich fall into temptation and a trap and into many foolish and harmful desires that plunge men into ruin and destruction." (*See,* 1 Timothy 6:6, NIV) Emphasis added.

Sure, who doesn't like nice clothes or fine foods? What person wouldn't choose to eat the finest meals everyday if it they could? This is not a bad thing. There is nothing negative about striving to better your position in life. Often times, it may be reflected in the car that you drive, or shoes that you wear, or foods that you eat. There is nothing wrong with that whatsoever. However, there is a fine line of which we must be cognizant. Striving to acquire riches or wealth at the expense of godliness is where many men and women fall short. Serving money can infect your way of thinking to the point of total self-destruction *and* cause a person to lose sight of God's intended meaning for their lives.

But, here is the great thing. The spiritual truth doesn't mean that God wants you to be poor, or in lack of anything! In fact, it's the complete opposite. A Bible scripture directly on point reads, *"And my God will meet all your needs according to his glorious riches in Christ Jesus."* (Phillipians 4:19, NIV). You see, God wants you to trust *him*. He wants you to love him above and beyond all earthly treasures. He wants you to have faith in *him* and *he* will provide you with all that you need in life. Consider this carefully:

"But seek *first* his kingdom and his righteousness, and all *these things* will be given to you as well." (Matthew 6:33, NIV) Emphasis added.

What do you think is meant by the words "these things?" It means that all of the material things that you may desire should come secondary to earnestly seeking God. In good consciousness, I can't tell you to an absolute certainty whether God will supply *you* with every material good that you desire because there is only one God, and as we saw earlier, *he* weighs the motivations of your heart. However, in my spiritual understanding of God's Word, I strive to practice a faith that is unwavering that God will supply *me* with *everything* that I need, and even some things that I *don't* need nor ever could have dreamt of! You see, that is an issue of *faith*, not selfishness, or greed. How about this one?

"No one can serve two masters. Either he will hate the one and love the other, or he will be devoted to the one and despise the other. You cannot serve both God and Money (Matthew 6:24, NIV).

Again, God's message is one of love and faith. Releasing your own "security blanket" is not easy for some people. When I say "security blanket," I am not referring to a sum of money. Instead, I am referring to the submission of your will to God's Word. In other words, the real issue returns to *faith* and the same spiritual principles that we have addressed throughout this book. Do you have enough *faith* to believe that what is *unseen* will generate what is *seen*? It's the same principle from before! The spiritual drives the natural. The spiritual realm is the parent; the natural realm is the child. The natural realm is subject to the spiritual realm. In other words, if my *hope* is that God will supply all of my financial needs, it is my *faith* that fills that hope. My faith in God's promise that He will supply all of my needs is what I meditate on. I put my faith in God. And if your faith is working in conjunction with love, obedience, honor, (and the rest of the Pillars found in the 7-Pillar Model for Daily Living), then you will be blessed beyond measure, financially, spiritually, emotionally, and any other kind of way that you can imagine. Let's look at one more:

"Store up for yourselves treasures in heaven, where moth and rust do not destroy, and where thieves do not break in and steal. *For where your treasure is, there your heart will be also.*" (Matthew 6:20-21, NIV) Emphasis added.

*"For where your treasure is, there your heart will be also."* That's profound. Think about it carefully. The things, activities, people, jobs, hobbies, and projects that you treasure in your life - that is where your heart is also. If a person's heart is in their paycheck, their bank account, their stock portfolio, or their worldly possessions, then it is no wonder why they feel as if their heart has stopped beating when a so-called "financial crisis" occurs. For all intents and purposes, that is where

their heart is so it makes perfect sense. But God loves us so much that he tells us, he warns us, of the dangers of the love of money or earthly possessions. And the part that should really get your attention is that the "proof is in the pudding!" In other words, the occurrences of persons who have committed acts of suicide because they have suffered a monetary loss happen all too frequently! The real tragedy in such cases lies in people's lack of knowledge because the spiritual truth is available to us all if we *pay attention to God's Word.* The World's system of thinking belies the spiritual truth. It contradicts the Kingdom's way of thinking and it's to the detriment and destruction of so many, and in my opinion, unnecessarily so.

Recall, if you will, this familiar scenario that I set forth near the start of this book.

A rich man is walking down the street and is approaching a homeless man, who is also crippled, hungry, and lame, sitting on the sidewalk in front of him. The rich man is carrying $10,000 total – $5,000 in each pocket. As he walks past the homeless man, the rich man reaches into his left pocket and pulls out $5,000, gives it to the homeless man, and continues on his way.

Five minutes later, a woman of very modest means is walking down the same street and approaching the same homeless, crippled, hungry and lame man sitting on the sidewalk. The woman of modest means is down to her last $10 – carrying $5 in each pocket. As she walks past the homeless man, she reaches into both of her pockets and pulls out a total of $10 (the sum total of her monetary possessions), gives it to the homeless man, and continues on her way.

Perhaps you will remember that this fact-pattern was proffered for the purpose of illustrating *greed* as an issue. The initial interrogatory was, *"Who gave more (the rich man or the woman of modest means)?* Well, in the context of hearing God's voice, an additional issue is *obedience*. Let me provide a personal example.

Not too long ago I was reading Luke 16:19-31. It is the story of "The Rich Man and Lazarus." I urge you to read this short story on your own, but here is the gist of what happens.

There was a rich man who possessed and enjoyed all the luxurious things that life had to offer. Also, there was a man named Lazarus, a beggar covered with sores and who longed to eat whatever crumbs fell from the rich man's table. The time came when the beggar died and they carried him to Abraham's side in heaven. The rich man also died and was tormented in hell. When the rich man looked up and saw Abraham far away, with Lazarus by his side, the rich man called to him saying, "Father Abraham, have pity on me and send Lazarus to dip the tip of his finger in water and cool my tongue, because I am in agony in this fire." (*See*, Luke 16:22-24, NIV). In reply, Abraham told the rich man, "Son, remember that in your lifetime you received your good things, while Lazarus received bad things, but now he is comforted here and you are in agony." (Luke 16:25, NIV).

Now, I only provided you with a portion of the story to give you a context in which to operate. After meditating on this Word concerning Lazarus, my Spirit led me to write the following:

"Do something to help the poor, the hungry, the crippled, and the lame. Help them! Remember them! Do something...everyday.

Share or give what you have or what you can. Help Lazarus! Ease his suffering in this life!"

By faith, I know that this was the Spirit of the Lord speaking to me. I know that this was his voice. As a result, I make a conscious effort to take note of each and every "Lazarus" that I see on the street during the course of a given day. More often than not, I will give whatever I can afford to give to that person, that "Lazarus" who is sitting on the sidewalk, in a train station, in the park, or on the street. It doesn't have to be a million dollars and there doesn't need to be a guarantee, from "Lazarus" to you, that he or she will spend the money on food rather than on something else. Giving (as I heard God's voice telling me to do), is an act of *obedience* that comes out of *faith*. Believing that you have heard God's voice *is* an act of *faith*! Obeying what he told you to do is an act of *love*. Understand what I'm telling you.

Hearing God's voice is by *faith*. Obeying God's voice is *love*. You can't talk about *hearing* without mentioning *obeying* because they go hand-in-hand. Similarly, you can't talk about *faith* without mentioning *love* because they also go hand-in-hand. Hearing is to Obedience, as Faith is to Love. The *power* of God is released in your life when you obey what you heard from God. And that obedience is a reflection of your love for God. Jesus said, "*If you obey my commands, you will remain in my love, just as I have obeyed my Father's commands and remain in his love.*" (John 15:10, NIV). That is why *faith* and *love* are "power twins" in the life of a Christian. Your love drives your faith. Your love for God is exhibited by your obedience to his Word, and his spoken Word is heard by faith.

In regard to "Lazarus" and obeying God's spoken words to me, there are times when I may not have much to give. There are times when the money that I have is already accounted for and allotted for other expenses. But that should *never* stop me from giving *something*. The very dime of a dollar may help someone in need even if that dime, to you, is insignificant. It could mean the difference between a warm cup of coffee on a cold night or freezing to death. You see, *disobedience hardens your hearing*. Disobedience to what God puts in your spirit to do will harden your ability to hear God's voice in the future. Operating under the World's system of thinking, people will have you putting a higher priority on the $5, $10, or $15 dollars in your pocket than on a human life suffering who is lying right next to the place where you're standing. The World's way of thinking puts such a high premium on the value of money that human beings won't normally part from it unless they are receiving something *quid pro quo*. This is how we know that the World's system is not in line with God's system. The Bible says to, "Love your neighbor as yourself." (*See*, Mark 12:31, NIV). And no matter where you live, there are people in your town, in your city, who are in need. When you see "Lazarus," what will *you* do?

I want to be clear. Many people give and help those less fortunate purely from a giving heart and God sees that. But, according to the Kingdom of God's way of thinking (which has its power rooted in love), giving to "Lazarus" should be an *everyday* occurrence. Maybe once in a while you, the reader, may give spare change or a dollar or two to someone less fortunate than you. That's not the issue. The issue is does it weigh on your heart to give something *every single time* you pass a "Lazarus" on the street? Do you at least take notice and consider what is in your pocket, or your purse, that you could give? Or do you fail to notice "Lazarus" at all? The World's mentality puts a higher price tag on the acquisition of money than it does on helping a person in need through a selfless act of kindness. Consider this carefully. What would people say if you gave $100 dollars to a random homeless hungry person on the street? What if it was $500 or $1,000? The point is that money becomes a real sensitive issue with most people in connection to releasing it for a cause that may not better *their* standing in some way. But, by faith, I know that God spoke to me:

"Do something to help the poor, the hungry, the crippled, and the lame. Help them! Remember them! Do something…everyday. Share or give what you have or what you can. Help Lazarus! Ease his suffering in this life!"

And although the relinquishing of money in order to help someone else's suffering is viewed skeptically and with a cautious eye within the World's system of thinking; by faith, I obey God's voice in doing what he told me to do.

On another note, many of you have gifts and talents that you are not utilizing to their fullest extent. Some of you have had an idea for a new business for months or years and have never taken the steps to get it underway. A few of you have wanted to do things that are totally within your grasp, but have stood in a place of *fear*, rather than *faith*, because you have operated according to the World's system of thinking. Remember:

The Kingdom of God's way of thinking is *faith-based* and the Kingdom's power is rooted in *love.*

The World's way of thinking is *fear-based* and the World's power is rooted in *selfishness.* The Kingdom of God's power is love and faith. The World's power is money.

If you are walking with God, seeking him and his righteousness daily, and making every effort to put yourself in a position to hear from him, then what he tells you to do often times goes against what the World would have to say about any given situation. It could be ending a relationship. It could be investing in a new business idea. It may be paying your tithes in church. You have to enter into a place of obedience knowing that your decision and actions, which line up with God's Word, may not be understood or supported by people who have not heard God's voice. In fact, you may even face ridicule, mockery, and derision by others. People often make fun of what they don't understand because it makes *them* feel more comfortable with the situation. In this life, you have to get to a point where you can be *gentle* and *respectful* to opposition, but at the same time, *rigid* in your thinking. Remember: (1) gentle & respectful, yet (2) rigid in your thinking. The Bible says,

"Always be prepared to give an answer to everyone who asks you to give the reason for the hope that you have. But do this with *gentleness* and *respect*, keeping a clear conscience so that those who speak maliciously against your good behavior in Christ may be ashamed of their slander." (1 Peter 3:15-16, NIV) Emphasis added.

This scripture substantiates God's call for you to be gentle and respectful to the "haters" of the world who may laugh, doubt, or sneer at you for obeying what God told YOU to do. Although you should be gentle and respectful, you also must be **rigid** in your thinking. When you get a Word from God and you put the wheels of obedience in motion and people surrounding you begin to oppose you, just remember what the Apostle Paul said:

"I care very little if I am judged by you…" (1 Corinthians 4:3, NIV)

You see, you've got to get to a place in your life where you stop seeking so desperately the acceptance of other people. That is a dangerous place to be because you have now turned over all *your* power to somebody else. And since I told you candidly that I did not write this book for monetary profit or political correctness, you shouldn't mind the frankness with which I am speaking to you. The next time someone is giving you grief because you are walking with God, or because you choose to go to church, or simply not follow them, just remember this question that I pose to you: *Why do you care so much about what somebody else thinks who might be going to hell?* Think about it. God is the one and only authority. The Word and instructions that come from hearing *his* voice should be your primary concern.

Take this book, for example. I firmly believe that God has given to me a message to convey. He has entrusted me with a *truth* that came out of his Word and that has the power and potential to help anyone who reads or hears it. I had never planned on writing a book based on the principles of successful Christian living. I had never planned on writing a book *at all*. But, after hearing the gospel of Jesus Christ and learning of God's grace and mercy concerning me, seeking his truth earnestly from that point on by staying in His

Word, then personally experiencing the hearing of God's voice and the instructions that He had for me, my spirit led me to write this book page by page. You see, God has equipped us all with talents that many of *you* are not tapping into. But, it takes for you to stay in the Word long enough to hear his voice, and then to obey whatever it is He told you to do. And you cannot sit in a place of *fear*. You must act in *faith*! Everything in the Kingdom of God operates by *faith*. Believing that God exists is by *faith*. Believing that God is a rewarder of those who earnestly seek Him is by *faith*. Expecting God to speak to you after you have meditated on his written Word long enough is by *faith*. Asking God to speak to you is by *faith*. Hearing God's voice is by *faith*. And when you get the experience of hearing God's voice *one time*, then from that point on you can exhibit a *hope*[11] that God will take you in the right direction *every time* (assuming that you proceeded in obedience of course). This is not always easy and can be very challenging if God is speaking to you about an uncomfortable circumstance or situation in your life.

For instance, maybe there was a situation where someone hurt you and your spirit is trying to tell you something regarding that person. Listen to that voice. Listen to your conscience. If you are a person who has a relationship with God and are steadily reading his Word, you can trust what your conscience is telling you to do. God told us, *"My peace, I leave with you; my peace I give you."* (*See,* John 14:27, NIV). The Holy Spirit, which God has given to you,

---

11    *See,* Romans 5:3-5 (NIV) [If we can just persevere while in the midst of trouble, God will speak to us. This is the *experience* that we want because from that point on, that *experience* will produce the *hope* that God will always be there to guide us. And what is the substance that fills our hope? *Faith!* Now, you are getting it!

will be grieved (*i.e.* uneasy) if a decision that you have made is not the right decision. There is no confusion, anxiety, or restlessness attached to the peace of God. But you must develop and continue to cultivate a relationship with God so that you will know when the Spirit is trying to show or tell you something.

You will hear God's voice by *faith*. His Words or instructions often require *courage*, on our part. His spoken Word will *line up* with the *written* Word and frequently *go against the World's* way of thinking. In my case, if I was operating according to the World's way of thinking, it would have been much more profitable, financially, to write and publish a book that appealed to a broader mainstream audience rather than a book about Jesus' love for you and me. Under the World's system of thinking, I shouldn't be discussing a topic as dark and dreary as rape or sexual abuse. A lot of people would say, "Who's going to read that?" Perhaps the most noteworthy fact can be attributed to the circumstances under which the book was written. I'm an American citizen, living in China, writing a book about Christianity, under a communist government rule who pledges its spiritual allegiance to Buddha. Ironic, isn't it? But that's how God works. He will set you in the midst of everything that is opposed to him, establish you there, and use you to educate and win non-believers to Christ through your natural gifts, talents, and abilities, and to be an example to others for Christ.

Here is my point. God allows you to go through certain difficult experiences in life so that you can help someone else in this world facing the same or a similar circumstance. True success is measured by whether you can make what happened to you, happen for somebody else. On that note, it comes full circle.

The Kingdom of God's way of thinking is *faith-based* and the Kingdom's power is rooted in *love.*

The World's way of thinking is *fear-based* and the World's power is rooted in *selfishness.* The Kingdom of God's power is love and faith. The World's power is money.

Read God's Word. Acquire *knowledge* from it and get *understanding.* Remember, you will know when God speaks to you, because (1) it will require faith (2) it will require courage (3) it will line up with his *written* word, (4) it will go against the World's way of thinking, and (5) *the peace of God will rule in your heart.* Let's take a look at this last and important factor below.

### 5. WHEN GOD SPEAKS TO YOU, *THE PEACE OF GOD WILL RULE IN YOUR HEART.*

Every time I talk about the "peace of God" in your heart, I am referring to the peace that is provided by *the Holy Spirit.* Even if you have never been a person of deep religious or spiritual faith, chances are you believe that people possess an inner voice that speaks to their conscience when facing certain decisions. Some people may refer to the inner voice as "instinct." That's fine. Whether you label the inner voice as "instinct," your "conscience," or your "sub-conscience," the function of all three effectively is the work of the Holy Spirit.

Shortly before Jesus was crucified, he informed his disciples of the impending events on the horizon. Specifically, Jesus said to his disciples,

"When *the Counselor* comes, whom I will send to you from the Father, *the Spirit of truth* who goes out from the Father, he will testify about me." (John 15: 26, NIV) Emphasis added.

"But I tell you the truth: It is for your own good that I am going away. Unless I go away, *the Counselor* will not come to you; but if I go, I will send him to you." (John 16:7, NIV) Emphasis added.

"I have much more to say to you, more than you can now bear. But when he, *the Spirit of truth*, comes, he will guide you into all truth. He will not speak on his own; *he will speak only what he hears*, and he will tell you what is yet to come. (John 16:12-13, NIV) Emphasis added.

This is the same Spirit that lies inside of you. It's God's Spirit. And let me remind you of God's Word regarding the Spirit that lies inside of you.

"We have not received the spirit of the world but the Spirit who is from God, that we may understand what God has freely given us." (1 Corinthians 2:12, NIV)

"Don't you know that you yourselves are God's temple and that God's Spirit lives in you?" (1 Corinthians 3:16, NIV)

"We know that we live in him and he in us, because he has given us his Spirit." (1 John 4:16, NIV)

"God has not given us a spirit of fear, but of *power*, and of *love*, and of a *sound mind*." (1 Timothy 1:7, NIV) Emphasis added.

I want you, the reader, to understand how truly blessed you are to have a Spirit inside of you that is the very Spirit of the Lord Jesus Christ. Before he was crucified, Jesus said a pertinent statement to which practically any person can attest. He said,

"In this world you will have trouble." (*See,* John 16:33, NIV). Immediately following that statement, Jesus added, "But take heart! I have overcome the world." (*See,* John 16:33, NIV). So, what am I saying to you? What is the real issue to be identified and expressed in spiritual language?

### LET THE SPIRIT GUIDE YOU

It's as simple as that. Jesus has already defeated all the works of the enemy and he has given his Spirit to you. By faith, and the same Spirit of truth which resides in me, the author, I believe this to be true. And if it is true, then tell me why must YOU feel that you are fighting your battles alone and that you must take every matter into your own hands? This is where many of us get ourselves into deeper trouble than we are already in.

The Spirit operates in opposition to the flesh. When I say "the flesh," I am referring to our propensies as human beings to succumb to the gratification of our natural bodily urges or emotions (*e.g.* lust, anger, envy, to name a few) due to a particular mindset that is in opposition to God's Word. Let us now turn to the scriptural authority on living our lives according to the Spirit, rather than by the flesh.

"So, I say, live by the Spirit, and you will not gratify the desires of the sinful nature. For the sinful nature desires what is contrary to the Spirit, and the Spirit what is contrary to the sinful nature. They are in conflict with each other, so that you do not do what you want. But if you are led by the Spirit, you are not under law." (Galations 5:16-18, NIV)

Life by the Spirit (or, "being led by the Spirit") is the issue when discussing having the peace of God rule in our hearts. And if we are to be *led* by the Spirit, then the real underlying sub-issue is *trust*. This is a crucial point and I pray that the Spirit will lead you to a place of understanding.

No one of us is perfect. There is a reason why even a long-time believer in the Word can stumble, fall down, or even fall away. This happens when we stop leaning on God. *Don't ever stop leaning on God.* It's a seemingly simple concept that, if not done, can lead to absolute chaos in your life. You see, when we lean on God, we are saying that we are *trusting* in his Word. Sometimes, in the midst of a difficult period, you simply don't know what to do and you allow worry and stress to take over in your physical body. Other times, when we are in the middle of troubling times, our first inclination is to act, or react. Think about it. I'm sure you can remember one time, if not several, when you acted or reacted prematurely to a situation. Perhaps, your husband, wife, boyfriend, or girlfriend said or did something that you didn't particularly appreciate and you said, or did, something in heated response. Or maybe you made a phone call, sent an email, paid a visit, or even sent a text message to someone which you later wish could have retracted. On occasion, we all face professional-related decisions regarding our places of employment such as whether to stay or leave. Perhaps, it's a rather straightforward situation of not liking your boss, a co-worker, or a subordinate, and trying to get through an entire workweek with that person without losing the last bit of self-control onto which you a holding.

It's the normal, average, daily situations like these, in which the Spirit will lead you. By submitting your own will to that of God's will, you are really saying that all of your natural fleshly habits and desires were put to death on the cross with Jesus when he died. And now, it is Jesus who lives, and can be seen, in you! This is the power of the Holy Spirit. People with the hardest of hearts can be made anew into some of the kindest, most loving people you could ever meet if they accept Jesus into their life, and are truly being led by the Spirit. It is the reason why being equipped with the *actual words of God*, ready to use on a moment's notice, can get you through any and all situations during the course of a day.

For example, being led by the Spirit will allow you to tolerate, be kind to, and even compliment a person on your job that you disfavor. Being led by the Spirit may result in a display of generosity, on your part, benefiting someone else who genuinely doesn't understand why you are being so kind to them. People will question what it is that got into you that made you into a totally new person! It may be between a wife and husband, or girlfriend and boyfriend, two co-workers, or even someone in your own family. And if you try to explain exactly what it is that has caused such a noticeable change in your personality, demeanor, or attitude, people who are *not* being led by the Spirit, or who simply don't know God, generally won't and can't understand fully. Let me show you why:

(13) "This is what we speak, not in words taught us by human wisdom but in words taught by the Spirit, expressing spiritual truths in spiritual words.

(14) The man *without* the Spirit does not accept the things that come from the Spirit of God, for they are foolishness to him, and he cannot understand them, because they are *spiritually discerned.* (1 Corinthians 2:13-14 NIV) Emphasis added.

You must understand that the Holy Spirit is awesome. There is no other way for me to put it. As you have been made aware, it is a Spirit of power. The Spirit has the ability to transform whomever it touches. The reason for the transformation is due to the very thing we are discussing. A person who is "led by the Spirit" or who "lives by the Spirit" is a new person operating within the Kingdom of God's system of thinking (based in love) rather than the World's system (based in selfishness). Figuratively, they have taken off the old self and put on the new self. Being "born again" has its roots in this concept. Right now, I want you to recall that at the beginning of the book, I set before you the following promise:

"By the end of this book, you will have acquired *the absolute imperative for* happiness, fulfillment, *peace*, and prosperity through knowledge, understanding, *discernment*, sound judgment, and most of all, wisdom." (*See*, p.7).

You see, becoming knowledgeable in God's Word is the beginning of genuine happiness, fulfillment, peace, and prosperity. Also, it is the beginning of *spiritual discernment* (*i.e.* the ability to perceive, decipher, distinguish, analyze, understand, and anticipate using your spiritual eyes and ears). For example, your co-workers who can't and don't understand the positive change that they have seen in you at work *or* why you haven't made your usual daily comment about strangling your over-demanding boss, are probably *lacking* the spiritual discernment to recognize the transformative power of God's Spirit which is now leading you. When a person advances in spiritual maturity to the point of operating consistently in these five (5) areas *(knowledge, understanding, discernment, sound judgment, and wisdom)*, that person is simultaneously being led by the Spirit in everything that they think, say, and do.

Jesus gave to us, among other things, five (5) *specific* things of greater worth than money, diamonds, or gold. He gave us his Word. He gave us the Truth. He gave us his Spirit. He gave us *his* Peace. And He gave us Life! Look at these five again. He gave us:

His Word

The Truth

His Spirit

*His* Peace

Life

Now, here's the incredible part. The five things that are on this list are not mutually-exclusive. *They are one and the same!* Pay close attention to the clarification below as you read relevant statements from Jesus taken from the New Testament:

**SPIRIT = TRUTH** ⇨ (16) "I will ask the Father, and he will give you another Counselor to be with you forever – the *Spirit of truth*." (John 14:16-17, NIV) Emphasis added.

**SPIRIT = TRUTH** ⇨ "…But when he, the *Spirit of truth*, comes, he will guide you into all *truth*." (*See*, John 16:13, NIV) Emphasis added.

**SPIRIT = LIFE** ⇨ (63) "The *Spirit gives life*, the flesh counts for nothing.

**WORD = SPIRIT *and* LIFE** ⇨ 64) The *words* that I have spoken to you are *spirit* and they are *life*." (John 6:63-64, NIV) Emphasis added.

**SPIRIT = TRUTH *and* LIFE** ⇨ "*I* am the way and    the **truth** and the **life**." (John 14:6, NIV) Emphasis added.

**SPIRIT = WORD** ⇨ (26) "But the Counselor, *the Holy Spirit*, whom the Father will send in my name, will teach you all things and *will remind you of everything I have said* to you."

**SPIRIT = *HIS* PEACE** ⇨ (27) "*Peace* I leave with you; *my peace* I give you." (John 14:26-27, NIV) Emphasis added.

**SPIRIT = *HIS* PEACE** ⇨ (22) "But the fruit of the *Spirit* is love, joy, *peace...*" (*See*, Galations 5:22, NIV) Emphasis added.

Accordingly, the *Word* of God *is Spirit and Life*. Additionally, we know that the Holy *Spirit* is the *Spirit* of *Truth*.[12] Moreover, the *Spirit* reminds us of the *Word* of God that was taught to us through Jesus. The *Life* that is in Christ Jesus is the *Spiritual Truth*. The fruit of being led by the *Spiritual Truth*, which is the *Word*, is *Peace*.

So, the person who is *led by the Spirit* is: (1) the person whose mind and heart is in synchronization with the spiritual truth (*i.e.* God's Word), which produces peace; *and* (2) the person who runs the race with the expectation of receiving the crown of eternal life. You see, the race is not given to the swift, but rather to the person

---

12    Throughout the gospels of Matthew, Mark, Luke, and John, Jesus spoke to his disciples and to his followers. In your reading, take note of *Jesus' repeated usage of the phrase, "I tell you the truth..."* For example, in the book of Mark, the following scriptures illustrate several examples of Jesus' usage of this phrase while speaking to various people:  Mark 3:28; Mark 8:12; Mark 9:1; Mark 9:41; Mark 10:15; Mark 10:29; Mark 11:23; Mark 12:43; Mark 13:30; Mark 14:9; Mark 14:18; Mark 14:25; Mark 14:30. Jesus uses this phrase thirteen times in the book of Mark. His Word *is* truth!

who is *prepared*. Preparation begins with humility. Humbling yourself to the point of realizing that there is something greater and much larger than you and the things you encounter in your daily routine.

However, as you are already aware, life is not a simple equation. People, (including individuals with an established faith in God), sometimes want things *how* they want them, *where* they want them, and *when* they want them. People get impatient. They allow their current perception of their situation to dictate their mindset. In other words, people begin to *worry*. They worry about money. They worry about their job. They worry about their weight. They worry about their future. They worry about their health. They worry about their kids. They worry about their loneliness. They worry that they're not married. They worry that they're divorced. They worry, worry, worry.

On the other hand, there are people who wallow in *hurt*. People who remain stuck in a holding pattern because some man, woman, girl, or boy, hurt them. There are people who can't truly move forward emotionally because they are constantly reliving the pain of yesterday. These people frequently divulge all of their dramatic tales of how "so-and-so" hurt them in order to garner sympathy or empathy from whoever will listen.

Then, there are the people in *fear*. People who, year after year, fail to confront the devils and demons in their life because they are in a place of fear. There are people who justify being wronged and mistreated because they fear *losing* the person who wronged or mistreated them and subsequently being alone. Many of these people have completely lost their voice rather than speaking up for themselves due to remaining in a place of fear.

Finally, there is the largest group of people to which most of us have been a member at some time in our life, including me. These people have experienced at least one, if not several, events that bring *worry, hurt, and fear* all at once! Well, guess what? These are common elements of life to which no one person is immune. But, the issue is what are you going to do? Sit there, and let the devil walk all over you and torment you, or *fight the right fight, with fighting faith?* The right fight is exercising your ability to say in the middle of your worrisome, hurtful, or fear-causing situation,

"Wait a minute. I'm going to *lean on God* and I'm never going to stop leaning on God no matter what has happened in the past or may happen in the future."

This is where our discussion returns to the Peace of God. Peace is highly underrated. I once heard a well-known, international spiritual leader say the following words. "When I was young, I prayed for joy. Now that I am older, I pray for peace." Some of you, young and old alike, can relate to the message conveyed in that statement. Peace is the polar opposite of chaos. Peace means the perpetual absence of worry. For my part, peace is happiness because without it, life can be a miserable existence.

Remember, there is a 5-star principle that underlies the 7-Pillar Model for Daily Living: *(1) Knowledge (2) Understanding (3) Discernment (4) Sound Judgment (5) Wisdom.* The person who practices all five, consistently, is a person who is *blameless* in the sight of God. But, don't get too comfortable. These five areas should be likened to a journey, not a destination. A person may consider himself a believer and follower of Jesus Christ and the Word of God and may practice all five faithfully, but he will never attain them *in full* For a human being to believe that he has attained *all* knowledge, or *all* understanding, or *all* wisdom is nothing short of self-deception.

The Bible says that, "…all have sinned and fall short of the glory of God." (*See*, Romans 3:23, NIV). (And of course we may rest assured that we can depend on the scripture for direction because "all scripture is God-breathed and is useful for teaching…and training in righteousness." (2 Timothy 3:16, NIV)). Interestingly, even so-called "non-believers" of the world tend to concur with arguably one of the greatest English poets of the eighteenth century, Alexander Pope (1688-1784), who said, "To err is human, to forgive divine." In short, no one person is perfect and the overwhelming majority will agree.

*However,* becoming a hearer *and* a doer of God's Word results in a shifting mindset that equips you with the spiritual *knowledge* and *understanding* to *discern* spiritual issues rooted in natural problems, thus enabling you to exercise *sound judgment* in your actions and reactions, which *is wisdom*.

This is your measuring stick for being *blameless* in the sight of God. But, understanding this *5-star principle* which *underlies* the Model for Daily Living requires more. You see, these 5 are actually the *by-product* of adhering to all 7 Pillars of the Model! Although your end-objective is to be blameless in the sight of God through behavior that reflects spiritual knowledge, understanding, discernment, sound judgment, and wisdom, that objective can *only* be achieved if you *first* adhere to the 7 Pillars of the Model, on a consistent basis. In other words, there is a *hierarchical relationship*. (This is very important so bear with me as I explain in greater detail).

Imagine if you will, a pyramid. A pyramid has three parts: (1) a base or foundation, (2) a middle section, and (3) an apex, top, tip, or point. (*See*, Illustration "*A*"). I want you to visually ingest the structural design of the pyramid.

**Illustration "*A*"**

**BLAMELESS**

**KNOWLEDGE, UNDERSTANDING, DISCERNMENT, SOUND JUDGMENT, WISDOM**

*7 Pillars of the Model for Daily Living*

The pyramid, shown in *Illustration* "A", not only provides a visual aid to the 5-star principle that underlies this section (*i.e.* peace ruling in your heart), but also illustrates a fundamental overview of the entire book. YOU are at the base of the pyramid. Your daily objective is to utilize the tools provided by the 7 Pillars of the Model to help you conquer all of the worry, hurt, and fear in your life. In adhering to the 7 Pillars, (the first of which is *faith*), your ever-increasing knowledge (which originates out of the Word of God), and Spirit-assisted understanding and discernment, enable you to practice sound judgment in handling all of life's challenges. The actions, reactions, thoughts, and decisions that you exercise with spiritual-based sound judgment are tantamount to wisdom.

By operating successfully at the base of the pyramid (*i.e.* adhering to the 7 Pillars of the Model), you are guaranteed to *eliminate* or *reduce* a considerable portion, if not all, of your *pre-existing* worry, hurt, and fear because you are unquestionably a new person in Christ who is now led by the Spirit as opposed to the flesh. Not to be overlooked, you are also guaranteed to *avoid* a considerable number of disastrous pitfalls and painful situations that you would have otherwise walked right into absent the protection afforded by the wisdom that comes from the Spirit-filled Word of God. You see, the real work comes at the base of the pyramid. If done faithfully, the resultant wisdom acquired will not only equate to *peace* in your daily routine, but will also merit you the title of "*blameless*" in the same, which will give you the *confidence* to ask God whatever you wish in this life, and it will be given you, *and* to stand in the day of judgment upon our Lord's return and receive the prize of eternal afterlife with God in heaven.

*When God speaks to you, peace will rule in your heart.* Recall earlier in the book, I talked about the patriarch Abraham and how, by *faith*, he heard God's command to leave his home country and subsequently, how he *courageously* set out on a journey in obedience to the Lord's voice. In particular, I drew attention to the inherent benefit of being removed from certain distractions in relation to your ability to *hear* what God has to say to you. The biggest distracters surrounding us can be the wrong friendships or relationships in our lives which have an influencing effect on our actions, emotions, goals, and dreams. Keeping this in mind, I turn your attention to Illustration "*B*" and Illustration "*C*". As I've explained to you on multiple occasions, it was through my own difficult situation that I, the author, turned to God and began to experience revelation through God's Word. This time of devotion was the beginning of a tremendous growth period. A time of study and learning that ultimately resulted in the enlightenment for this book, the message contained herein, and a new, innovative idea for a business. This is what some Christians call "breakthrough." It was the start of God getting my undivided attention. The important point that I submit to you is that it was made possible because, as difficult as it was, my usual surrounding distractions were simply not there. Circumstances were such that I necessarily changed addresses in order to assist my friend, thus leaving my hometown behind. Understand that I'm not suggesting for everyone to pick up and move in order to hear God's voice. What I am suggesting is that sometimes we get to a breaking point due to life's embattling trials where we look up and suddenly realize that we are in a place of solitude simply because of what we are going through. It is *that* place where your hearing becomes sharper because your focus becomes clearer, and you can then make your breaking point your turning point.

Having said that, the habit of writing "inspirational letters" (*e.g.* Illustrations "*B*" and "*C*") initiated while I was in *that* place that I just described to you. I didn't begin writing the "letters" at the start of my coming to Christ. It wasn't until several months into my reading and studying the Word diligently and earnestly that I began to "hear" these inspirational letters in my heart. (You may recall in earlier pages my "pre-coming to Christ belief" that I had always possessed a talent for writing. I had always written inspirational pieces and poems. But now, I write for God. I have labeled it the "Be You, For Me" effect).

As I read more of God's Word and my understanding increased, my written works increased. Even today, I continue to write these letters whenever my Spirit leads me to do so. Time and time again, after studying the Word of God, I become inspired to write. By faith, I know that *this* is the voice of God. This is *why* I told you at the start of this book to *take notes*. Get into the habit of writing things down. As you get closer to God, He will speak to your heart. And who knows? God may lead you in the future to use those same notes to not only bless you, but also to be a blessing to someone else!

The Spirit has taught me the importance and significance of not just writing notes in relation to the Word *of* God, but also writing down the Word *from* God. Remember, God's spoken Word will *line up* with his written Word. In addition, His spoken Word will require *faith*, it will require *courage*, it will *go against the world's* system of thinking (*i.e.* it will be love-based rather than based in selfishness), and *peace* will rule in your heart. Well, when I hear God's voice in my heart to write, I write. The content of what is on the paper comes by *faith*. The act of getting a pen, conveying the message being given to me on the sheet of paper and not questioning these actions to the point of discouragement and disobedience, takes *courage*. Writing these "inspirational letters" in response to God's instruction knowing that other people who saw me doing this would probably laugh or think I was crazy is exactly what I mean when I say you'll know God speaks to you because it will *go against the world's* system of thinking! And that brings us to *peace* ruling in the heart. Although I always write an "inspirational letter" while sitting *alone* after reading the bible, these same "letters" have now been immortalized in published form in English, Spanish, Portuguese, Italian, and Chinese; sold and purchased by people in various countries, and hopefully helping scores of people around the world. This brings an immeasurable sense of peace to my mind and my heart – all originating from spending time in the Word of God and hearing and obeying his voice.

So, here is what I ask of you. In preparation for reading the two "inspirational letters" below, refresh your memory on the following concepts:

Your daily objective should be to utilize the principles provided by the 7 Pillars of the Model for Daily Living to help you combat and conquer the *worry, hurt, and fear* in your life.

By operating successfully at the base of the pyramid (*i.e.* adhering to the 7 *Pillars of the Model*), you are guaranteed to *eliminate* or *reduce* a considerable portion, if not all, of your *pre-existing* worry, hurt, and fear because you are unquestionably a new person in Christ who is now being *led by the Spirit.*

There is an inherent benefit in being removed from certain distractions in relation to your ability to *hear what God has to say to you.*

The biggest *distracters* surrounding us can be *the wrong friendships or relationships* in our lives which have an influencing effect on our actions, emotions, goals, and dreams.

You are guaranteed to *avoid* a considerable number of disastrous pitfalls and painful situations that you would have otherwise walked right into absent the protection afforded by the wisdom that comes from the Spirit-filled Word of God.

Becoming a hearer *and* a doer of God's Word results in a shifting mindset that equips you with the spiritual *knowledge* and *understanding* to *discern* spiritual issues rooted in natural problems, thus enabling you to exercise *sound judgment* in your actions and reactions, which *is wisdom.*

Now, read the corresponding "inspirational letters" below using your *spiritual eyes* and *spiritual ears.*

Inspirational Letter #1 – Friendships

Inspirational Letter #2 - Discernment

## FRIENDSHIPS

Don't just give of yourself freely to Everyone and/or Anyone.

It affects what you would be able to give to others in the future

It can alter your destiny – your immediate and/or long-term course of action

Proverbs: 12:26: "A righteous man is cautious in friendship…" *(Friends / Acquaintances)*

Do you really need this person in your life?

What are THEY doing in their own lives?

Is it consistent or contrary to *your* path, goal, and vision

Set Boundaries on Personal Relationships that are *"rootedly"* casual.

Do they love Jesus?

What fellowship do you have with someone not also seeking the Lord?

You have *no* business being with (or entertaining) people who God didn't bring into your life! Disobedience leads you astray from the will of God for your life. This includes missing out on the person (or people) He willed for you to meet because you were entertaining the wrong person's company.

Fight the Right fight, with fighting Faith!

## DISCERNMENT

The Lord puts certain people in your path. Other encounters are *not* of the Lord. All good and perfect things are from above. Certain people, certain relationships, certain acquaintances, certain encounters are of God. Others are not. As a rule, *peace*, the Peace of God, is present when God puts people in your life. There is a Peace about it. But other times, those encounters that are not of God — there is an absence of the peace that comes from God. There is "uneasiness." Listen to the voice. You have come to recognize and know God's voice. Pay attention to the Holy Spirit — the Spirit of Sound Thinking.

*The issue is Discernment.* You must be able to discern which encounters, people, activities, invitations, potential friendships, etc. are from above, from the Lord. In your spirit, you can feel whether you have peace or not. Don't grieve the Holy Spirit by ignoring the voice and do not put the Lord your God to the test.

*"-Be Rigid, If Not Rude"*

Shut the door and lock it on those situations that are not of or from God. Don't allow a thought to become a stronghold, a distraction, and pull you out of the will of God. *The enemy wants to disrupt your mindset to disrupt your destiny.* But, your spiritual weapons are working for you.

*Knowledge, Understanding, Discernment, Sound Judgment,* and *Wisdom*

Praise God for the Spiritual Truth. Operate in Love. Love drives Faith. Have Faith in God. And be discerning. All good things are from the Lord.

Remain in Him, and He will remain in you.

And remember…when you allow those encounters, friendships, or relationships, to become long-lasting, those are the very same friendships / relationships that are difficult. They don't have the peace of God attached to them. They are like dead-weight that you disobediently remained in out of complacency or familiarity. Fight the right fight, with fighting faith!

These two "letters" are the result of what *I* heard using *my* spiritual ears. It doesn't matter who you are, you will agree that it's difficult to deny the truth. Never apologize for the spiritual truth. I have faith that someone, somewhere, was affected by the message contained in those two letters. Although the two letters were written separately with approximately a month and a half in between, I present these two letters together because there is a common underlying issue that can be extracted from both: *discernment in friendships or relationships.* When viewing this issue against the backdrop of the existence of certain distractions in our everyday lives, it becomes a pertinent point with respect to your ability to *hear God's voice* concerning direction for your life. Thankfully, I experienced it in my own way. And every word written in this book, including the "inspirational letters," is merely an example of *my* ability to hear God's voice concerning direction for *my* life. What I'm telling you is that if God works for me, he will work for you. I now obey God's instruction regarding "discerning friendships" and the resultant wisdom has afforded me a much greater measure of one of my most prized possessions. Peace.

So remember, when God speaks to you,

It will always require *faith*

It will require *courage*

It will *line up with his written word*

It will *go against the world's* way of thinking, and
*peace* will rule in your heart

May God be with you as you continue on to the Second Pillar
of the 7-Pillar Model for Daily Living: *depart from sin.*

SECOND PILLAR:

# Depart from sin

Truth is often difficult to hear when it applies directly to you. At times, some people become offended when truth is cast their way because they interpret it as unfounded judgment. Similarly, in the area of spirituality (or, religion), one person's truth offering may be construed (or misconstrued, depending on the point of view) as judgmental behavior. Most people aren't too receptive to the moral judgment of their daily deeds and actions. Think about it. No one enjoys being judged and rightfully so. The Bible cautions, "There is only one Lawgiver and Judge, the one who is able to save and destroy. But you — who are you to judge your neighbor?" (James 4:12, NIV).

Exercising a fundamental respect for other people's beliefs is a principle that should be practiced by all. It is possible to hold tightly to your belief without degrading someone else's belief. In my humble opinion, if this principle were universally applied on a global scale, perhaps we would see a decrease in conflicts between nations, as well as *within* nations. At the root of any civil war within a state's borders lies a fundamental disrespect for difference. But, difference is not tantamount to deviation. Life's perspectives should not be viewed as a "sum-zero" game, especially in the area of spiritual belief. What *you* believe is what works for *you*. What I believe may work for me. But it is the mutual respect for any difference of belief that fuels a harmonious existence.

The 7 Pillars of the Model for Daily Living are a product of what the Lord placed in my heart to share with the world. Whether it speaks to *you*, in particular, is not of my immediate concern. My primary responsibility is to provide you with the *spiritual weapons* that will help you obtain a lasting measure of success, happiness, and peace. The first pillar is *faith*, as discussed in previous chapters. Nothing in the Kingdom of God operates without faith. Conversely, everything in the Kingdom of God operates by faith. The Pillars are not mutually exclusive. They work together. Your faith must always be working even as you delve into the particulars of the Second Pillar: Depart from Sin. As your exposure to the Word increases, I have faith that the Lord will increase your *spiritual knowledge* correspondingly. And may the light of the Lord also lead you to the deepest depths of insight (*i.e. spiritual understanding*).

### You are God's temple / You are the house

The *foundation* for the Model's success lies in the second Pillar: *depart from sin.* There is an important reason why I have chosen to capitalize "*depart from sin*," as opposed to using lower-case letters.

I want you to grasp that *departing from sin* is its own Pillar. It is just as important as any other Pillar of the Model. It is an imperative to the hope of receiving God's peace and his blessing and it must not be taken for granted simply because it seemingly conveys the obvious. Humble yourself. In the same way that *faith* had more levels than you initially imagined, *departing from sin* also is a multi-tiered Pillar which, if given proper deference, will provide guidance in various areas of your daily lives and decision-making processes. That's the interesting part about this book. The Pillars of the Model interlock. They are interwoven and blatantly stated, cannot be separated if you are to receive results. Contextual learning is learning at its finest, so let's put it into perspective.

Imagine that you are studying for an important exam which is comprised of two sections. The first section requires that you write an hour-long essay. The second section mandates that you complete 100 multiple-choice questions. To attain the *best* results, it wouldn't be prudent to prepare by only writing essays everyday prior to the exam. Similarly, it wouldn't be very effective to only answer multiple-choice practice questions, without writing simulated practice essays. In other words, you wouldn't study for only *one* part of the test. For best results, you would prepare for everything that you will face on the exam. Well, life is no different. You will be handicapped going into life's battles without properly equipping yourself with *all* of your spiritual weapons. What good is a newfound *faith*, if you continue to commit some of the same old "sinful mistakes" that have been detrimental to your health - spiritual and natural – in the past?

Let's take another example using sports. Tennis, basketball, futbol (or, soccer), badminton, baseball, volleyball, water polo, table tennis, etc., are a classification of various sports that all have something in common. In each of these sports, there is an "offensive" component and there is a "defensive" component. If you have ever played or watched any of these sports, you know that a team, and/or an individual player, fluctuates back and forth between offense and defense. Well, in each of these examples, offense and defense require a different set of skills. What good is it to the team, and/or the individual player, if the coach has only provided instruction on one component, and not given instruction on the other component? All offense and no defense will result in a loss. Similarly, a great defensive showing with little or no offense will lead to a losing effort. Speaking candidly, one might say that practicing the *wrong* way is a waste of time. Your spiritual ears should be tingling right now. Practicing the *wrong* way is another way of stating the converse of the very principle of which you have become so familiar. Practicing the *wrong* way is equal to fighting the *wrong* fight. In doing so, you go into the game of life ill-equipped and what happens? You lose. Not because you weren't willing to play hard and compete, but because you were ill-equipped and lacking the right knowledge and understanding to bring you the victory in all of life's various battles. That's not how we play the game. And that's not how we *prepare* for spiritual battle. Remember, the race is not given to the swift, but to the person who is *prepared*. It's the person who knows what to do when trouble comes, who will outlast a Satanic attack or troublesome spots in their life. That is the person who obtains the crown. So, be sure to give your humility to "*departing from sin*" in the same measure as you did for "*faith*." Then, you will be equipped with the full armor of God and His power may be manifested in you as the Word informs us.

*Departing from sin is the foundation for prosperity.* Someone may ask, "Well, what is sin?" For our purposes, sin is defined as "missing God's mark." It's as simple as that. To "miss the mark" means to depart from God's Word as it pertains to you. Now, at this juncture, there are two ways I can go with this. I can tell you all the ways that people generally "miss the mark" in their lives by listing a number of sinful acts, *or* I can explain to you the incredible value that God places on each and every one of us. I choose the latter on the reasoning that it is more profitable to focus on the present and future rather than the past.

### You are the temple, you are the house.

What do I mean by this? The Bible clearly states:

"Do you not know that *your body is a temple of the Holy Spirit*, who is in you, whom you have received from God?" (1 Corinthians 6:19, NIV) Emphasis added.

"Don't you know that *you yourselves are God's temple* and that God's Spirit lives in you? If anyone destroys *God's temple*, God will destroy him; for *God's temple* is sacred, and *you are that temple.* (1 Corinthians 3:16-17, NIV) (Emphasis added)

*Guard the house!*

*You are the temple. You are the house.* God's Spirit lives inside of you. Your challenge, duty, responsibility is to *guard the house*. I respectfully remind you, the reader, to receive the knowledge that you are hearing with your spiritual ears and spiritual eyes, not with your natural senses. Spiritual knowledge must be spiritually discerned with your spiritual eyes and ears, otherwise your understanding will be lacking.

You are the house of God. The Spirit of God lives within your heart. Like any other edifice, there are entrances into that edifice. Every building has a way to get inside, if not multiple ways to get inside. The temple that is your body is no exception to this rule. The entrances to the temple that is your body are several. Let's take a detailed look at each "doorway" into our bodily temple and what steps we must take to effectively safeguard the house against the enemy, who is Satan.

### LUST OF THE EYES

*Lust* is a term of art that is much broader than its obvious sexual connotation. *Lust* is an intense appetite to fulfill selfish gratifications; an intense longing. *Intense* is defined as existing in extreme degree. As you may recall, there are two systems of operation in existence. There is the "Kingdom of God's way of thinking" and there is "The World's way of thinking." Remember,

- The Kingdom of God's way of thinking is *based in faith* and the Kingdom's power is rooted in *love*.
- The World's way of thinking is *based in fear* and the World's power is rooted in *selfishness*. The Kingdom of God's power is love and faith. The World's power is money.

*Lust* is rooted in selfishness, not love. It opposes the Spirit and is designed to lead you up, out, and away from the will of God for your life. Of course, when I say the will of God, I mean the Word of God. *Lust* may take the form of *temptation* to gratify a sexual desire, but it may also take the form of an intense longing for *anything* that is within our visual sight. A person can be in *lust* for tangible things such as money, a house, a car, clothes, jewelry, or even a certain goal or objective. If you don't deal with *lust*, *lust* will deal with you. But before you can deal with *lust*, you have to be able to articulate the real issue using spiritual language. People who have issues of *lust* in their lives don't automatically have an addiction to sexual activity, or an addiction to an intoxicating substance. Nor does a person dealing with *lust* necessarily require an intervention to lessen their desire for money, houses, jewelry, or any of the other things mentioned above. The real root of *lust* is *selfishness*. If you deal with selfishness, you deal with *lust*.

*Lust* is designed to lure you, seduce you, away from standing on God's Word. If Satan can get you to operate outside of God's Word, then that means your *spiritual weapons* are not working for you. *The Word of God is your spiritual weapon.* You may recall that Jesus told us,

"The words I have spoken to you are Spirit and they are life." (*See,* John 6:63, NIV)

In other words, the Word of God *is* your spiritual weapon. Without it, you are ill-equipped to fight off the wiles of the devil which so often takes the form of *lust*, which when coupled with temptation, can give birth to sin if your spiritual weapons are not in place. Understanding that *selfishness* is the root of *lust* is only the beginning of knowledge. Now, you must turn your attention to the most common way that *lust* enters the mind, body, and heart — *through the eyes.*

Your *eyes* are a sensory gate. Often times, people don't realize that the *images* that they take in visually with their eyes *become thoughts* which are planted in the mind. Read it for yourself:

"Your eye is the lamp of your body. When your eyes are good, your whole body also is full of light. But when they are bad, your body also is full of darkness. (Luke 11:34, NIV)

The question is what is it that *your eyes* are taking in? What are you seeing? What *images* are you looking at? To make it plain, what *television* shows are you watching? What *movies* are you seeing? What pictures or images are you looking at on the *internet*? What things are you putting directly before your eyes? And don't think for one second that this message is only for men rather than women, or people under the age of 35 rather than over the age of 55. As stated above, sexual temptation is only one form of *lust*. To limit the discussion accordingly would do a great disservice to the message underlying *departing from sin.*

In my life, I've met women who have harbored an intense longing for shoes! Women love shoes! Italian women, Spanish women, Portuguese women, Chinese women, American women (and a host of women from countries too numerous to list); a great deal of women have an intense longing for shoes. Now, I am not suggesting that a person's affinity for shoes is inherently wrong, let alone a sin. What I am suggesting is that *temptation is an intense pressure applied to your thinking.* Whereas a failed attempt to combat the temptation to buy a pair of shoes may only result in a jovial sense of defeat, a failed attempt to combat the temptation to cheat on your husband may result in a lifetime of regret. You see, the issue is not the *object* of your temptation. The real issue lies deeper than the surface where the root of the problem is located. Because the spiritual realm precedes the natural realm, it is to the spiritual realm that we look to decipher the real issue. That issue is *selfishness*.

How many women readers would affirmatively state that they have either known a man, dated a man, married a man, or raised a man who *lusted* after women, albeit in the form of an actual woman or, some fantasy image as presented through mass media? Men are visual. I don't think that is a point of contention for anyone. As human beings, women attempt to search for explanations in the natural as to why men behave a certain way. In my view, that's pointless and a waste of time. Think about it. If you are of the mentality that most, if not all, men are dogs, and that's the deepest you can go in your assessment as to why men behave the way that they do, then you as a woman are just as shallow in your thinking as they are. *Lust* is not exactly a new phenomenon. Its implications are dispersed throughout the Bible in no uncertain terms. So, if men today are still repeating the same issues as men in biblical times, then that clearly says something. It says that there is a common element in human nature that has its roots in a more profound explanation than simply "man is part canine."

You may note, however, that my intent is not to come down too harshly on the younger generation. Wisdom often comes with age, experience, mistakes, and pain. Far too often, a divide exists between generations separated by a flowing river of judgment. Though experience may be correct when speaking, words of wisdom are often lost on youth not out of disrespect, but rather out of an inability to understand what experience is saying. Real knowledge, understanding, and wisdom come from the Lord, not from men. The Bible tells us,

"For the Lord gives wisdom and from his mouth come knowledge and understanding." (Proverbs 2:6, NIV)

A young person in their late teens, twenties, or even early thirties may not have lived long enough to face the kind of opposition that a person of age has already lived through time and time again. Trials and tribulations bring humility, *to some*. Humility is the place where true learning begins because it is at that point where you accept the reality that you don't know everything and that you need help. A young person may very well understand right from wrong in the natural sense, but only the experience that comes with age can provide the platform for contextual learning that allows spiritual understanding to occur.

What you must begin to understand is that *selfishness* is the root of *lust*. If you deal with *selfishness*, you deal with *lust*. *Willpower won't work*. Let me say that again for those of you who missed it. *Willpower won't work!* It's not enough. Jesus tells us,

"Watch and pray so that you will not fall into temptation. *The spirit is willing, but the body is weak.*" (Mark 14:38, NIV) Emphasis added.

People get down on themselves because they fail to resist *temptations* that are common to mankind. Many of you have told yourselves on numerous occasions that you are going to stop doing something, but you continued to do it anyway. That's exactly what Jesus meant when He said, "the spirit is willing, but the body is weak." You see, being led by the natural body, as opposed to being led by the Spirit, will get you into trouble every time. But, just because you succumbed to temptation in the body doesn't mean that you are a terrible person. Instead, it means that you are likely not fighting with *spiritual weapons*. And if you are not fighting with *spiritual weapons*, then you are not *fighting the right fight*. And let me be clear. I am referring to *lust* and *temptation* involving sexual activity outside of marriage, drinking alcohol, doing drugs, partying, stealing, cheating, infidelity, pornography, the love of money, excessive shopping, greed, over-eating (*i.e.* over-eating to the point of being *excessively* and *unhealthily* overweight), and any other activity that has mastery over you.

Of course, it takes a humbled person to admit when he or she has lost control. It takes a humbled person to admit that he or she even has a problem. This is why there can be no growth without a dose of humility, and you will continue to lose the battle until a healthy admission is set forth. Think about *selfishness* in these terms. Sex outside of marriage, drinking alcohol, doing drugs, partying, stealing, cheating, infidelity, pornography, the love of money, excessive shopping, greed, and over-eating (*i.e.* over-eating to the point of being *excessively* and *unhealthily* overweight), all have one thing in common. *These activities gratify you.* It's as simple as that. They all gratify a desire that is personal to you. And if you are wise enough to not be offended by the spiritual truth, then you will agree.

At this point, you should be wondering, "Well, how do I deal with *lust*?" "If willpower isn't enough, then what do I do?" "What's the answer?" The answer is that you must look to *the root* of the problem and address *the root. love versus selfishness.* Remember,

- The Kingdom of God's way of thinking is *based in faith* and the Kingdom's power is *rooted* in *love*.
- The World's way of thinking is *based in fear* and the World's power is *rooted* in *selfishness*. The Kingdom of God's power is love and faith. The World's power is money.

You see, it's all about your *mindset*. You have to *change your mindset.* When I say "mindset," it means your *way of thinking.* As seen above, there are two systems at play: the Kingdom of God's system and the World's system. *Selfishness* is attached to the World's system. *Lust* is rooted in *selfishness. Selfishness* is a spiritual power, not a natural one. You cannot see, hear, taste, twouch, or smell *selfishness*, yet you know it exists. It is a spiritual power that operates against the Kingdom of God's system. The reason why *willpower doesn't work* is because willpower is an attempt to defeat the wiles of the devil, a dark spiritual force, using your <u>own</u> devices as opposed to God's devices. We cannot defeat Satan *on our own*, and glory to God, we need not try. That is why Jesus came into the world. Jesus has already defeated Satan and has given all authority to us to trample on all of the works of the enemy. Don't forget, Jesus told us,

"I have given you authority to trample on snakes and scorpions and to overcome all the power of the enemy; nothing will harm you." (Luke 10:19, NIV)

*Love tramples selfishness.* You've got to find something or someone greater than yourself to be accountable to. That something or someone is God. Being *led by the spirit* is for the purposes of putting to death the desires of the flesh. Submitting to God's Word, which is Spirit, pulls you out of submission to *lust* and human *temptation.* You can't serve two masters. You cannot do both. It is impossible. Pay close attention to the following scripture because it is directly on point to the issue at hand:

(5) "Those who live according to the sinful nature have their *minds set* on what that nature desires; but those who live in accordance with the Spirit have their *minds set* on what the Spirit desires.

(6) *The mind* of sinful man is death, but *the mind* controlled by the Spirit is life and peace;

(7) *The sinful mind* is hostile to God, it does not submit to God's law, *nor can it do so.*

(8) Those controlled by the sinful nature *cannot please God.*

(Romans 8: 5-8, NIV) Emphasis added.

It's all about your *mindset.* The nature of your mindset determines your action! Either you are with God or you are against Him. Jesus told us,

"He who is not with me is against me." (*See,* Matthew 12:30, NIV)

Your *mindset,* or way of thinking, has to be based in *love,* rather than in *selfishness.* Please recall the following from page 13 in this book:

"In order to fight the *right* fight concerning all of the many challenges that you face every single day, it will benefit you ten-fold if you master the ability to *identify and express* the true underlying issue using spiritual terminology, rather than natural terminology."

Going out carousing on Saturday night with friends, cheating on your partner, an alcoholic or drug relapse or just "casual" recreational drinking or drug use, overeating, excessive shopping, stealing, are due to a *mind being set on the gratification of self* rather than the pleasing of God.

The Bible tells us that "*God is love.*" (*See,* 1 John 4:16, NIV). Your *mind set* has to be *based in love,* which means based in God. A mind that is based in God is based on God's Word because the Word is God. (*See,* John 1:1, NIV). You see, when you are more concerned about doing what is right in God's eyes rather than pleasing yourself for that moment, then you are being led by the Spirit. Those who are not led by the Spirit cannot please God. In much the same way, those who are not being led by the Spirit tend to do what *they* want to do, and often end up doing some things that they *didn't* want to do! Read it for yourself:

(18) "...For I have the desire to do what is good, but I cannot carry it out.

(19) For what I do is not the good I want to do; no, the evil I do not want to do – this I keep on doing.

(20) Now if I do what I do not want to do, it is no longer I who do it, but it is sin living in me that does it." (Romans 7:18-20, NIV)

Did you read that carefully? Doesn't that sound like *you,* or at least your "evil twin?" Let's be honest. How many people on a daily basis around the world try *not* to do something, and then do exactly what they tried not to do? And for how many decades and centuries do you think that law has been in effect? It's nothing new! Yet, there are vast sums of people who never figure it out.

If you have wanted to lose 10, 20, or 30 pounds for 10, 20, or 30 years, yet haven't gotten the results that you've desired for so long, that can only mean one thing. You have got to find some reason greater than yourself to lose the weight! That's the key! If you can't stop drinking, looking at pornography, partying with your friends on the weekend, smoking cigarettes, doing drugs, having sex, spending money, overeating, stealing, God's Word is the only spiritual weapon powerful enough to defeat that spirit of *selfishness* that is the root of all things *lustful.* The power of *love* (which also means the power of God since God *is* love) is greater than any other force in existence, spiritual or natural. And guess what? God gave his Spirit to *you* so that *you* could be *led by the spirit and be strong in the Lord.* Please note, I didn't say *be strong on your own.* That would be willpower, and as we have seen, *willpower is not enough.* "*Alcoholics Anonymous*" meetings being held around the world are filled with people everyday who try to exercise willpower. It's not that their spirit isn't *willing*, it's that the body is weak. We must be strong *in the Lord*, and only then can we conquer *anything!* The Bible tells us,

"Finally, *be strong in the Lord* and in his mighty power." (Ephesians 6:10, NIV) Emphasis added.

Therefore, if you are *led by the Spirit,* then your obligation is to live according to the Spirit. If you are led by the Word of God (and God's Word is Spirit), then you will do what the Spirit (God's Word) tells you to do. In doing so, you will put to death the misdeeds of the flesh and you will not do what it is that you do not want to do. You see, the person who is led by the Spirit no longer operates under the obligation to fulfill the desires of the flesh. That person is no longer under that law. Instead, he is under grace – God's grace. It's the only way. But I'll tell you something. These words are spiritual truth. What I am sharing with you is *revelation knowledge.* The world can't accept it because the world doesn't understand it. It is a spiritual truth that is spiritually discerned. May he that hath ears to hear, let him hear.

So, I ask you again. What is it that you're seeing? What are you taking in with your eyes? What is your husband taking in? What are your kids taking in? Your eyes are a sensory gate that must be guarded. *You are the temple. You are the house. Guard the house so you can be strong in the Lord!* Jesus and the Apostle Paul say on countless occasions:

- *"You must be on your guard."* (*See,* Mark 13:9, NIV)
- *"So be on your guard;* I have told you everything ahead of time." (Mark 13: 23, NIV)
- *"Be on guard!* Be alert!" (*See,* Mark 13:33, NIV)
- *"Be on your guard…"* (*See,* Matt. 10:17, NIV)
- "Watch out! *Be on your guard* against all kinds of greed…" (*See,* Luke 12:15, NIV)
- "So *be on your guard!* Remember that for three years I never stopped warning each of you night and day with tears." (Acts 20:31, NIV)
- *"Be on your guard;* stand firm in the faith; be men of courage; be strong. Do everything in love." (1 Cor. 16:13-14, NIV)
- "Therefore, dear friends, since you already know this, *be on your*

*guard* so you will not be carried away by the error of lawless men and fall from your secure position." (2 Peter 3:17, NIV)

These warnings are not meaningless. *You are the temple. You are the house. Guard the house! Be on your guard. Guard your eyes*! Do not let anything into the house, through your eyes, that is contrary to the Word of God. Protect the house. Guard the house so you can be strong *in the Lord*! I cannot overemphasize the significance and importance of this point.

In the First Pillar: *faith*, we discussed how God speaks through dreams and visions. Dreams are an important mode of communication for those who are able to *spiritually discern* God's voice and *hear* what it is that he is saying. Yes, in this world, people will chastise, label as "crazy," or ridicule those who say that they can *hear* God's voice. Yet, as Christians, we *hear* God's voice because we are his sheep. Like a herd of sheep that follow the voice of the Shepherd, the sons and daughters of God also know God's voice. A marvelous illustration of our ability to *hear* God's voice can be found in the following parable:

1. "I tell you the truth, the man who does not enter the sheep pen by the gate, but climbs in by some other way, is a thief and a robber.

2. The man who enters by the gate is the shepherd of his sheep.

3. The watchman opens the gate for him, *and the sheep listen to his voice.* He calls his own sheep by name and leads them out.

4. When he has brought out all his own, he goes on ahead of them, *and his sheep follow him because they know his voice.* (John 10:1-4, NIV) Emphasis added.

You see, when you live by your natural senses *only*, you are not tapping into your true power. God is Spirit. The Word of God is Spirit. We are Spirit. The most powerful forces in the universe are spiritual. Love, hate, envy, greed, forgiveness, anger, joy, kindness, self-control, patience, faithfulness, jealousy – these are forces that you cannot see, touch, taste smell or hear. They are forces that are imperceptible to your natural senses. Yet, we all know the power of love and the power of hate; the power of jealousy and the power of patience; the power of anger and the power of kindness. These forces, some light and some dark, are spiritual in nature. They are either the fruit of the Holy Spirit, or the fruit of an evil spirit. Depending on which side you are referring to, light or dark, we see the fruit of the Spirit manifest itself on a daily basis in our surroundings.

For example, the senseless killing of a human being by another human being is a fruit of the evil spirit. Gang violence amongst youth in various countries is often times the product of anger and frustration, turned outward. The resultant thefts or murder is a fruit of the dark spiritual force. Food and medical supply contributions between nations is often based in love and kindness. These are the fruit of the Holy Spirit. Here is the point. What you see with your eyes in the natural sense is only the fruit of a deeper issue. This is why I am teaching you to look beyond whatever problem arises in your life in the natural sense. *Look deeper.* Whatever events or occurrences that are happening or have happened in your life are merely the manifestation of a spiritual force behind those natural events. When you address *the root* of a problem, the branches will change.

In the parable above, God is the shepherd and we are his sheep. *Jesus is the gate* by which we have access to the Shepherd.

(7) "I tell you the truth, *I am the gate for the sheep.* All who ever came before me were thieves and robbers, but the sheep did not listen to them.

(8) *I am the gate; whoever enters through me will be saved."* (*See,* John 10: 7-9, NIV) Emphasis added.

God is the shepherd. We are his sheep. Jesus is the gate. That leaves only one more entity in the parable, the thief. Satan is the thief. Here is what Jesus says about the evil spirit, Satan.

*"The thief comes only to steal, kill, and destroy."* (*See,* John 10:10, NIV)

You must understand something. The biggest lie that Satan can get people to believe is that he doesn't exist. These are the very people who don't understand the forces behind what they see with their natural eyes when desperate circumstances arise. Satan does exist. He doesn't have a body. He is an evil, dark spiritual force. Because he doesn't have a body, he is always trying to get some-*body*. This is how he works. One way that Satan can enter your life (*i.e.* your mind and body, or "the temple" or "the house," is through what you take in through your sensory mechanisms (*i.e.* eyes, ears, mouth, etc.). In the First Pillar: *faith*, we touched upon how Satan can also enter through your emotions, thoughts, and feelings. We will discuss that in greater detail in the pages to follow.

For now, it is absolutely imperative that you understand that it is God's sheep who *hear* his voice. Those who ridicule, question, criticize, and don't believe are not his sheep, and therefore cannot *hear* his voice. Jesus told the unbelieving Jews of that time in no uncertain terms,

"…you do not believe because you are not my sheep. My sheep listen to my voice; I know them, and they follow me." (*See*, John 10:26-27, NIV)

As sure as the sun rises day to day, God has spoken to me, the author, repetitively in dreams about this notion of *guarding the house*. Even prior to my spiritual awakening upon coming to Christ, I would have these recurring dreams involving lucid imagery relating to this specific message. At that time, my spiritual ears were not yet in tune, so I could not *hear* God's intended message through these recurring thematic dreams. It wasn't until I began to grow spiritually through reading God's Word and spending time meditating on God's Word that I could *spiritually discern* a deeper message found therein. Remember, Jesus spoke to his disciples and to his followers mainly in parables. He spoke in the form of stories that were full of imagery. Similarly, all of the dream sequences found throughout the Bible, Old Testament and New Testament, were chalked full of imagery and symbolism. This is because God speaks to our hearts, not our ears! If he spoke to our ears, then anyone and everyone would hear and understand him. This has never been the case. His meanings are *spiritually discerned*, and only those who are being *led by the Spirit* can *hear* him and understand him.

In Genesis 4:7, God told Cain,

"…*sin is crouching at your door; it desires to have you*, but you must master it." (*See,* Genesis 4:7, NIV) Emphasis added.

Here, God's words to Cain evoke images of a structure, a *house*. This should not be taken lightly. *You are the house.* Just like any house erected in the natural, you too have doorways that lead inside.

You may recall that in the First Pillar, *faith*, I shared with you two of my own personal dream sequences and also their corresponding interpretations through *my* spiritual discernment. Well, in this instance, I believe that the imagery of your body as the *house* of the Lord is sufficient to convey my intended message. Such a powerful image, if you receive it, should effectively increase the value that you place on yourself! You and I are no different. You are God's creation just as I am. God's love is available to you just as it is to me. Your physical body has the same value as mine. God loves you as He does me. God wants to guide and protect you as His will is to guide and protect me. Some of you may even be aware that God has given his Spirit to you, just as he has given it to me. Now, I am simply reminding you that God's Spirit inside of you translates to you being the Lord's temple. You are the house of the Lord. I'll say it again. *you are the house*! And just as I must *guard the house* against the infiltration of wrong influences that enter by way of "worldly" images, movies, conversations, music, substances, emotions and feelings, *you too* must *be on guard* and protect what God has entrusted to you.

How many times have you told yourself that you would *not* allow some event in your life to occur, yet that event still occurred? Then, in hindsight, you realized the point at which you should have either said something, taken a stand, walked away, or performed whatever action would have appropriated a different result. You see, too many of us "guard the house," but *leave a window open*! Please listen carefully with your spiritual ears. It does you no good to tell yourself that you will be on guard against any seemingly "bad" men or women that try to come into your life (or, remain in your life), yet you sign-up for, or remain, on three or four different singles/dating matchmaker websites or frequent two or three different clubs every weekend. It does you no good to say that you will eliminate curse words from your everyday conversational speech, then, proceed to listen to music that is filled with insolent language or continue to hang around people who rattle off curse words like sailors. Honestly, what benefit do you receive by perpetually confessing that you need to lose weight, and yet, continue to walk past the same restaurants, donut shops, and pastry stores on your lunch break that tempt you by sight and smell? This is nothing short of self-deception. It's what I call, "leaving a window open."

God's Word, written and spoken, leads to success in all areas of life for those who *hear* and *obey*. Any reader of even just a few select passages in the gospels of Matthew, Mark, Luke, or John can clearly see that just because Jesus speaks to a person, doesn't mean that they *hear* him. By "hear," I am referring to the ability to spiritually discern an intended meaning. Hearing in the natural is not the equivalent of hearing in the spiritual. Always pay attention to the element of *spiritual discernment,* because that is what you are striving to attain. The Bible says, "…the Lord is my helper…" (*See,* Hebrews 13:6, NIV). Well, *hearing* God's voice *helps us* in our lives to avoid situations and pitfalls altogether that otherwise would so easily ensnare us (assuming that we *obey* what we heard).

To *depart from sin*, you must first discern God's Word for you regarding who you are in Christ. *You are the temple. You are the house. Be on your guard! Guard the house!* This means to take time in your daily lives to think. Think about the hobbies and the activities in your weekly routine that leave you susceptible to the wrong influences. Take the time to consider the things that you think about *the most* in any given week. It could be a person, place, or thing, but pay attention to what consumes *your thoughts* during the course of any given week. You see, anything that you take in through your senses has the potential to become *a thought*. Thoughts have the potential to become *strongholds*. And strongholds, in the mind, if they are of the wrong influence, can be detrimental, if not totally destructive.

For example, the young 25 year-old man who listens repeatedly to spiritually-dark music filled with imagery of hate, destruction, and evil now harbors *thoughts* surrounding the message found in the music. As *thoughts* become implanted in the human mind, they become *strongholds* which a person may then carry out to fruition, or act upon, in response to what has rooted itself in the mind. Interestingly, the American legal justice system recognizes this principle to some extent, but under a different name:  the criminal defense of insanity. The general idea is that a defendant's culpability for his criminal actions may be lessened, or mitigated, if there is a showing that his mental state was impaired at the time the crime was committed. Well, regardless of my opinion of the American legal justice system, I submit to you that the basic principle has some validity because...

**WHAT YOU THINK AFFECTS WHAT YOU DO.**

*Your mind is the battleground.* Your thoughts determine your actions. What you read, see, smell, touch, and hear determine your thoughts. In other words, for my readers who excelled at mathematical equations, visualize the following:

$A$ = Sensory in-take (*i.e.* images, words, conversations, pictures, etc.)

$B$ = Thoughts

$C$ = Actions

In life, $A = B$. The things that you take in by your senses become a thought.

In life, $B = C$. The thoughts in your mind often become your actions.

Therefore, $A = C$. *The things that you take in by your senses determine, or have a major effect on, the actions that you take.*

Naturally, we tend to view this truth in light of all the negativity in the world and understandably so. Think about it. All too often in the cases where a person has committed an act of murder or some other heinous crime, there was some simultaneous element of "mind influence" that shaped the culprit's way of thinking. Perhaps, it was a so-called "religious doctrine." Maybe the person possessed a certain ideology involving ethnic or race relations. Or, perhaps there was the presence of an intoxicating substance. In all these cases, one thing holds true. There was a sensory in-take of something influential that determined, or had a major effect upon their subsequent, and regrettable, actions.

Who hasn't heard of the notion of being "brain-washed?" Well, obviously you cannot wash someone's brain in the literal sense. However, you can influence their thoughts by putting certain images and words into their mind. It's a simple, but powerful concept that is exemplified best through children. If you placed 50 five year-old children, from 50 different countries, in one room, what would be the end result (besides a noisy room)? Would they play together or would they hate each other? They would play. If you placed 25 fifty year-old men from 25 different countries in one room, what would be the end result? Would they co-exist peacefully or would there be adversarial tensions? Here is the point. Information received determines what we think. What we think (even about other people) determines our actions. So, the million-dollar questions are:

- What are you taking in with your senses?
- What are you allowing to become a *though* in your mind?
- What *thoughts* are nesting and becoming *strongholds*?
- How are these *strongholds* manifesting themselves in your daily or weekly *actions*?

Previously, we talked about the importance of your *mindset* and *setting your mind* to line up with God's way of thinking. Now, we are discussing how a person's mind becomes set! Or, put another way, what things are coming through their senses, becoming thoughts and strongholds, and causing them to either commit sinful acts, or just causing them to fail in whatever situations they need to rectify or improve? You see, this is not judgment. I'm not judging you. I am telling you how you can improve your self-control in whatever area of your life you may need it. And someone may ask, "How do I know that the words of this book are influenced by God or the Holy Spirit?" The response is simple.

Remember, the five ways to determine whether God's voice is attached to something or not:

1.  It requires *faith*
2.  It requires *courage*
3.  It will *line up with God's written word*
4.  It will *go against the World's way of thinking*
5.  *Peace will rule in your heart*

**Faith:**    Faith is a belief. Everything in the Kingdom of God operates by faith. Every suggestion, comment, and principle in the Model for Daily Living *requires faith*! You are the house of the Lord. *You are the house.* You must believe God's Word that he has given us his Spirit as a deposit, a guarantee, of the fulfillment of His eternal promises to come.

**Courage:** *Guarding the house* takes courage. Having the *discipline* to assess and locate the areas of your life that essentially are open "windows" and "doorways" for wrong influential information to enter your mind, nest, and become *strongholds requires courage*!

**Line up with written Word:**    The Bible says,

- "The weapons we fight with are not the weapons of the world. On the contrary they have divine power to *demolish srongholds.* We demolish arguments and every pretension that sets itself up against the knowledge of God, and we *take captive every thought* to make it obedient to Christ." (2 Cor. 10: 4-5, NIV)

- This scripture illustrates the power of our spiritual weapon, which is the Word of God, to tear down, trample, defeat, destroy, and arrest every *thought* and *stronghold* that goes against God's

Word and sets itself up in the minds of people.

- *You are the house!* Don't let foolish arguments, superficial desires, or images that cause *fear* remain in front of your eyes or your ears. *Guard the house!*

**Against the World's way of thinking:** This is an easy one. Remember, there are two systems of thinking in effect: the Kingdom of God's way of thinking and the World's way of thinking.

- The Kingdom of God's way of thinking is *faith-based* and the Kingdom's power is rooted in *love.*
- The World's way of thinking is *fear-based* and the World's power is rooted in *selfishness.* The Kingdom of God's power is love and faith. The World's power is money.

  1. In the U.S, all of the graphic images or content that are "worldly" in nature originate from the World's way of thinking. In this day in age, just turn on your television and watch any "made-for-television" movie or situational-comedy show. Count how many times you hear God's name, or some form thereof, taken in vain. I respectfully challenge you to do this. Count how many times you hear a television character or personality say, "God" or "Jesus Christ." Depending on the movie or television show, there is a good chance you may even hear *profane language attached to* the name of God or Jesus Christ.

  2. This is merely one example of the very images, words, conversations, messages, and pictures that you should guard against! *You are the house!* What you take in by way

of your senses often times becomes *a thought*. If those thoughts are strong enough, they become *strongholds*, which have the power to affect your actions. For the younger generation, it's called "pop culture." It's music, movies, trends that comprise popular culture. For the older generation, it's a matter of *demolishing strongholds* that have already become *habitual*; the recognition and courage to remove, add, or re-arrange little things to prevent or guard against things that affect the mindset.

3. Whether you are young, old, or middle-aged, seeing yourself as *the house of God* and *guarding the house* against destructive images that are a commonality in worldly culture *goes against the world's way of thinking*.

**Peace ruling in your heart:**    Self-control is a powerful spiritual weapon with results that can also be seen in the natural. *You are the house. Guarding the house* against high calorie in-take, for example, and food and beverages with little nutritional value, or too much sugar and salt can prolong your life! It can result in a 10, 20, 30, 40, or 50 pound weight loss! I don't know too many people who wouldn't be "at peace" with a prolonged healthier life and a few pounds off the midsection. Going a step further, there is a peace that comes along with the power to go God's way rather than the way of the masses. God is concerned not just with our actions, but our thoughts. *Guarding the house* means guarding your *thought life* and the Word of God assures you that the Lord "will keep in *perfect peace* him whose *mind* is *steadfast* because he trusts in you." (*See*, Isaiah 26:3, NIV). Plainly stated, *hearing* and *obeying* God's Word to *honor your body and mind* as the *house* and *temple* of *God* brings peace because...

- You won't die of *cirrhosis of the liver* from *bringing alcohol into the house.*
- You won't die from an *overdose on cocaine or heroin* by in-taking fatal *drug substances into the house.*
- You won't die from a *stress-induced stroke or heart attack* caused by years of *emotional abuse that has resonated in the house.*
- You won't die *alone* because your partner or spouse has left you due to an addiction to pornography or inappropriate lustful behavior which has *taken root in the house.*

*Guarding the house* equates to guarding what you allow your natural senses to take in, which in turn prevents you from having the wrong *thoughts*, and subsequently taking the wrong *actions*. When you eat healthy foods and take in foods rich in nutrients and energy, you feel better on the inside. When you take in unhealthy foods, your insides feel worse. So why would you guard against unhealthy food, but not guard against unhealthy and impure conversation for instance? Both will impact you negatively *on the inside*. Eating unhealthy foods will affect your body. Hearing unhealthy words will affect your mind. In other words, the former relates to your natural body or being, which is temporary in nature, and will eventually pass away no matter what you take in. The latter pertains to your spiritual body or being, which is eternal in nature, and may potentially find everlasting life through Christ Jesus. For many, most, or all, the promise of eternal life as God's son or daughter is a *peace-loving promise that rules in the heart. You are God's temple. Your are the house. Be on guard. Guard the house!*

Remember, everything presented to you through the 7 Pillars of the Model for Daily Living is underscored by the 5-star principle: (1) Knowledge (2) Understanding (3) Discernment (4) Sound Judgment (5) Wisdom. As you move through the next several pages of the Model for Daily Living regarding the topic of GETTING PAST HURT, may the Spirit of the Lord be with you and may the content therein be a source of enlightenment and strength in your daily life.

## THIRD PILLAR:

# *Getting past the hurt*

*Hurt* is something that many people have felt in their life. Getting past a broken heart is a very serious topic that deserves proper time and teaching. Everyone is familiar with *hurt* that comes from disappointment, lies, cheating, or even death. Often times, dealing with *hurt* means that you have suffered a *loss* of some kind. It may be a relationship partner. It may be a family member. It may be job. It may be a best friend. It may even be the loss of a hope or a dream.

In this day in age, divorce rates around the world are sky high. It's not uncommon for husbands and wives to separate within two or three years from the inception of the marriage. It's become commonplace for young men and women to meet, start dating, and begin a relationship built on *lies* regarding where they've been in the past, who they've been with in the past, and why they've done what they have done in the past. It never ceases to amaze me the sheer numbers of people who say that they just want to *be loved* unconditionally, yet they are afraid to *give love* unconditionally for *fear* of getting *hurt*. As people get older and accumulate more life experience, they often become wiser, smarter. But where matters of the heart are concerned, this is not always the case. With age and experience, some people become *more fearful* of *getting hurt*. Some people become more closed, less trusting, less open, and less honest for *fear* of leaving themselves susceptible to *hurt* simply because they were *hurt* in the past.

Obviously, different people operate differently. But, *hurt* is not a visible characteristic. You cannot see *hurt* with the natural eye. (And please allow me to make an important distinction). *Hurt* is not the same thing as *disappointment*. At the start of the book, I cautioned you about the following:

"Words are important! Your words are all that you have to express your thoughts and feelings that arise out of any and all issues in your life. People often take for granted the art of vocal expression by trying to convey a certain message using the wrong words. Then, they assume that a listener will comprehend their intended meaning, although, in reality, their lackadaisical efforts to communicate effectively have "shortchanged" the listener."

*Hurt* is defined as injury, damage, or harm. *Disappointment* is defined as a failure to fulfill expectations or wishes. For our purposes, in discussing matters of the heart, *hurt* is of a higher degree than disappointment. Proceeding on that notion, if you are a person who is experiencing, or has experienced *hurt* in your life, then

I am talking to you. You know your own life. You know if you have had your *heart broken* by someone that you trusted. You know that a *broken heart*, and the *hurt* attached thereto, can be *paralyzing*. If you have ever dated, married, or loved someone in your life, and for whatever reason, the relationship ended, most likely, you experienced some level of *hurt*. If someone that you loved, trusted, or depended upon, *lied* or *deceived* you, and you later discovered the truth, then most likely, that person *hurt* you. This is our area of focus: *hurt* brought about by *lies* and *deception* and *how to get past it*. Let's take a look at the ramifications of *lies* and *deception*, and how the resultant *hurt* can affect your ability to see things clearly.

At the root of many breakups, legal separations and divorce proceedings, is some form of miscommunication. By miscommunication, I am not merely referring to a misunderstanding. I am also referring to the act of *misleading* or *misdirecting* another person through words and actions. Think about it. Lies result in the misleading of another person, which in turn, results in a misunderstanding or warped perception of reality.

When people enter into and *build relationships* on a foundation of *lies* and *deceptions*, eventually someone is going to get *hurt*. Whether it's the proponent of the lie or the person being deceived or misled, or both, depends upon the circumstances involved in that particular situation. You know your life and which side of the line you fall on. You know if you've lied to someone and *hurt* them, or if you have been lied to, and been hurt by the lie. I can't begin to tell you the number of people that I have spoken to around the world that fall on either side of the line. In other words, I can't give an accurate accounting of the scores of people that I've spoken to that have been affected by *hurt*. I think of my friends in the United States, China, Chile, Brazil, Spain, France, Mexico (to name a few), and the stories that I've heard surrounding a *broken heart* spurred on by *lies* and *deception*. Admittedly, it fascinates me to the extent that nothing binds us all together more tightly than the condition of the human heart. You don't need an interpreter to explain *hurt* and you don't need to be a citizen of a certain nation to experience *hurt*. *Hurt* is felt by all and no one person is immune to it.

What you probably *didn't* know is where *hurt* can lead you, if you're not careful. Pay close attention!

### HURT LEADS TO ANGER, AND ANGER TURNED INWARD LEADS TO DEPRESSION

How many of you have ever been hurt, gotten mad, and then gotten sad? Unfortunately, this is the progression that often takes place in people's lives. Depending on the degree of the HURT, this can be a very dangerous place to be for the following reasons:

- *Hurt* can make you *bitter*
- *Bitterness* can make you *sick* (*i.e.* stress)
- *Hurt* leads to *anger* (this is very dangerous, especially for men)
- *Anger* (especially in men) can lead to absolute *chaos* (*e.g.* violence; breaking the law)
- *Anger* turned inward leads to *depression* (also leads to stress-induced illness)

You see, *hurt* feelings *rob us* of the blessings God intended for us for our lives. You must figure out how to take the *hurt* out! Don't build upon a foundation of *hurt*. If *hurt* is in your life, you won't ever make a good decision. You will never make the *right* decision *hurt*. *Hurt* is counter intuitive in nature. When a person has been deeply *hurt*, what seems to be the best decision is always the wrong decision. *Hurt* keeps you from going forward. It keeps you stuck, stranded in one place. You may *think* that you're going forward, but if you are operating in *hurt*, your forward progress is stunted. It's an illusion. You have to learn how to forgive and dismiss what people have done to you. You cannot continue to make references to the *hurt* of the past. The greatest lesson any person can learn about *hurt* is how to deal with it, how to respond to it, and how to get past it.

Let's face facts. *Hurt* people are sometimes unpleasant to be around. They have a tendency to weave their past into the conversation. Some make you have to read their mind and others wear their heart on their sleeve. *Hurt* people lose the motivation to fight against negative emotions. *Hurt* people are sometimes depressed and wallow in self-pity.

**HURT PEOPLE CONTINUE TO TRY TO MAKE LOGICAL SENSE OUT OF AN ILLOGICAL LIE.**

*Hurt* people hold on for dear life to something that was never true. *Hurt* people allow their hearts to remain attached to something that never existed, or doesn't exist anymore. The dangers of letting your heart be tied to a *lie* or a *deception* cannot be overstated, especially those people who are tender-hearted, trusting, and most of all fighters and believers in *true* love. *Hurt* people can hang onto a lie as if it were truth, thus *living a lie*. This is precisely why I told you in previous paragraphs, *you cannot build on a foundation of hurt.* It will *never* be right. You must take the hurt out.

*Hurt* people make bad decisions. *They make decisions to protect their feelings instead of their future.* When you're in *control of your emotions*, you make decisions that protect your future. The number one enemy of people around the world is that they allow their emotions to be in charge of their life. *Self-control is a gift from God to get you to your destiny.* Your emotional *hurt* cannot be in charge of your life.

Now, at this point, you may be feeling a bit sad or discouraged because of the weight brought on by simply *discussing lies, deception* and *hurt.* Don't fret. Contextual learning is learning at its finest and it was necessary to paint a detailed picture to which we could all relate. If you've been *hurt* and suffered a *broken heart,* then you now have a context in which to operate. You can now call to memory *natural* events that have transpired in your own lives that have caused *hurt.* Notice what I just said. *natural events!* What have I been telling you from the start of the book?

### IDENTIFY YOUR ISSUE *AND* EXPRESS IT CORRECTLY!

To "fight the *right* fight" concerning all of the many challenges that you face every single day (*e.g. hurt*), *identify and express* the true underlying issue using *spiritual* terminology, rather than natural terminology.

**Natural language:** Your husband, wife, boyfriend or girlfriend *hurt* you. They lied to you. They deceived you. They cheated on you. They emotionally abused you. They physically abused you. They treated you badly. *They hurt you!*

### REAL ISSUE IN SPIRITUAL LANGUAGE: (TRUST)

The person that hurt you betrayed your trust. They did not tell *the truth*. The *truth* is the polar opposite of a *lie*. Jesus says, "I am the way, and *the truth*, and the life." (*See*, John 14:6, NIV). Jesus also tells us that Satan is the father of *lies*, there is *no truth* in him, and when he *lies*, he speaks his native language. (*See*, John 8:44, NIV). God hates liars. Strong words, I know, but they are not my own. The Bible clearly says,

"There are six things the Lord hates, seven that are detestable to him:

- haughty eyes
- *a lying tongue*
- hands that shed innocent blood
- a heart that devises wicked schemes
- feet that are quick to rush into evil
- a false witness who pours out *lies*
- and a man who stirs up dissension among brothers
  (Proverbs 6:16-19, NIV) Emphasis added.

If you are beginning a relationship with someone, your spiritual eyes and ears should be working for you to *discern* if this is the right person for you or the wrong person. *Lies*, especially, at the *start* of a relationship are *not of God*. God detests a lying tongue. Therefore, you know that a relationship that begins on a foundation of *lies*, *deception*, and *untruth* does *not* have the *peace of God* attached to it. And as I stated earlier, *hurt people continue to try to make logical sense out of an illogical lie*. They hang onto the lie which means they hang onto a relationship that does not have the peace of God attached to it. This is a very dangerous place to be. The reality is that people, all over the world, are *hurting*. But if you can't identify and express the real issues, then you can't apply a solution that will *get you past the hurt.*

*Jesus is the Truth.* The Word of God is *truth.* You can *trust* God. You can *trust* his Word. That's why when you have a relationship with the Lord, you have *peace.* It's because there is nothing false, misleading, untrue or deceptive about God's love for you. One way that we know God's peace is *not* attached to a certain relationship is if there are lies and deception present. We also know that people are not perfect and that at some point, *forgiveness* must enter the picture, just as Jesus Christ forgave all of us. *Forgiveness* is a sub-issue of *getting past hurt.* For now, let's focus on mastering the way to overcome *hurt.* *Getting past hurt* involves one thing and one thing only: taking authority over your emotions.

### Taking authority over your emotions

Real destruction or success doesn't come from the outside, but from the inside. A broken heart brought about by lies and deception is an external event. It is something that happened *to* you. But, it is the response that comes *from* you that determines the real outcome. When you have been *hurt,* you *must* learn to take authority over your emotions to retake charge of your life. People so often turn over the controls of their life (*i.e.* their heart) to someone else and feel completely helpless when they are lied to, deceived, or let down in a major way. It is at this point where many people *feel* as if they have no control over their emotions. They cannot separate their head from their heart and often times remain stuck in an emotionally hurtful situation. What you may not realize is that remaining in a place of *hurt* shortchanges our ability to receive the blessings that God has intended for our lives. Essentially, hurt people assign the highest priority to the *hurt* that they are experiencing and place everything else second. This is why many people give up. They give in. It's because they are now viewing life through a lens of emotional pain rather than putting the pain in its rightful place.

I want to be clear. I am not, nor have I ever been, a proponent of denial. If someone or something has *hurt* you, don't pretend it never happened! Denial simply means ignoring the truth and that will not help you in any way. What I am suggesting to you is that God is bigger than any *hurt* that you could possibly feel. God is bigger than any pain that you may go through. Don't deny the pain of *hurt*; focus on the medicine. How do you get past a hurtful situation? *Getting past hurt* is achieved by *Taking authority over your emotions*. This is the root issue that is for everybody! Now, let's take a closer look at the word *"emotion."*

**Emotion** – an emotion is a mental and physiological state associated with a wide variety of feelings, thoughts, and behavior. Emotions are subjective experiences, often associated with mood, temperament, personality, and disposition. The English word 'emotion' is derived from the French word '*emouvoir.*' This is based on the Latin '*emovere,*' where *e-* (variant of *ex-*) means 'out' and *movere* means move.[13]

For your comprehension, allow me to reiterate for the sake of clarity. The word, "emotion" comes from the French word "*emouvoir*," which is derived from the Latin "*emovere*" – which can be broken down into two parts:

---

13     *See,* www.answers.com/topic/emotion; (Wikipedia: Emotion)

- *"e"* means out
- *"movere"* means move

So, in using your spiritual eyes and ears, consider the meaning of the word *"emotions"* in relation to your daily life. Do you see it? *Emotions,* as they pertain to you, have the ability to *move* you *out* of the will of the God for your life. This is an extremely important point. *Emotions,* as they pertain to you, have the ability to *move* you *out* of the will of the God for your life. If you cannot control your emotions, then you are susceptible to disorder and chaos coming, or remaining, in your life. Emotions *cannot* take authority over us. We must take authority over our emotions. If you can control your emotions, you can do anything! The person who can control their emotions can do *absolutely* anything. The Bible says,

"Better a patient man than a warrior, a man who controls his temper than one who takes a city." (Proverbs 16:32, NIV)

In other words, *self-control* over your emotions is mightier than the sword. The ability to control one's emotions is more powerful than one who can overtake a city in battle.

When you don't have control over your emotions, your emotions are leading *you*. People who can't control their emotions often times want to control someone else. Perhaps, some of you can pinpoint a situation in your own life where that has occurred. Or maybe, you know someone to which this applies. Either way, it is imperative to understand that we as human beings have emotions, but our emotions must not have us! By the very definition of the word, we know that our emotions can potentially *move* us *out* of God's plan for our lives. Automatically, that should put you on high alert because *true* and *lasting* success and prosperity are only found when you are operating *within* God's will for your life.

Often times, emotions are feelings on the inside usually rooted in pleasure or pain. Of course, that is an oversimplification of the definition, but it is accurate in light of the purpose of this Pillar which is to illuminate the common pitfalls that plague so many of us in our daily routine. Being led by emotions that are connected to pleasure or pain, is where many people get themselves into trouble because it's *those* feelings that *move* you in a certain direction and can cause a person to act without *sound judgment*.

Please recall the Second Pillar and that the notion of *guarding the house* was directly affiliated with protecting and controlling your *thought* life. In other words, *guarding the house* means to monitor and be discretionary with what you take in with your natural eyes and ears because negative content often leads to wrong *thoughts*. *Thoughts* become *strongholds*, which can only be demolished by the spiritual weaponry that is the Word of God. Well, *thoughts* and e*motions* are related. What you *think* can easily influence and determine what you *feel*, thus the importance of getting your "*thinking*" to line up with the Word of God. You *must* read your Bible and meditate, ponder, and think upon what God says. If your *thoughts* line up with God's Word, then your *emotions* will line up with your *thoughts*, and your *emotions* will also be in line with God's Word. Visualizing the circular image is helpful.

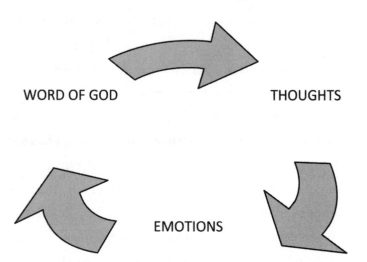

WORD OF GOD                              THOUGHTS

EMOTIONS

Everything begins with God's Word. The spiritual precedes the natural. When you are *not* in tune with God's Word, then your emotions will *move* you *out* of God's will for your life. Alternatively, when you *have* the Word of God in your mind, in your mouth, and in your heart, then your "spiritual thoughts and feelings" move you *toward* God.

Satan is "the father of lies," and there are three ways that he tries to get to you:

- he makes *suggestions* to you
- seduces your *emotions* and your *feelings*
- whispers things to you by putting *thoughts* in your mind

I have told you before and I'll tell you again that he is limited in what he can do because Satan has no physical body! Therefore, he is *always trying to get some body*! His evil spirit can only do harm in the natural sense if he is able to enter and use a natural body. That is why he is constantly trying to attack us through our thoughts, feelings, and emotions. They are his way in. Don't forget, *You are the house!* Essentially, when you *guard the house diligently*, you are not only *on guard* against the improper images, pictures, songs, and conversations that this World has to offer – you are also *on guard* against allowing your *emotions* to take authority over you!

You have already been made aware that *the house* has windows, doorways, and entrances just like a real physical structure in the natural sense. Your eyes, ears, and mouth are the most common way in. However, your *emotions* are also a doorway! If you don't know your position as a son or daughter of God, the enemy can absolutely torment you through your *emotions*. *Fear, anger, lust, envy, loneliness, discouragement, worry, hurt*, etc, are all *emotions* that lead many people down a path of destruction and cause them to have a very stressful life. The *emotion* of *fear* is arguably the strongest negative-based emotion that a human being can harbor. Its antithesis is *faith*. The *emotion* of *fear* is a doorway. *Satan's way into your life is through fear.* If you tolerate *fear* for even one second, you are giving the devil an entryway into your life to wreak havoc, confusion, disorder, and chaos.

*You are the temple. You are the house. Be on guard. Guard the house!*

Doorways include *emotions*. The Bible warns us,

"Do not let the sun go down while you are still *angry*, and do not give the devil a foothold." (See, Ephesians 4:26, NIV) Emphasis added.

Doorways include *emotions*. But I remind you in love, if you cannot cite the real or root issues in your life, and learn to express them in spiritual language, you are in danger of fighting the *wrong* fight.

Of course, nobody is perfect. Jesus is the only man to walk the Earth who was without sin. While here on Earth, he was the walking, talking, breathing, Word of God. The Bible says,

"*The Word became flesh* and made his dwelling among us." (*See,* John 1:14, NIV) Emphasis added.

"For we do not have a high priest who is unable to sympathize with our weaknesses, but we have one who has been tempted in every way, just as we are — *yet was without sin.*"(Hebrews 4:15, NIV) Emphasis added.

Jesus, the Lamb of God, who was sent by the Father to take away the sins of the world, was indeed, *human*, and had *human emotions*, the same way that you and I have *emotions.* Yet, Jesus was without sin. This means that Jesus *had* emotions, but His emotions *did not have him.* He was led by the Spirit rather than by the natural. And, the good thing is that we have a God who can relate to what it is that we feel. For example, Jesus knows firsthand what it's like to be *hurt* or *angry*, yet he remained *blameless.* On this truth, common sense dictates that *we* should do whatever Jesus did in order to *take authority over our emotions*, and also be without sin. Who among us hasn't gotten *angry* from time to time? But, the Bible says,

"Do not let the sun go down while you are still angry." (*See,* Ephesians 4:26, NIV)

Think about it. Have you ever had an argument with someone in the evening or at night before going to sleep? It's a terrible feeling. It may not even be an argument. It may merely be something that upset you prior to falling asleep. *Anger* is an *emotion* that cannot be out in front, leading you. If anything, *emotions* must be the trailer, the thing that is found in the rear. Again, it does no good to *deny* that upsetting things do happen in life, things that may bring *fear*. The issue is how will you *respond*? Look at the scripture again, but this time take note of the word in italicized-type.

"Do not let the sun go down while you are *still* angry." (*See*, Ephesians 4:26, NIV)

You see, the word "still" suggests that there should be a *change of emotion* prior to going to bed. It doesn't purport to abandon the human emotion altogether, but rather to *take authority over it.*

When Satan attacked Jesus' *emotions*, Jesus exercised authority and maintained *authority*. Here is a prime example. Just prior to the betrayal of Jesus by Judas, Jesus and his disciples went to a place called Gethsemane. Jesus was well aware the hour of his betrayal was upon him, and he was overwhelmed with emotions of distress and sorrow. The Bible says,

(32) "They went to a place called Gethsemane, and Jesus said to his disciples, 'Sit here while I pray.'

(33) He took Peter, James and John along with him, and began to be *deeply distressed* and *troubled*.

(34) '*My soul is overwhelmed with sorrow to the point of death,*' he said to them." (*See*, Mark 14:32-34, NIV)

Here, Jesus was distraught to the point of death and understandably so since he knew that he was about to be delivered into the hands of his captors and crucified. Now I ask you. When was the last time *you* were distraught and distressed to the *point of death?* An emotional onslaught so great, that Jesus felt sorrow to the point of death. That's heavy. Now, I won't make light of some situations that many of you may find yourselves in from time to time. Stress, lack of money, worry, heartache, depression, sickness, can all cause a heavy emotional sadness that leaves us vulnerable to be led by our emotions rather than making right decisions based on what is best for our lives. But turning our attention back to Jesus, the real question becomes... *what did Jesus do when his emotions were attacked?*

Answer: (1) *He went forward* and *he prayed*

Let's take a closer look.

(34) "*My soul is overwhelmed with sorrow to the point of death,*" he said to them. 'Stay here and keep watch."

(35) *Going a little farther, he fell to the ground and prayed...*"

(*See,* Mark 14:34-35, NIV) Emphasis added.

Jesus, at the point of being overwhelmed with a level of sadness that could kill him did two things: he went forward, and he prayed.

Some of *you* are at a point of sadness in your life. Someone has carried around a heavy heart about *something* for weeks, months, years, and maybe even decades. Somebody has been emotionally abused, physically abused, carries regrets, has made bad choices, entered wrong relationships, battled addictions, struggled with weight, and finds him or herself in a life that has taken a wrong turn. Someone is stuck, stranded, unhappy, unfulfilled, and feels as if they have no peace, no joy, no love, no security, and no hope. Well, I have two things to say to you.

GO FORWARD AND PRAY

Remember, the word *"emotion"* comes from the French word *"emouvoir,"* which is derived from the Latin *"emovere"* – which can be broken down into two parts:

- *"e"* means out

- *"movere"* means move

Satan attacked Jesus' emotions at Gethsemane to try to *move* Jesus *out* of the will of God for *his* life, which was to die on the cross for our sins. You see, no one took Jesus' life. Jesus *laid down* his life on his *own authority*. But you must know the Word to know the truth. Jesus said,

(17) The reason my Father loves me is that *I lay down my life* – only to take it up again.

(18) *No one takes it from me*, but I lay it down *on my own accord*.

*I have authority to lay it down and authority to take it up again.* This command I received from my Father. (John 10:17-18, NIV) Emphasis added.

Jesus was given *authority* to lay down his life on the cross for our sins. Satan attempted to bombard Jesus' emotions with distress and sorrow *to the point of death* regarding what was to come. And although Jesus had the authority, Satan attempted to get Jesus to give up that authority and give in to his emotions. Satan wanted Jesus to relinquish his authority under the weight and pressure of sorrow, distress, and troubled emotions in hopes that Satan would *move* Jesus *out* of God's intended purpose for his life. Under emotional attack, Jesus *took authority over his emotions by going forward*, and *praying. Blessed is the man who outlasts a satanic attack that bombards his way of thinking. Blessed is the woman who withstands a satanic attack that grips her emotions.* Remember, the race is not given to the swift, but to the man who is *prepared*. You've got to know what to do *before* trouble comes.

And let's not overlook a key element regarding Jesus *taking authority over his emotions*. The will of God for Jesus' life was to spread the gospel truth and take away the sins of the world. He was sent to Earth to execute a plan that was already established for his life. His dying on the cross allowed our sins to be forgiven. His dying on the cross gave us the opportunity to find eternal life in Christ Jesus. So, what am I saying? What is my point? The point is that *Jesus' taking authority over his emotions* kept him on *the right path* for his life. This didn't merely affect *him*. It affected others: you, me, and the whole human race. What you must understand is that *your* ability to *take authority over your emotions* and stay within the will of God for *your* life, will affect somebody else's life! Maybe it's a friend, a family member, a relationship partner, or someone you don't know. The product of being "*kingdom-minded*," as opposed to "*self-minded*," is that *other* people will be blessed as a result of the *authority* that you exercise in *your life* in the name of the Lord.

In this world, the unfortunate reality is that people get *angry* and kill one another. Political leaders harbor *hatred* in their hearts and commit acts of genocide. Mothers *worry* and abandon babies. Young people *fear* and get abortions. Men *lust* and commit adultery. Women *fear* and tolerate abuse. People *stress* and suffer high blood pressure. Men surrender their *authority* and submit to being labeled an alcoholic or drug addict. People *envy* and lie, cheat, and steal. People harbor *greed*, abduct women and children, and engage in human trafficking.

### EMOTIONS, EMOTIONS, EMOTIONS
*Take authority over your emotions!*

Let's be clear. I'm under no disillusion. Although the *spiritual truth* is available to everyone, not just *anyone* will receive it, will want to hear it, and frankly, can even understand it. Although Jesus tells us repeatedly, "follow me" (*See,* Matt. 4:19; *See* also, Mark 2:14; John 1:43), not everyone will be enlightened by the *spiritual truth*. Not everyone in the world will endeavor to be like Jesus. The Bible clearly states,

(29) "For those God foreknew he also predestined to be conformed to the likeness of his Son, that he might be the firstborn among many brothers.

(30) And those he predestined, he also called; those he called, he also justified; those he justified, he also glorified. (Romans 8:29-30, NIV)

The fate of the masses I cannot speak to because I am not the Lawgiver, nor the Judge. What *is* clear to me is that there is cause to *rejoice* if you are one of those whom God "foreknew," "predestined," "called," "justified," and "glorified." There is cause to REJOICE if you are concerned with being "conformed to the likeness of his Son." *To be like Jesus* means to *take authority over your emotions.* You can't be like Jesus if you *don't take authority over your emotions.* If you are in his Word, then you are in him and he is in you. His Word is Spirit (*See,* John 6:63, NIV). Jesus gave you his Word, which means that you also have his Spirit. And God did not give us a Spirit of fear, but a Spirit of power, of love, and of self-discipline. (*See,* 2 Tim. 1:7, NIV).

Now, we know that Satan is always trying to *move* you *out* of the will of God for your life. Somebody might say, "Well, what is the will of God for my life?" The will of God is printed out for you in 66 books of the Bible. But you have to know what the will of God says! Satan tries to move you by attacking your feelings and emotions. The enemy whispers to you and before you know it, you're saying to yourself,

"I *should* go to church (or bible study), but I don't *feel* like it."

But the will of God says,

"*Let us not give up meeting together, as some are in the habit of doing,* but let us encourage one another – and all the more as you see the Day approaching. (Hebrews 10:25, NIV) Emphasis added.

Then you get to church (or bible study), and say to yourself,

"I'm not giving my tithe or offering this week. Or, maybe I'll just give *half* of it."

But the will of God says,

"*Bring your whole tithe into the storehouse.* Test me in this and see if I will not throw open the floodgates of heaven and pour out so much blessing that you will not have room enough for it. (*See,* Malachi 3:10, NIV) Emphasis added.

Satan wants to *move* you *out* of the will of God for your life, and some of you allow him to do so! Just because the *feeling* comes or shows up doesn't mean that you have to submit to it! Let me say that again. Just because you *feel* something doesn't mean you have to act on it. Someone might reply, "Well, that's easy to say, but much more difficult to do." Well, let me show you exactly the source of power that will allow you to *take authority over your emotions.*

Jesus told us without a hint of uncertainty,

(19) "*I have given you authority to trample on snakes and scorpions and to overcome all the power of the enemy; nothing will harm you.*" (Luke 10:19, NIV) Emphasis added.

You already have the authority, but unless you know who you are in Christ Jesus, you don't know the *authority* that you have. In other words, you are fighting life's spiritual battles without your *spiritual weapons*. The *authority* can only be found *in the Word*! *Jesus* is the word made flesh! (*See*, John 1:14). The *authority* is in him! If his Word is in you, than he is in you and also the *authority* to trample on snakes and scorpions and overcome *all* the power of the enemy. And like I said before, how many of you have come across some snakes and scorpions in your life? *We need our spiritual weapons*!

So, the real issue has been laid out for you. How do you *overcome hurt* in your life and how do you *take authority over your emotions*? You now know the source and power of your *authority* (*i.e. where it comes from and what it can do*), but the question is: How do I *activate, ignite, spark, turn on, bring to the forefront, my authority*? More specifically, how do I enlist my *authority* when my heart is broken; when I've lost my job; when the doctor informs me that I'm sick; when I've been subjected to emotional and/or physical abuse; when I'm afraid; when I'm worried; when I'm lonely; when I'm hurt; when I'm angry; or when I'm depressed? When the enemy is doing his best to bombard my way of thinking with haywire *emotions* and *feelings* that seem heavier than I can bear, how can *I take authority over my emotions* at that moment?

Answer: *the shield of faith*

You must put up the *shield of faith*.

When you put on the *full armor of God*, you put on the following:

- the belt of truth
- the breastplate of righteousness

- your feet are fitted with the readiness that comes from the gospel of peace, and
- the helmet of salvation

(*See*, Ephesians 6:14-17, NIV)

In addition to all of this, you *take up the shield of faith*, with which you can extinguish all the *flaming arrows* of the evil one. The *flaming arrows* are those haywire emotions and out-of-control feelings of *fear, anger, hurt, lust, depression, discouragement, worry, sickness, jealousy*, and *rage*. Remember, the devil preys upon your *emotions* by trying to seduce your thoughts and feelings. These *flaming arrows* (or, *fiery darts*) have the potential to strike and do much damage in our lives, as we have seen with people who are led by their *emotions*. But the *shield of faith* will quench all the flaming arrows, or fiery darts, of the devil.

What is the *shield of faith*? It's the *Word of God*.

When you feel like your heart has been stepped on by some guy or girl, man or woman, who *hurt* you, *lift up the shield of faith* and quote Luke 10:19 with confidence:

"God gave me *authority* over *all* the power of the enemy; *nothing* will harm me."

When your *emotions* start coming apart and you begin to *worry* about your lack of finances, lack of love, lack of health, and lack of peace, *lift up the shield of faith* and quote Matthew 6:33 boldly:

"Seek ye *first* the kingdom of God, and his righteousness; and all *these things* shall be added unto you."

When you're suffering and feeling weak and downtrodden because your relationship didn't work out or is going through a difficult period, or because you have lost *hope* in ever finding a lasting relationship, *life up the shield of faith* and quote Jesus' words in 2 Corinthians 12:9 without pause:

"*My grace is sufficient* for you, for *my power is made perfect in weakness.*"

You see, when those flaming arrows and fiery darts (*i.e. suggestions, thoughts*) start flying at you, *put up the shield of faith. The effect or result is that you will value more what the Word of God says about you than what people, or your situation, say about you.*

*Lifting up the shield of faith* is exactly what Jesus did when he was led into the desert to be tempted by Satan for forty days. (*See,* Luke 4:1-13). The Bible says that Jesus ate nothing during the forty days and at the end of them was hungry. (*See,* Luke 4:2). When the devil said to Jesus, "If you are the Son of God, tell this stone to become bread," Jesus *lifted up the shield of faith* and said, "*It is written: 'Man does not live on bread alone.'*" (Luke 2: 4) Notice Jesus' *first three words:* "*It is written.*" Jesus, in the face of an emotional satanic attack, quoted the Word of God.

Then the devil led Jesus up to a high place and showed to him all the kingdoms of the world and said to him, "I will give you all their authority and splendor, for it has been given to me, and I can give it to anyone I want to. So if you worship me, it will all be yours." (*See,* Luke 4:5-7). Jesus responded by *lifting up the shield of faith* and said, "*It is written: 'Worship the Lord your God and serve him only.'*" (Luke 2: 8) Again, notice Jesus' *first three words:* "*It is written.*" Under pressure applied to his thinking and feeling, Jesus quoted the Word of God.

Finally, the devil led Jesus to Jerusalem and had him stand on the highest point of the temple and said to him, "If you are the Son of God, throw yourself down from here. For it is written, 'He will command his angels concerning you to guard you carefully; they will lift you up in their hands so that you will not strike your foot against a stone.'" (*See,* Luke 2: 9-11). (Before we even get to Jesus *lifting up the shield of faith,* take note of how Satan used the words, "It is written" in his attempt to *move* Jesus *out* of the will of God. Satan knows the Word of God and will twist it, bend it, and flip it around in his attacks against you! But, if you don't know *the truth,* then you will fall for *the contradiction.* You must *know* and stand on *the Word of God).* Jesus answered by *lifting up the shield of faith* and replied, "*It says: 'Do not put the Lord your God to the test.'*" (Luke 4:12)

We open ourselves up to be defeated by *hurt and fear* when we *don't know* God's Word. I guarantee you, if you spend time in the Word of God, getting to know the Lord and his will for your life, it will equip you with the emotional fortification to never be defeated by *hurt* or *fear* again. God's Word will give you direction on how to deal with all of the *emotions* that are common to man. The Word will show you how to *overcome lust.* The Word will help you to *overcome a broken heart.* The Word will show you how to *take authority over your emotions* When you give God's Word *first priority* in your life, you will be led by his Word (*i.e.* The Spirit of God), rather than led by your human *emotion.* The Spiritual must precede the natural in *all* things.

As we move closer to the conclusion of this Pillar, let's quickly review what you have learned. In order for us to find true and lasting prosperity, as followers of Christ, we *must depart from sin*. We are *all* born sinners. No one is perfect. But God's grace is available to us through His only Son, Jesus Christ, who was sent to Earth to teach and preach the good news that our sins may be forgiven if we believe in him. Indeed, we obtain the promise of eternal life through Jesus Christ, but there is much more to it than that. God wants us to have a *good life*! Jesus says that he came so that "we may have life, and have it more abundantly." (*See*, John 10:10, NIV). That means, God wants you to have a *good life*, and not just an average, humdrum, so-so, run-of-the-mill, anything-will-do, life. There is a *fullness of joy* that is in him that can only be *revealed* through the Holy Spirit. And that *"revelation knowledge"* can only come by *spending time* in fellowship with the Holy Spirit. How do we do that? We do that by spending time in God's Word. Remember, the words spoken by God *are* spirit, and they are life. (*See*, John 6:63, NIV).

But when we are caught up doing the things that appeal to the *natural man* and the *natural woman*, in opposition to the Holy Spirit and in contrast to God's Word, then we cut ourselves off from the blessings that God has in store for our lives. There is an old saying that "ignorance is bliss," which means that there is no accountability, responsibility, and worry attached to something that you don't know. In other words, you can't blame *me* for something that I didn't know. Well, allow me to enlighten you. *Ignorance* is possibly the biggest enemy in the life of a believer *or* a non-believer. What you *don't* know *can* hurt you! In reality, that should not be a difficult concept for anyone because it applies in the spiritual *and* in the natural. Ignorance of the spiritual truth is no exception and no excuse. I like what Jesus said in regard to ignorance. He said,

"*Are you not in error because you do not know the Scriptures or the power of God?*" (See, Mark 12:24, NIV)

The truth is that if you *aren't* concerned with your *faith* in God, then you really won't care too much about a discussion on *departing from sin.* I know this to be true, at least for some people, because I recall a time in my life when I didn't care. There is a thick cloud of disillusionment in the world today that does not allow so many people to see the spiritual truth, God's truth. In that place, you can't see God's truth. You're probably not reading the Bible, and you're likely not spending any time getting to know God for yourself. It's your choice to continue on this path and it's *no one's right to judge you* for doing so. But, if there was a better way to live, I'd certainly want someone to tell *me.*

For believers and followers of God's Word, we *are* concerned with *departing from sin.* And the more you know of God's Word, the more accountable you are to abide by it. "Ignorance is bliss" goes completely out the window – it doesn't apply. We must "hear" and "*do*" what the Word says. (*See,* James 1:22, NIV). We must stay in the Word of God continuing to fellowship with the Holy Spirit so that we may limit the "slips" and "stumbles" that may occur in our walk with Christ. *Departing from sin* is the foundation of receiving God's blessing! When we fail to *depart from sin*, it causes us to feel *guilt* and *condemnation* and we don't feel *confident* of *God's presence* because of our misdeeds. This is so important. I know that somebody understands what I'm talking about but perhaps, you've never been able to put it into words. Let me state it again clearly.

*Failing* to *depart from sin* brings *guilt* and *condemnation*, and causes us to *lose confidence* in *God's presence*.

This is *why* a person who is a believer in Christ, who goes to church and studies the Bible, but nonetheless commits error through some measure of sin, feels *guilty* and removed from God's good graces. Even though God said, "I'll never leave you, nor forsake you," the presence of sin undermines the *confidence* that we have in *God's presence*. It takes away the *confidence* that enables us to *lean on God* in confusing times, to go to him in prayer and *ask God* for whatever we need. Don't ever forget, the devil is a "thief" who comes "to *steal*, kill, and destroy." (John 10:10, NIV). Well, when we fail to *depart from sin*, we allow the enemy to *rob us* of the *confidence* that we should have as children of God. Without that *confidence*, we're effectively *blocked* from the many blessings that God wants us to experience.

Ok. I understand that nobody likes to be called a "sinner." Nobody likes to be chastised and labeled as someone who is living in sin. (I don't like it either). Thus, the phrase *depart from sin* may be offensive to some people. However, I have said repeatedly, you must accept God's Word *humbly*. Humble yourself. The Bible tells us,

"He who ignores discipline comes to poverty and shame, but whoever heeds correction is honored." (Proverbs 13:18, NIV)

The Word also tells us,

"Whoever loves discipline loves knowledge, but he who hates correction is stupid." (Proverbs 12:1, NIV)

Strong words, but they are not my own. Open the Word and read them for yourself. Words of discipline are *always* difficult to hear, for *everybody*. The Bible says,

"No discipline seems pleasant at the time, but painful. Later on, however, it produces a harvest of righteousness and peace for those who have been trained by it." (Hebrews 12:11, NIV)

So my advice to you is simple. Forget the "labels." Labels tend to offend people in such a way that they close their ears to hearing the truth because they *feel* that they are being judged. Well, don't let that *feeling of offense* guide you. Let the Spirit guide you. You have feelings; feelings don't have you. The Word of God tells us what we *should* do and what we *should not* do. You can call it whatever you want.

I suddenly remember my Shakespeare:

"A rose by any other name would smell as sweet."

– William Shakespeare, *Romeo and Juliet*

Regardless of the name, "sin," "partying," "recreation," or otherwise, it is still the failure to abandon the above that determines whether we will receive the prosperity that comes from God.

Stop cursing and using profane language.

"Nor should there be obscenity, foolish talk or coarse joking, which are out of place, but rather thanksgiving." (Ephesians 5:4, NIV)

"Don't let any unwholesome talk come out of your mouths…" (*See*, Ephesians 4: 29, NIV)

Stop having sex outside of marriage, viewing pornography, and just being "wild."

"But among you there must not be even a hint of sexual immorality, or of any kind of impurity…because these are improper for God's holy people. Such a man has no inheritance in the kingdom of Christ and of God." (*See*, Ephesians 5:3,5, NIV)

Stop qualifying your "YES" and your "NO" with curse words. "Simply let your 'Yes' be 'Yes,' and your 'No,' 'No'; anything beyond this comes from the evil one." (Matthew 5:37, NIV)

In other words, *stop saying "hell yes"* and *"hell no,"* (or some other version of this which is much stronger). Just say "Yes" and "No." Anything else comes from the prince of *this* world. Set your mind on heavenly language, not "worldly" language.

"Set your minds on things above, not on earthly things." (Colossians 3:2, NIV)

Stop drinking mixed alcoholic beverages (vodka, rum, tequila, whiskey, margaritas, martinis, etc.) red wine and white wine.

(29) "Who has woe? Who has sorrow? Who has strife? Who has complaints? Who has needless bruises? Who has bloodshot eyes?

(30) Those who *linger over wine*, who go to sample bowls of *mixed* wine." (Proverbs 23:29-30, NIV) Emphasis added.

*Don't attach savoir faire[14] to drinking wine. Don't think you're a renaissance person cultured in worldly etiquette because you are adept at wine tasting! It's a lie! It's a trick! It's a trap!*

(31) Do not gaze at wine when it is red, when it sparkles in the cup, when it goes down smoothly!

(32) In the end it bites like a snake and poisons like a viper.

(33) Your eyes will see strange sights and your mind imagine confusing things.

(34) You will be like one sleeping on the high seas, lying on top of the rigging.

---

14    *Savoir faire* is defined as "the ability to say or do the right thing or graceful thing." *See,* www.answers.com.

(35) 'They hit me,' you will say, 'but I'm not hurt!' They beat me, but I don't feel it! When will I wake up so I can find another drink?" (Proverbs 23:31-35, NIV)

I hope that you see what I'm trying to do. It's one thing for me to say *depart from sin*, and it's another thing for me to say *stop drinking*, or *stop cursing*. We all live in the same world and face the same issues. What applies to you also applies to me. In other words, whatever medicine I prescribe to you, I must also take my dosage on a daily basis, that is, if I want to be on the *path to the good life* and ultimately earn a place in heaven.

This Pillar, *depart from sin*, teaches you *how* to *overcome lust*; *how* to *overcome hurt*; *how* to *take authority over your emotions*; and to lay a foundation for the prosperity that comes from God to be manifested in your life. You want God's prosperity, not the world's prosperity. You want God's wealth, not just the world's wealth. You want money and riches that are from God, not from somewhere else. There is an *honor* that comes from God that cannot come from men or women. God tells us,

"Those who *honor* me, I will *honor*, but those who despise me will be disdained." (1 Samuel 2:30, NIV) (Emphasis added)

Praise God for your diligence and humility! As you continue on to the *fourth pillar*, may the Holy Spirit *reveal* the *knowledge* and *understanding* that will lead to *discernment, sound judgment, and wisdom* in your daily lives concerning *departing from sin*.

Now, it is time to move forward to the next pillar in the 7 Pillars of the Model for Daily Living. The *fourth pillar is honor*.

# FOURTH PILLAR:

## *Honor*

*Honor.* Here is a word that doesn't surface in most people's vocabulary on a daily basis. *Honor* is a word that can be used to denote a noun or a verb. The Fourth Pillar, *honor*, will provide clarity as to what it means *to honor* someone. Specifically, we will focus on *honor* in the context of what it means to *honor* God in our everyday life. Let's begin with a few synonyms of the verb *'to honor.'*

### To HONOR – RECOGNITION; REVERENCE; DEFERENCE; HOMAGE[15]

*"Recognition* implies *acknowledgment. Reverence* implies profound respect mingled with love, devotion, or awe. *Deference* implies a yielding or submitting to another's judgment or preference out of respect or reverence. *Homage* adds the implication of accompanying praise.[16]*"

Now, let's simplify things as much as possible for clarity and understanding. When we *honor* God, we give him recognition by showing deference to his Word. We yield our own desires and our will in submission to his Word out of reverence. Simply stated, to *honor God* is to *acknowledge God and give eight to His Word.* When you *acknowledge* someone, you give deference to the words that they speak. You give recognition to their judgment and you yield to their word. It's important for you to grasp that *honor* is more than mere respect. Remember my rule regarding words:

---

15    *See,* Merriam-Webster's Online Dictionary, www.merriam-webster.com.
16    *See,* Merriam-Webster's Online Dictionary, www.merriam-webster.com.

Words are important! *Your* words are all that you have to express your thoughts and feelings that arise out of any and all issues in your life. People often take for granted the art of vocal expression by trying to convey a certain message using the wrong words. Then, they assume that a listener will comprehend their intended meaning, although, in reality, their lackadaisical efforts to communicate effectively "shortchanged" the listener.

To *honor* means to *acknowledge*. To *honor* means to give someone the right to speak into your life and attributing *weight* to their words. To *honor* means that you give *priority* to another as it concerns *your* life, *your* decisions, and *your* actions.

What I *don't* want you to do at this point is to assume that what you are about to read in this Fourth Pillar is the obvious. On the contrary, there is nothing *obvious* about knowledge that can only be *revealed* by the Holy Spirit. Humble yourself, and you will be blessed by the content of this Pillar. More importantly, may the Spirit of the Lord touch your *heart* so that *the ear of your heart hears* God's truth as it pertains to the significance of *acknowledging* him in all that we do, hearing his Word, and obeying what we are told. Contextual learning is learning at its finest, so let's add a dose of reality to the situation.

Don't you love it when your wife, husband, girlfriend, boyfriend, friend, family member, co-worker, subordinate, or even your boss, cares what you think? When someone cares enough about your opinion to ask what *you* think *they* should do, it suggests the presence of *honor*. There is an *acknowledgment*. Whether that person actually *gives weight* to your opinion, instruction, comment, or reply is a separate issue. Nevertheless, the *acknowledgement* shows that this person esteems your opinion enough to ask what you think. Who among us doesn't feel appreciated when people ask our opinion, especially when there is a difficult decision to be made, or there is a problem that needs to be resolved? Moreover, when the person in need of advice or direction is a loved one or someone that you deeply care for, there is an affirmation of the *trust* that exists between you and that person. In other words, the act of acknowledgement serves to strengthen the bond of trust between you and that individual. Maybe it's something relatively insignificant like your husband asking you what color tie he should wear to an interview. Or, perhaps your wife wants to know your opinion on whether she should take the promotion offered at her current job (a job that she strongly dislikes), or change jobs and take a slight pay cut, but be happier in a new and different line of work. It could be that your boyfriend wants to know what you think about his idea to start a new business. Or, possibly, your girlfriend asks for your insight on returning to school to attain a higher educational degree. You see, there is something about being "included" in another person's decision-making process that affirms, strengthens, undergirds, and propels the relationship to a higher level of trust and commitment.

Why should our relationship with God be any different? Here is the one and only God, who loves you as his own, wanting to be *involved* in your life. Just think of all the decisions, big and small, difficult and simple, that you make in the course of a day or a week. My question to you is, "how often do you *involve* God with your daily decision-making processes?" Inevitably, your answer will fall into one of three categories: always, sometimes, or never.

The Book of Life tells us,

(5) "Trust in the Lord with all your heart and lean not on your own understanding;

(6) *in all your ways acknowledge him,* and he shall direct your paths." (*See*, Proverbs 3:5-6, KJV) Emphasis added.

We must learn, and not forget, to acknowledge God in our daily decisions. Have *faith* in God. You can't say that you have *faith* in God, but rarely, if ever, consult him concerning the things that are going on in your life. You can't say that you *love* God, but there is no acknowledgment, recognition, or deference shown to him as the head of your life. You *honor* those whom you *love.* The person, or people, in your life whom you *involve* and *consult* regarding the varied decisions that you encounter are often those whom you *love.* By *acknowledging* their presence and seeking their counsel, you are effectively showing *honor.* This is how you verify if your *love* for someone is authentic, you "check" the *honor.*

To *honor* God means giving him the right to speak into your life, and giving his words *weight.* It means that God has *first priority* in your life. It means *Him first* in all that you do. In the morning when you wake up, it's *Him first.* Giving thanks in prayer for waking you, for his grace and mercy, and just being in tune with the Spirit *before you begin* your day. When I say "before you begin," I mean before you eat breakfast, before you shower, before you make a phone call, open an email, or do anything else, give God the "*firstfruits*" of your energy, your mind, and your thoughts. It's *Him first*. You see, when you give God's Word *first priority* in your life, then he in turn will attach *first priority* to *your* words! The Lord declares,

"*Those that honor me I will honor,* but those who despise me will be disdained.)" (1 Samuel 2:30, NIV) Emphasis added.

I don't know about you, but I want the *honor* that comes from God. God's *honor* will have *God's peace* attached to it, his *pleasures* attached to it, and his *fullness of joy* attached to it. In other words, receiving the *honor* that comes from God is where we begin to enter into a place of *real* success. Seeking God's *honor*, as opposed to the *honor* that comes from men, is something you should think about. *Yes! There is an honor that comes from God only!*

"How can you believe if you accept honor from one another, yet make no effort to obtain *the honor that comes from the only God?*" (John 5:44, NIV) Emphasis added.

So, now you are aware that there is an *honor* that comes from God *only*. We work tirelessly in our lives to receive the *honor* that comes from men, but not from God. Think about it. We work to the point of *stress* to please our bosses, our managers, our supervisors, and our department heads, but do we give that same effort to please the one who gives and sustains our very life? Think about the "politics" that some people are willing to play in order to be viewed in a more favorable light by another human being – an honor that, candidly speaking, may or may not be forthcoming! But if you seek God's *honor*, he can and will *honor* you like no one on Earth can *honor* you.

There are four (4) areas of your life that I challenge you to consider:

1. Your time
2. Your conversation
3. Your body
4. Your money

### HONOR GOD WITH YOUR TIME!

Time is everything. How you *spend your time* on Earth determines your position in life, and in death. In other words, how your time is spent on Earth determines where you will spend your time after you leave this Earth. *Time spent wisely* brings a harvest of good fruit. *Time spent foolishly* results in a harvest of bad fruit. *Time spent* living according to God's Word brings eternal life. *Time spent* immersed in sin, with no repentance, leads to death. We live in a world that equates time with money. And you are already aware that "the world" has a way of thinking that is not in line with the Kingdom of God's way of thinking.

The Kingdom of God's way of thinking is *faith-based* and the Kingdom's power is rooted in *love*.

The World's way of thinking is *fear-based* and the World's power is rooted in *selfishness*. The Kingdom of God's power is love and faith. The World's power is *money*.

The World's mentality says that "*time is money*." The World tells you that the most important thing that you could do with your time is earn money. This line of thinking suggests that *money is top priority* in the world in which we live. Right now, I want you to be clear on something. There's nothing inherently wrong with earning money. There is nothing wrong with having rooms stocked with treasure chests full of money. The possession of money is not the issue. *The issue is priority.* What has *priority* in *your* life?

The World's *mindset* equates time with money. Well, I submit to you here and now that *time is more valuable than money.* Let me say that again.

*Your time is more valuable than your money*

Having God's *honor* bestowed upon you will not only result in financial stability, wealth, and success in this life, it will bring you the "incomparable riches of his grace" that is salvation and eternal life with him in heaven. (*See*, Ephesians 2:7). You see, when you *set your mind* to put *Him first*, you will *acknowledge* him *first*, in all that you do. In putting *Him first*, you are giving God's Word *weight* as it pertains to your life. In other words, you care what God has to say about your situation more than what anybody around you has to say about your situation. And we already know from the *First Pillar: Faith* that,

There is *power* tied to God's voice, *if* you (1) can engage the Word *of* God long enough to receive a word *from* God; and (2) if you *obey* what he told *you* to do.

It's the *power* that is tied to God's voice that encompasses his *honor* toward you! You must attribute *weight* to what God has to say to you about your life in order to receive the *honor* that comes from the Lord. And to do that, you must first, *acknowledge* him, *involve* him, *consult* him, and *seek his counsel, in all things.* Your *first priority* must be him! (Money is a mere by-product of his *honor* toward you). So, what does putting *God first* require? It requires a *mindset* that is in line with the Kingdom of God, and not in line with the World. More specifically, it requires a *mindset* that is faith-based and rooted in *love*, rather than rooted in selfish ambitions.

What do you do with *your* time? Are you spending quality time reading God's Word and meditating on what God has to say about *your* life? The Bible, amazingly, has an adequate answer for everything that we encounter in our lives. Everything! But, you've got to *labor* for it. You can't be a lazy Christian and expect to receive the *enlightenment* that God freely gives to us through the Holy Spirit. It won't happen because there isn't enough *time spent* in devotion to gaining the *understanding* that comes from his Word. You've got to *practice the presence* of the Holy Spirit through *time spent* in God's Word. Try it! Do your best to be cognizant on a daily basis to check with God on all the little things that you think of, ponder, or worry about during the course of a day. If you get into the practice of *acknowledging and honoring God* in the little decisions, greater are the chances that he will *acknowledge and honor you* in the bigger decisions. This is the *"faithful over the few, ruler over many"* test. Jesus told us,

"Well done, good and faithful servant; *you have been faithful over a few things, I will make you ruler over many things."* (See, Matthew 25:23, NIV) Emphasis added.

And because you've passed the *"faithful over the few, ruler over many"* test, God will begin to *honor* you in ways that are beyond your limited imagination. But, *the seed* is the Word of God, studied, pondered, and meditated on; *acknowledging* him and his Word in your life.

If you think about it logically, is it really a smart move on our part as human beings to be too busy for God? As I stated earlier, people go to great lengths to receive the *honor* and *praise* from their friends, family, co-workers, and bosses. Sometimes, it's out of insecurity; sometimes it's out of *fear*. As Christians, it's time we gained perspective on the spiritual truth. *Fear*, in the *biblical* context, means to *revere*. Well, we have already provided four synonyms for *Honor: recognition, reverence, deference,* and *homage. Revere* is the root word of *Reverence*. So, to *honor* God is to *revere* him. To *revere* him is to *fear* him.

I love what Jesus said in Luke 12: 4-5. He said,

(4) "I tell you, my friend, do not be afraid of those who kill the body and after that can do no more.

(5) But I will show you whom you should fear: fear him, who *after* the killing of the body, has the power to throw you into hell. Yes, I tell you, fear him. (Luke 12:4-5, NIV) Emphasis added.

Remember, this is *Jesus* talking! Jesus, who begins practically every sentence, every story, every parable with the words, "*I tell you the truth…*" Now, it matters little to me what status, position, or title you hold in life, those words written above spoken by Jesus, about who God is and his omnipotent power, *should* get your attention…and quickly! Maybe it's just me, I don't know. Anyone that has the power to throw *me* into hell *after* my earthly body is dead is someone who I do not want to offend. But again, maybe that's just me.

*Honor* God with *your time.*

### HONOR GOD WITH YOUR CONVERSATION

If you really want to check your *honor*, just identify what it is that you *talk about the most* during the course of any given week. What comes out of your mouth is a product of what is in your heart. This is a very profound and specific topic that will be discussed in later chapters, but we will touch upon it now in the context of *honor*.

What subject(s) do you tend to gravitate toward *the most* in your conversation? Is it a relationship, that guy or girl who you've been dating on and off for 3 years? Is it your job, your health, your family, or perhaps, your finances? Whatever things you discuss, whether inwardly to yourself, or outwardly to another person, are the things that occupy your heart. The issue is whether we are *honoring God* with our conversation, at all?

I'm not so much referring to refraining from course speech. Yes, as Christians, we should *honor* God in our *way* of speaking. The Bible says,

"Do not let any unwholesome talk come out of your mouths, but only what is helpful for building others up according to their needs, that it may benefit those who listen." (Ephesians 4:29, NIV)

That's right. Whether you are a believer or a non-believer, we need to be more aware of whether our words are uplifting to someone else, or do our words tear people down. God's sons and daughters should speak words that encourage, motivate, and uplift the spirits of anyone who listens. It sounds like a small thing, but our words have such power to either edify or destroy.

"With the tongue we praise our Lord and Father, and with it

we curse men, who have been made in God's likeness. Out of the same mouth come praise and cursing." (James 3:9-10, NIV)

It's true. Think about it. Out of the same mouth come words that are positive, loving, honorable, and respectable to others, or they are sharp, cutting, degrading, and demoralizing. We may *honor* God simply by the nature of our words. We believe this to be true.

However, the real focus and purpose of this section has to do with *honor* in relation to *time spent acknowledging God* in your conversation. It's not a complicated, deep, confusing concept. When you are speaking to another person during the course of any given day, do you ever mention God's name in the conversation? I am *not* asking if you begin to "witness" to someone or attempt to convert them to your belief. I'm also **not** asking if you try to engage a perfect stranger in conversation about the goodness of the Lord. Those are good things, of course, but "religion" is not the issue. The issue is whether you use your mouth, your tongue, to simply give God *recognition, acknowledgment,* or *credit* for *anything* during your conversation with another person? Here's a great example.

A few months ago, I was watching an American collegiate football game on television. After the game ended, the quarterback of the winning team gave a brief television interview, broadcasted live, where he was speaking about the victory that his team had barely managed to pull off over their opponent. The two teams playing were college teams, so the age range of the players was approximately 18 to 22. In other words, they were young adults. When the sports broadcaster asked the quarterback to give his account of the last few plays of the game, the quarterback did so eloquently and exuberantly. But between every two or three sentences, the quarterback would simply say, "Praise God." The more excitement he showed about their win, the more energized he would say, "Praise God." And it was evident to me that his words weren't merely "filler words." He meant it.

In that brief example, I want you to see that the words "Praise God," were simply a part of his conversational speech. It wasn't offensive to anybody. It wasn't said in a proselytizing manner that could be mistaken for advocating religion. It wasn't overstated. Here was an 18-year old young man, giving a postgame television interview to millions of viewers around the world, simply giving God the *credit* and *honor* for the victory that he had just won. That, to me, was much more impressive than the victory itself and it spoke to the character of that young man.

How many times in *your* daily life do *you* give God the *honor* when *you* experience a victory? How many times do you *acknowledge God* when there is someone listening? Here we are, creations of the Lord our God, and many of us don't even mention his name in our daily conversations. How would that make *you* feel if the objects of *your* affection never even called out *your* name in the presence of other people? For my readers who are parents of teenagers (ages 13-17), how does it make *you* feel when *your* kids are ashamed of *you* when they are in the presence of their friends? Remember, my words are not judgmental here. That's not my intent. The intent is to get you to open the spiritual eyes and spiritual ears of your heart and realize that *God cares* whether or not you *acknowledge him* in your everyday life!

I like what Jesus said in his prayer to God, *his* Father, before he was betrayed by Judas and subsequently arrested by a detachment of soldiers, officials from the chief priests, and the Pharisees. Jesus said,

(25) "Righteous Father, though the world does not know you, I know you...

(26) I have made you known to them, and will continue to make you known in order that the love you have for me may be in them..." (*See*, John 17: 25-26 NIV)

Did you hear that? "Righteous Father, though the world does not know you, *I know you*." I love that. You have to love that. "Though the world does not know you, *I know you*." These are the words that Jesus spoke out loud! These are words of *acknowledgement* in the presence of his disciples! Put simply, this is Jesus giving *honor, recognition, reverence, deference, homage,* and *acknowledgment* to the Lord our God, our creator, and our Father through words spoken from his mouth. And then Jesus says that He will "*continue* to make [God] known in order that the love [God has] for [him] may be in them."

This is the model for how I want to speak in the presence of listeners. God has been too good to me for me *not* to speak aloud telling of his goodness, grace, and mercy so that his love which is in *me*, may also be in *someone else*. In the words of my young football friend, "Praise God."

### LIP HONOR *VERSUS* HEART HONOR

Of course, many of you have heard the phrase, "talk is cheap." Words don't cost anything. Words are free. For example, I may tell a million people that I can lose 50 lbs. (or, 50 kg.) in 50 days. I can boast that I'm a great athlete that knows how to lose unwanted excess weight by exercising and dieting, and that I can shed a large number of pounds within a relatively short amount of time. I can advertise my methods to those who listen. I can guarantee results beforehand and convince friends and strangers alike to believe that I am knowledgeable on how to lose 50 lbs. (or, 50 kg.) in 50 days.

But, until I actually initiate *change* in my life (*i.e.* change my eating habits, change my daily schedule to include exercise) and **sustain** the effort that it takes to drop the weight, all of my "big words" have little to no meaning. Well, the same idea applies to us and the ways in which we *honor God*.

Professing our love and devotion to Christ and his Word *vocally* is great, as we discussed in the previous section. I want to be clear on that. But *saying* and *doing* are two very different things. *Saying* you love someone, and *showing* that you love someone, are not the same. Although this is probably a concept that most people are familiar with, it takes on a new perspective when viewed in the light of your own relationship with God. In the Bible, it was the prophet Isaiah, (and later, Jesus) who said,

"These people honor me with their lips, but their hearts are far from me." (Matthew 5:8)

*What is love without honor?* I'll save you some time and give you the correct answer. The answer is *nothing*. *Love* without *honor* is *nothing*. For *love* to be worth something, *honor* has to accompany it. *honor* must be there too. Remember, the verb '*to honor*' means to *acknowledge*; giving someone the right to speak into your life and giving their words *weight*; assigning *priority* to someone (or their words) as it concerns *your* life, *your* decisions, and *your* actions.

Men, you say you love your wife, but what good is that love if you don't *listen* to her? Women, you say you love your husband, but you give more weight to what your mother or your girlfriends say than to what he's trying to tell you. Frankly, that's not love or honor. So, perhaps an appropriate question would be, how can we *honor God*, if we are not *honoring the people* God has put into our lives?

*Honor carries weight!* To *honor God* means that his Word carries so much weight that nothing else anyone says or does will detract you from standing on his truth. A real problem for many people is that they care too much what other people say and think about them. The bottom line is that you can't *honor God unless* you put *Him first*! Otherwise, your loyalties are divided and no one can serve two masters. (*See*, Matthew 6:24). It just doesn't work that way.

Are you beginning to see the interlocking nature of the Pillars of the Model? I told you that no one Pillar is mutually exclusive. To *honor God's* Word, you have to *know* what he said. You have to read the Word of God (*i.e.* the Bible). His Word tells us to *depart from sin*, and we put our *confidence* in living according to words spoken from a God whom we cannot see. In doing so, we *change* our lives around, leaving sin behind and turning to a life of righteousness. And the Word says that "the righteous shall live by *faith*." (*See,* Habakkuk 2:4). As we begin to *hear* and *obey* God's commands, laws, and decrees for our lives, we are showing our *love* for Him, which is driven by *honor*.

You see, *obedience* is an act of *honor*. The obvious example involves *honoring your parents*. It doesn't matter what age you are, when you *acknowledge* your parents (*i.e.* give them the right to speak into your life, and attribute *weight* to their words), you are *honoring* them. In your adult life, *honoring your parents* does *not* necessarily require that you follow their advice, but it *does* require showing a measure of *recognition* of their opinion. The Bible says,

"Give ear to your father whose child you are, and do not keep honor from your mother when she is old." (Proverbs 23:22, NIV)

What about the matter of *convenience*? When we do what God says only when it's convenient for *us*, or when *we* want to do it, that is *not honor*. This is a big one! Many of us, believers and non-believers don't ever want to do something when it's inconvenient for us! I'm no exception. We want to do things when WE are *ready* to do them, on our time, and not on somebody else's time. But, this can be a very harmful and damaging mentality for an obvious reason, and also a reason that may not be so obvious.

I began the discussion of *honor* with a foundation of establishing a *Him first* mentality. It's reasonable to say that it is obvious that we should put God first in our lives, even at the expense of our own inconvenience, simply because that's what his Word tells us to do. But, this response is a C+ answer at best. Although it is correct, it is also incomplete. The A+ answer considers what potential dangers await the person who only serves God when it is *convenient for him*. This is the guy who suddenly finds himself in need of help and he truly needs guidance and direction as to what to do, what decisions to make, and what actions to take. But, because he is *conditioned* to seeking God's counsel only when it's convenient for *him,* there is no solid relationship of *trust* between that person and the Lord. I'll repeat what I said earlier in this Pillar:

If you get into the practice of *acknowledging and honoring God* in the little decisions, greater are the chances that he will *acknowledge and honor you* in the bigger decisions.

*Confidence is a major issue!* When troublesome and desperate times show up at your doorstep, there are people all over this world that *believe in God,* but they *don't* truly know how to *turn to him* and *find the power and the answers* that they so desperately need. I've seen this with my own eyes in the lives of Christian people. But when you *practice honoring God,* whether it's convenient or inconvenient to you, it boosts your *confidence* that you can lean on him during the times when you're tired and hurt.

More importantly, the people that *honor God only* when it's convenient from *them,* run a serious risk of not understanding the *real power* that lies in God's Word. This is the danger spoken of above that is *not* so obvious. You can't say that you *love* and *honor* the Lord, but then when troubling times come, you allow depression to set in, speak words of defeat to yourself, and get ready to give up, cave-in, and quit. Sometimes, *it's when those difficult challenges come* where *honoring God becomes* seemingly inconvenient! Think about it. When you get laid-off from your job and money is scarce and worries start to set in, you may think twice about *honoring God's Word* which says, "Bring the *whole tithe* into the storehouse..." (*See,* Malachi 3:10). A person who recently lost their job may deem it "inconvenient" to pay monetary offerings and tithes to the Lord, in church, when they aren't sure how they're going to pay their rent on the first of the month. But, it's the guy who *acknowledges* God's Word; gives it *recognition*; attributes *weight* to it; and shows *deference* to it – even in the face of seeming inconvenience – that exhibits real *trust* in God's Word and whom God will honor because he honored him. (*See*, 1 Samuel 2:30). Moreover, this is the man who practices what he has heard. He doesn't stop at "hearing," but he continues on to "obeying." *Obedience is an act of honor.* And the *confidence* level of the man who *honors God* in the face of an inconvenient trouble increases because we know from the *first pillar* that everything in the Kingdom of God operates by *faith*.

"And without *faith* it is impossible to please God." (See, Hebrews 11:6).

So, when the fiery darts and flaming arrows of life come at you (*i.e.* difficult divorce, relationship "melt-down", internal family fights, friends desert you, unsatisfied with your job, low finances, etc.), it's the person who *honored God* through the good times *and* the bad times that will have the *confidence* to turn to him, and have the *faith* that he will, in turn, *honor* them right on out of the emotional or financial pit that they're in.

We make things more complicated than they are. Put *Him first*, and good things will follow. It's as simple as that. The moment the word "but" enters into the picture, you're in trouble.

- I would read the Bible, *but* I don't have a lot of time.
- I would go to church, *but* now is not the right time.
- I would like to learn more about God, *but* I don't believe in religion.
- I would give an offering and tithe, *but* I don't go to church.

- I would go to church, *but* I don't know where to find one.
- I would go this Sunday, *but* I have something to do Saturday night.
- I do believe in God, *but* the doctor said there's no cure.
- I have faith in God, *but* I'm going to stay in this unhealthy relationship.
- I know God can do anything, *but* will he do it for me?

When we put *Him first*, we are saying that *there is no limitation* that can be put on God. There is no shackle that can be put on our focus to put *Him first*. In *honoring God first*, there is nothing that holds a higher *priority* than his Word. And if the most important thing in your life is God's Word, then somebody please tell me why would you be worried to the point of sickness about money?

You see, our focus is on *Him first*! There is no "but." And if you put *Him first*, without condition, then you will have every *confidence* that He will put *you first* and take care of all of your needs. It's the realization that there is nothing bigger than God. There is nothing more important than his Word. And life takes on a whole new meaning when you are *enlightened* to see and understand that God's power and his love are available to you, twenty-four hours a day, seven days a week. Worry cannot be first. Loneliness cannot be first. Sickness cannot be first. Depression cannot be first. Regret cannot be first. Fear cannot be first. Inconvenience cannot be first. Excuses cannot be first. Self cannot be first. It's *Him first*, and everything else will be added unto you. (*See*, Matthew 6:33). Lip honor *versus* heart honor. This is *heart honor*.

These words are rich. When something of value is being offered or made available, it doesn't need to be sold. To put it in layman's terms, you don't need to sell a "million-dollar idea." Value sells itself.

To those people who can recognize value when they see it, there is a benefit for those who *seize* the opportunity. Others may or may not recognize value, but either way, if they *fail* to seize it in a timely manner, there is nothing left but a missed opportunity, empty rationalizations, and regret. For others still, they may never recognize value, and that is an unfortunate reality that is beyond anyone's control.

Well, truth has value. *Truth is value.* Whether you recognize it or not is one issue. Whether you *seize* it or not is another issue. Those who only pay "*lip honor*" to God's Word are like the people who may or may not recognize value, because either way, they *fail to seize* the opportunity, and subsequently, will find themselves in a category of those who have "missed out." But, those who pay "*heart honor*" to God's Word are like the people who recognize value *and seize* God's Word while the opportunity is still available. The *value is in the truth.* And *who* is the *truth?*

"Jesus answered, *I am the way and the truth and the life.*" (See, John 14:6 NIV) (Emphasis added)

So, if the *value* is *in* the *truth,* and Jesus *is* "*the Truth,*" then we can determine what the *value* is by listening to what *he* says! And Jesus (otherwise known as, "*the Truth*") says,

(32) "Whoever *acknowledges me* before men, *I will also acknowledge him before my father in heaven.*

(33) But whoever disowns me before men, I will disown him before my Father in heaven. (Matthew 10:32-33, NIV) Emphasis added.

So, ladies and gentlemen, there it is. "*The Truth*" has spoken. The *value* in "*the Truth*" is that those people who *acknowledge him* in *this* life, *he will also acknowledge* before GOD *in heaven!* In case you missed that, we're talking about eternal life – not 50, 60, 70,

80, or 90 years like the average life span on Earth. *Eternal life!* And whether you receive *eternal life* or not is based on whether you recognize value in the truth and seize it! Put another way, whether Jesus *honors you* before God in Heaven is a direct result of whether *you honor Jesus* before men on Earth. And remember…

"Do not be deceived: God cannot be mocked. A man reaps what he sows." (Galations 6:7, NIV)

*Lip honor versus heart honor.* That is the issue. God sees everything. He can't be mocked. I urge you to put *Him first*, give *heart honor*, and He will lift you up in all that you do.

### Honor God with your body

What does it mean to *honor God* with our bodies? As an athlete, I've always had an appreciation for the capability of the human body. Some of the greatest professional athletes, past and present, are a testament to what physical feats the human body can accomplish. And if *you* have ever played or participated in a competitive sport at a high level, then you also know and understand the role of *the mind* in relation to the physical body.

Let's take the game of basketball, for example. Basketball is a sport that is loved and played all over the world. The sheer numbers of naturally physically gifted athletes that play the game of basketball, on a global basis, are too numerous to count. I have played with and against some of America's finest players and seen physical feats that would boggle the mind of the average spectator. But, *the greatest players of all-time* have something that sets them apart from the rest, above and beyond their physical abilities.

To illustrate my point, some of the greatest athletes that I have ever seen have never put on an NBA uniform. They have never signed a contract to play for an NBA team. I'm talking about guys who are either the physical equivalent, or *superior*, to many of the professional players you watch on television. These are guys that play on playgrounds and in gyms across America on a daily basis. Granted, not everyone was destined to be a big-time professional athlete. Some fall prey to the cruel lifestyle of the street and the neighborhood. Others are overtaken by injury. Many had no parental figure and lacked the "guidance" necessary to ensure that the young player did well in school, stayed away from bad influences, and took the right roads to success. Undoubtedly, all these things are factors. But, there is one more factor that tends to get overlooked by people who simply look on and appreciate the physical gifts that are displayed by the professional athlete – *the mind*.

Continuing in my basketball illustration, take the act of shooting free throws, for example. 90% of free-throw shooting is mental. 10% is physical. *The mind* is a *powerful* tool that can guide *the body* to accomplish amazing things. The true legends of sport are the ones who have the ability to focus, concentrate, and perform at the highest level irrespective of injury, pain, adversity, and pressure. In other words, they possess an unalterable *"mind control,"* which when coupled with superb physical abilities, spells greatness.

In the twentieth century, Muhammad Ali and Michael Jordan were probably the two foremost examples of *the power of mind control* in the context of sports. Prior to Ali's suspension in 1967, and before Jordan's first retirement in 1993, these two men displayed talents that have not been seen to this day, in their respective sports. Is the reason because there have been *no* athletes since these time periods to come along that possess equal or greater physical ability? The answer is a resounding "no." Here is my point. It is of greater utility to recognize that such athletic greatness must be viewed through the lens of *the power of the mind*, and not the body. The ability *to control* oneself through *the power of the mind* is a dynamic force to behold.

Now, I have given this example as a backdrop to *"honoring God with our bodies"* for the purpose of illustrating *the power of the mind* in relation to *controlling* what we do with our bodies. Consider the excellence of the two legendary athletes mentioned in the previous paragraph, and you have no choice but to acknowledge their unique mental and physical abilities. In this life, they are recognized as two of the greatest talents of all time. (And the role of sports has been integral in *my* life, so I can appreciate a statement such as this).

Well, consider something else. The Bible says,

"Physical training is good, but training for godliness is much better, promising benefits in this life *and* in the life to come." (1 Timothy 4:8, NIV) Emphasis added.

For all the accomplishments that may come from physical training, the Word tells us that training for *godliness* is much better because it holds benefits in this life *and* in the next. If you learn to apply "mind control" over your physical being in your everyday life, you will accomplish feats that you never knew you could accomplish. But here is the caveat. There's only *one way* to gain the *kind* of *mind control* that is necessary to be one of *"the greatest"* in the eyes of the Lord, and that *one way* is through Jesus Christ and the Word of God.

If you can learn to *set your mind* on the things of God, then your bodily actions will follow. The Bible tells us,

"For God did not give us a spirit of fear, but a spirit of power, of love, and of a *sound mind*." (2 Timothy 1:7, NIV)

To have a "*sound mind*" means that your "way of thinking" <u>lines up</u> with the Word of God. Put another way, your "way of thinking" is in line with godly thinking. Well, in *sports*, the physical feats of *the body* have a direct correlation to *the discipline* of "*mind control*." In LIFE, the discipline of "*mind control*" has a direct correlation to the *practice of temperance*, which is *"self-control"* You see, in sports, the mind controls how the body performs. That's the end of that. But, in life, the *Spirit* controls the mind, which controls how the body performs. A victory or loss in sports is fleeting, but a victory or loss in life is eternal. (May he that hath ears to ear, let him hear.)

Fighting the *right* fight is paramount. This is the only way that you will learn to *honor God with your body*. It's an absolute shame to hear of a man or a woman succumb to a bad habit or an addiction. I don't care what the bad habit or addiction may be. *You cannot control your body without learning how to control your mind! And you cannot control your mind unless you are operating within the power, the love, and the self-discipline of God's Holy Spirit* (which has been given to you freely, and lives on the inside of those who have accepted Christ into their life and put *Him first*).

People are trying to stop a 10, 15, 20-year drinking habit by going to *Alcoholics' Anonymous* meetings confessing their name followed by a self-deprecating admission of *"…and I'm an alcoholic."* In no way do I mean to disparage a person who is making an effort to address the issue of alcoholism, but a person who is in need of *results* must learn to fight the *right* fight or suffer defeat. No one is immune to the trials of life, but what are you doing going to an *Alcoholics' Anonymous* meeting, off and on for 30-something years? That's not success! That's not peace! That's not wholeness in life! Unfortunately, people operating within the World's mentality (as opposed to the Kingdom of God's mentality) are lacking the *truth*. The Word tells us, "Where God is, there is *freedom*."

"Now the Lord is the Spirit, and *where the Spirit of the Lord is, there is freedom*." (2 Corinthians 3:17, NIV) Emphasis added.

"If you hold to my teaching, you are really my disciples. Then you will know the truth, and *the truth will set you free*. (John 8:31-32, NIV) Emphasis added.

Bondage to substances and habits plague people all over the world and takes their very life away. Jesus warned us when he said, *"I tell you the truth, everyone who sins is a slave to sin."* (*See,* John 8:34, NIV). Some people literally die as a result of substance abuse and others live a life in which they may as well be dead because they've lost control over everything, including self-control.

It's time we *honor God with our bodies.*

The Bible says,

(1) "Therefore, I urge you, brothers, in view of God's mercy, to offer your *bodies* as living sacrifices, holy and pleasing to God – this is your spiritual act of worship.

(2) Do not conform any longer to the pattern of this world, but be transformed by the *renewing of your mind...*" (*See,* Romans 12:1-2) Emphasis added.

Read these scriptures again with your spiritual eyes and spiritual ears and focus on these five words in particular: *bodies, sacrifices, transformed, renewing,* and *mind.* In order for you to *honor God* with your *body,* you are going to have to *sacrifice.*

**Sacrifice** – the act of *offering* something to a *deity* in propitiation or *homage; forfeiture* of something highly valued for the sake of one considered to have a *greater claim* or value.

Here is the goal. To forego fleshly desires as a *living sacrifice* and *forfeit our bodies* to God who has a *greater claim* to us than we do on ourselves. People destroy their bodies on a daily basis under the impression that no one else has a claim to it. But, the Word says,

"You are not your own; you were bought with a price. Therefore honor God with your body." (*See,* 1 Corinthians 6:19-20, NIV)

God sent his only Son, Jesus Christ, to die on the cross as a sacrificial lamb to take away the sins of the world – sins that *all of us* have committed. You live because he died. Yet, we walk around in darkness not realizing *the truth.* The truth is that you were bought at a price! Your salvation is free, but it's not cheap. God has a greater claim on you than the desires of the flesh have on you.

At this point, someone might be thinking, "Well, that sounds nice and fine, but real *self-control* is not easy." I would be inclined to agree, *if* I were operating within the "World's system of thinking." *Self-control* is a fruit of *the Spirit* (*See,* Galations 5:22). The World's equivalent to self-control is *willpower,* or put another way, *mind control.* But the enemies that you fight against are not of flesh and blood, they are from a dark spiritual realm, and that's why willpower is not enough. Willpower is not a spiritual weapon because it's not rooted in the Word of God. The Word of God *is* Spirit (*See,* John 6:63). Willpower doesn't go deep enough. It can't reach the root of the problem. But the Word of God is "sharper than any double-edged sword" (*See* Hebrews 4:12) and it's the *only source of power* that will tame addictions and habits that the World deems to be irrepressible.

To be *transformed,* (*i.e.* changed), the Word gives the prescription on how to effect transformation in no uncertain terms – by the *renewing of your mind.* It's like I've been saying all along, *the mind controls the body, but the Spirit controls the mind.* You see, this is what the World's mentality *lacks - spiritual knowledge.* Knowledge which can only be *revealed* through *time spent* in fellowship with the Holy Spirit, also known as *revelation knowledge.* Of course, people who lack *faith* will criticize, judge, taunt, laugh at, or "make light of" the *faith* upon which the Kingdom of God operates. But, the one thing that *no one* can argue with is *results. Power* is defined as *the ability to get results.*

You see, everything that I'm teaching you is *not just talk.* Otherwise, this would be a tremendous waste of time and energy for me and for you. This is about *getting results.* Or put another way, *the power to get results.* I like what the Apostle Paul said,

"The Kingdom of God is not a matter of talk but of power."

(1 Corinthians 4:20, NIV)

It's commonplace for people to say that they want to *change.* People make commitments to *change* every week and then repeat the same old habit, activity, or decision without any lasting *change* ever taking place. You say "I'm going to kick that smoking habit."

You say, "I'm done with drinking." You say, "I'm going to refrain from sexual activity." You say, "I'm going to lose the weight and get healthier." You say, you say, you say…but,

*change isn't change until you change!*

And the only way to have the power to get *lasting* change is by the *renewing of your mind* with God's Word. It's the only way. And for those who doubt, let them doubt and remain in a powerless position to implement real *change* in their life. But, for those who *humble themselves* and put off the selfish nature which operates in contrast to the Kingdom of God, there will be an empowerment to get results. This is what we call, *the blessing*. It's the *empowerment to get results*. The results will come in the form of real *self-control* over your body through the *renewing of your mind* in the Spirit.

It's time that *you* start to *honor God with your body* through the *renewing your mind*. Get in the Word of God, stay in the Word of God, and discover the *power* of the Holy Spirit that will enable you to get the *results* that you want. Take on the attitude of the scripture that says,

"…I will not be mastered by anything." (*See*, 1 Corinthians 6:12, NIV)

Real power *is* self-control. Blessed is man who crucifies the flesh and practices temperance, which is *self-control*. My friends, it's time that we *honor the Lord with our bodies*.

## HONOR GOD WITH YOUR MONEY

The Bible tells us,

"For where your treasure is, there your heart will be also." (Matthew 6:21, NIV)

This scripture needs little explanation. You would be hard-pressed to find someone in the world that hasn't been introduced to the role that money plays in their respective culture and society. Some people might even say that "money makes the world go around." Money buys food. Money buys clothes. Money plays a part in determining your social status in life. Money *is* the world's power. And I *thank God* that I <u>don't</u> operate within **this** system of thinking. Money can ruin lives. Issues with money can cause people to willingly *end* their lives. It can cause dissension amongst brothers and spouses. It can cause people to commit criminal acts with no disregard for another's welfare.

Of course, there's a flip side to this argument. Money can be used to accomplish great charitable acts. It can feed and clothe the homeless. The acquisition of money can alleviate financial-induced worry and it can afford a level of peace. Money can supply the seed investment for great ideas, businesses, projects, and philanthropic visions. It can get you the best medical care and education. Simply stated, money allows you to do things that you otherwise would not be able to do if you didn't have it.

There is nothing inherently wrong with money. Truth be told, when you have money, it makes life easier in several regards. But where people get themselves into trouble is when they attach a value to money that is above all else. The Bible says,

"For the *love* of money is a root of all kinds of evil." (1 Timothy 6:10, NIV) Emphasis added.

*Giving*, without expecting something in return, is viewed favorably in the eyes of the Lord. Jesus said, "

"It is more blessed to give than to receive." (Acts 20:35, NIV)

The bottom line is that different people have different attachments to money. Some people release money easier than others, for what could be for any of a variety of reasons. But *honoring God with your money* involves much more than the act of *giving*. At this point, those who *humble themselves* are about to learn something that is of *great value* to their success in life.

*Tithing is not a part of your giving program; It's a part of your blessing program!*

Some people become wary when it comes to giving their money to the church for a variety of reasons. One reason may be that there is distrust as to where the money is actually going. A common question or concern is whether their money is going directly to the pastor or priest? Other people may feel that they work too hard for their money to simply surrender their hard-earned cash to a basket being passed around during a Sunday service or mass. But here's what I want you to do right now. Forget all of the various "religious classifications" that exist in the world. They're completely irrelevant. It doesn't matter if you consider yourself to be Christian, Catholic, or any other denomination; what you are about to read applies to *everybody*.

Offerings and tithes are different. A monetary *offering* to the Lord, in church, may be of any amount, paid on no particular basis of consistency. Whether a person goes to church three times in one year or thirty times in one year, that person may bring a monetary *offering* to the Lord whenever he or she has the notion to do so. Offerings are *not* the focus of this discussion.

*Tithes*, however, are *a systematic release of 10% of all your increase.* In other words, if your wealth has been increased by $100, then $10 goes to the Lord as a *tithe.* The concept is biblically-based and is found throughout the Bible. But, like anything else in life, a *lack of exact knowledge* hinders our understanding and can keep us out of the place of promotion that God has made readily available to us.

Remember from the previous section that "the *blessing*" is defined as *the empowerment for success.* The converse is also true. A "*curse*" is the empowerment for failure. In the Bible, God's *blessing* fell upon the patriarchs that systematically released their *tithe* to God! Specifically, Abraham (the father of our *faith*) and Jacob (also called, "Israel") didn't get *established* in their *blessing* until the release of their *tithe.* In the Seventh Pillar, *tithing*, we will take a closer look at Abraham and the prominent role that tithing played in his *empowerment to succeed.*

You see, *tithing* is *not* giving. According to God's Word, 10% of all your increase *already* belongs to God. *Tithing* involves *returning* to God what already belongs to him. Therefore, you must disabuse yourself of the notion that *tithing* is synonymous with *giving.* It's not. But rather, *tithing* is part of an *exchange.* The exchange that takes place between you and God is the release of the tithe *in exchange* for the blessing! In other words,

*Tithing is not a part of your giving program; It's a part of your blessing program!*

Or, put another away,

*Tithing activates the blessing.*

Remember, there are two systems in operation that are in stark contrast to one another. There is the Kingdom of God's system (or, the Kingdom's way of thinking), and there is the World's system (or, the World's way of thinking). They are not to be reconciled. They do not line up with each other. They are not in agreement with each other. You cannot operate in both systems simultaneously. They are as different as day is from night. The World's system of thinking is built on earthly knowledge and earthly wisdom which comes from men. The Kingdom of God's system of thinking is built on spiritual knowledge and spiritual wisdom which comes from God. The World's way of thinking does not support the Kingdom of God's way of thinking because the World operates under a different *system*. God has a system that is not like the World's system and you're going to have to choose which side of the line you come down on.

The Kingdom of God's way of thinking is based in *faith* and the Kingdom's power is rooted in *love*.

The World's way of thinking is based in *fear* and the World's power is rooted in *selfishness*

The Kingdom of God's power is *love* and *faith*

The World's power is *money*

Think about it carefully. Paying your *tithe* is the systematic release of 10% of all your increase. This involves the physical act of releasing money to God. To believe that *one-tenth* of all your increase already belongs to God, and that you are *returning* it to him, undoubtedly requires *faith*. Well, we know that...

The Kingdom of God's way of thinking is based in *faith*.

To believe that the release of the *tithe* is done *in exchange* for the *blessing (i.e. the empowerment for success)*, undoubtedly requires *faith*. Again, we know that...

The Kingdom of God's way of thinking is based in *faith*.

Believing that God's *blessing* will actually manifest itself in your life in the form of *results* upon the release of the *tithe* is a measure of *faith*. You know what comes next...

The Kingdom of God's way of thinking is based in *faith*.

The guy who is *afraid* to systematically release 10% of his increase attaches a higher priority to the *worry* of not having enough money to pay his bills, or get through the month, than to operating in *faith*. What do you think this represents in our understanding of the two systems?

The World's way of thinking is based in *fear*.

Some people, who say to themselves, "I *could* give 10% of my increase after every paycheck, but frankly, I need my money." This could very well fall on the side of...

the World's power is rooted in *selfishness*

Of course, not everyone has a lot of money. But if you have allowed such a notion to become the premise for your understanding of *tithing*, then you have completely missed the point. Obviously, you can't give what you don't have. *Honoring God with your money* should *not* be done out of *obligation* or *fear*. You see, some people are "put off" by the fact that someone expects them to give a certain amount. Some people feel bad or embarrassed because they simply don't have money to give, or they don't have an amount that they *wish* they could give. But, the important thing to remember is that God looks at *the heart*.

The Bible says,

"Each man should give what he has decided in his *heart* to give, *not reluctantly or under compulsion*, for God loves a *cheerful giver*.

(2 Corinthians 9: 7, NIV) Emphasis added.

If some people find it "uncomfortable" to release a small amount of money to a homeless person that they *see* on the street, most likely it will be a "painful experience" for them to systematically release 10% of all their increase to a God that they *cannot see*. This lends support to the premise that nothing works in the Kingdom of God *outside* of *faith*. Remember, the Bible tells us,

"For where your treasure is, there your heart will be also." (Matthew 6:21, NIV)

If your heart is in your money, then you will likely find it difficult to release it and you won't be a "cheerful giver," which pleases God.

God wants us to *trust* in *him*. It's a very interesting dynamic when you take the principle of *honor*, and the *Him first* mentality, and you set it beside the World's perspective of *money*. If you put *Him first*, then by default, you must put *self* second. That entails *acknowledging* God's Word which commands that we pay our tithes and offerings. To *honor God with your money* means that your money cannot have a first-place position in your heart! It's as simple as that. We'll discuss this in greater detail in later chapters. But for now, I want you to be cognizant that *God's promise of the blessing* is attached to the release of the *tithe*.

If you don't believe me, read it below. For the Lord God, himself, says,

"Test me in this, and see if I will not throw open the floodgates of heaven and pour out so much *blessing* that you will not have room enough for it." (*See*, Malachi 3:10, NIV) Emphasis added.

The Word also says,

(9) *"Honor* the Lord with your wealth, with the *firstfruits* of all your crops; then your barns will be filled to *overflowing,* and your vats will *brim over* with new wine." (Proverbs 3: 9-10, NIV) Emphasis added.

Tithing is not a part of your giving program; it's a part of your *blessing* program!

*Tithing activates the blessing*

It's time that we *honor God with our money*!

To *honor God* means *to acknowledge Him first* in our lives. *As* you have just seen throughout this Pillar, we may *acknowledge* him in several ways: (1) with our *time,* (2) with our *conversation,* (3) with our *bodies,* and (4) with our *money.* But merely asking God for his opinion, as it pertains to our lives, is not enough. If *honoring God* means *giving him the right to speak into our lives, and giving his Word weight,* what do we do once God has actually spoken? What do you do when God has given you an answer to your prayer? What do you do when that little voice on the inside of you (*i.e.* the Holy Spirit) tells you to choose a certain path; to let that ex-boyfriend or ex-girlfriend go; to stay in the difficult marriage and work it out; to quit smoking; to stop partying; to read the Bible; to find a church; to be less selfish; to be more loving; to start a new business; to reach out to your family, etc. – *what do you do?*

It would be an incomplete effort to address *acknowledging God,* and then fail to address what you *should* do once *He speaks to you* in regard to the issue that you brought to him! Simply put, you can't discuss *honor* without discussing the subject of *hearing and obeying*. In the next section, you will come to know and understand that real *honor* includes *perpetual obedience*.

### HEARING AND OBEYING

Let's address the obvious right now. Chances are that if a person says that he or she *hears* from God, then they will automatically become a candidate for ridicule. In this section, whenever I speak of *hearing* from God, I am not referring to an actual voice that can be heard with your natural ears. God speaks his Word to our *hearts*. Every time you see the word, "*heart*," I want you to imagine that God put the three letters "*e-a-r*" in the center of the word "*heart*" for a reason. He speaks to the *ear* of our *heart*. Likewise, each time you see the word "*heart*," I want you to also imagine that God put the first four letters "*h-e-a-r*" in the beginning of the word "*heart*" for a reason – so we can *hear* him. Now, proceed in humility and in *faith*.

Reading the Bible, for yourself, is vital to your empowerment for success. Without consistent meditation and the refreshing of God's Word in your mind and heart, you cannot remain in a place of *faith*. You may go to church, listen to spiritual music, or wear a gold or silver cross around your neck. You may do all of these things. But, if you don't have *the root,* which is a personal relationship with God, *based on his Word*, then you don't have anything. It's not a difficult concept to grasp, but we as human beings can be rather blind to the truth.

The reality is that many people *don't* feel a need to develop a *real* spiritual connection with God. If you're a person who has a decent life and you're content with your situation, then it is likely that you won't possess the frame of mind that *change* is needed. Sometimes, it isn't until we find ourselves in a place of trouble, hurt, or difficulty (*i.e.* emotional, financial, or physical) that we then turn our attention to the idea of a higher being, a higher power.

The fact is that not all people grow up going to church or believing in God from a young age. However, there does come a point in your life where you are faced with the question, *"What do I believe?" "Do I believe in God?"* By the time most people have reached adulthood, "society" (*e.g.* talk shows, movies, radio, internet, family, friends, etc.) has had such a major psychological impact on their thought processes that it's difficult for them to elicit a pure response that is not, in some way, a product of their environment. Since contextual learning is learning at its finest, let me give you a good example: China.

I wrote this book while living in Shenzhen, China. It's a great city and the people are warm and friendly. Historically, China's political and social views are firmly rooted in communism. In China, the *outward* expression of an individual's personal spiritual or religious beliefs is not legally-protected as it is in the United States. To my knowledge, China has no equivalent of America's First Amendment constitutional protection *vis-à-vis* religion. In China, this is the environment that has been in existence for ages.

However, there is a widespread misconception about China in regard to the daily environment that stems from its communist roots.

My experiences in China were first-rate. In fact, I think the United States could learn a lot from China. Like anything else, there's some good, and some bad. And even though certain expressions are legally forbidden, there is an undeniable movement towards Christianity and the belief in Jesus Christ, especially among the younger generations. Living in China was fascinating for many reasons, not the least of which was attending a Christian Bible study in one of China's largest legally-recognized Christian churches. It's one thing to share your belief in God on a weekly basis with people from your *own* country. It's a totally different experience to share your belief in God, *in agreement with*, people of a *different* country; a country which has, historically, suppressed the furtherance of that very same belief.

The moral to the story is simple. At some point, there have been significant numbers in the Chinese population that must have been faced with the question, *"What do I believe?" "Do I believe in God?"* In other words, despite the government's historical suppression of the outward expression of viewpoints regarding Christianity, the people in China are no different than the people in the United States. The fundamental question still applies, universally, no matter who you are, where you live, or what your countries' laws may be. *"What do I believe?" "Do I believe in God?"* It just so happens that certain governmental infrastructures are more tolerant as to the outward expression of those views. But the fact remains that the question exists for everyone and the answer will either reflect a measure of one's *faith*, or it'll be a product of a perspective that has been shaped by society. *hearing* the Word of God has much to do with the determination of what a person believes.

So, let's proceed on the premise that you are reading and meditating on the scriptures in the Bible, and that you are making an earnest effort to implement *change* in your life surrounding certain areas. On this premise, take a look at the following scenarios directly below.

How many of you are in a predicament *right now* that has to do with a relationship issue with another person? How many of you would be open to advice, direction, or even suggestions as to what you should do? How many of you feel a sense of *loneliness* in your life? (And remember, you can be *in a relationship* or *in a marriage*, and *still* feel a sense of loneliness). How many of you feel as if something is *missing* or that something is *broken* in your life regarding the issue of relationships? To those who have been disappointed in the area of *trust*, are you in search of a *new* relationship *before* the hurt has completely healed or subsided? How many of you who are *single* would say that you are *whole* in your "singleness." Or, would you say that you're looking for your "other *half*?"

You see, the Bible has answers for all of these questions. And where there are gaps in your intellectual comprehension of God's *written* Word, the Holy Spirit will reveal answers to the *ear* of your *heart* through his spoken word. But you must have enough *faith* in God, and exhibit enough *faithfulness* to continue reading his Word, for life's answers to be revealed. This is the basis of the personal relationship with the Lord through *time spent* in fellowship with the Spirit by reading his Word. Follow me closely.

I've spoken to young, single women who think that their personal lifelong decision to refrain from participating in promiscuous sexual activity is a "weakness" in regard to their pursuit to find a husband. For that, you needn't look any further than Proverbs 31:10 (NIV), which says,

"A wife of noble character who can find? She is worth far more than rubies. Her husband has full confidence in her and lacks nothing of value."

Similarly, I've spoken to women who have adopted a low self-esteem and a bruised self-image because of their belief that an "overweight" woman is not an attractive woman. For this, take a good look at Proverbs 31:30 (NIV), which reads,

"Charm is deceptive, and beauty is fleeting; but a woman who fears the Lord is to be praised."

I've known people to enter into relationships based on the *words* that their prospective partner *said* to them, as opposed to developing a *friendship* over time to determine if starting a relationship with the person is the right and prudent decision. In other words, it's not smart to enter into a relationship based *solely* on *words*, in hopes of alleviating *loneliness*. But rather, take time to examine the "fruit" that is being produced in their life and then determine if it matches up with their verbal confession. Anybody can *say* "Yes, I believe in God." But, what *evidence* in their life corroborates these words? Is there "fruit" of *love, peace, joy*, etc. in this person's life? For this, I like what Jesus said in Luke 6:43–45 (NIV).

(43) *"No good tree bears bad fruit, nor does a bad tree bear good fruit.*

(44) *Each tree is recognized by its own fruit. People do not pick figs from thornbushes, or grapes from briers.*

(45) The good man brings good things out of the good stored up in his heart, and the evil man brings evil things out of the evil stored up in his heart. For out of the overflow of his heart his mouth speaks."

These scriptures represent so much more than just "religion" as mankind defines that word. They are *life*! They are *health* to a person's spirit, body, and soul. They are a blueprint for successful living. If you're a *single* person entertaining a hope for a good and positive relationship in your future, now you can ask yourself in regard to the prospective mate, "Have I *really* taken the time to look at this person's life and locate the "fruit" of what they are saying? Now, you have a guide which tells you that "the good man brings good things out of the good stored up in his heart, and the evil man brings evil things out of the evil stored up in his heart." "No good tree bears bad fruit, nor does a bad tree bear good fruit." "Each tree is recognized by its own fruit." (*See*, Luke 6:43-45, NIV).

Therefore, if he has been divorced two or three times, that is not something to ignore. If she refuses to be *transparent* about a certain time period in her life, that's not something to ignore. If he's always talking about what he *intends* to do, but never *does* any of it, that's not something to ignore. If you have to find out from a *stranger*, something that *she* should have told you herself, that's not something to ignore. You see, whatever is on the inside of a person comes out in their life. It's the "fruit" that should be a primary concern rather than the appearance of the "tree." But, knowledge that you don't have, can't help you. Or, put another way, what you *don't* know, can hurt you.

Do you see just how much helpful information can be extracted from God's Word? His written word is the seed for spiritual knowledge, understanding, discernment, sound judgment, and wisdom, all of which *cannot* be attained by any other source. But, this is only the beginning. The goal is to stay in the Word *of* God long enough until you *hear* a Word *from* God. This is a principle to which you were introduced in the *first pillar: faith*.

God speaks to the *heart*. It may be a foreign concept to someone who is new to Christ. It can even be a bit confusing. But, if you will just continue reading God's Word diligently and earnestly until you get the *experience* of *hearing* God's voice, then you will begin to live life with an *expectation* (*i.e.* hope) that God will speak to your *heart* on a regular basis. This *hope* that God *will hear* your prayers may then be filled by your *faith* that God has *heard* your prayers.

In the *first pillar: faith*, we discussed 5 factors that apply when God speaks to you. Do you recall? Allow me to refresh your memory.

When God speaks to you, *it will always require faith*

When God speaks to you, *it will require courage*

When God speaks to you, *it will line up with his written Word*

When God speaks to you, *it will go against the World's way of thinking*

When God speaks to you, *peace will rule in your heart*

The problem comes when people begin to enter into a place of *unbelief*. They stop believing that God will speak to them. They let doubt enter in. In other words, they lose *faith*. And when *faith* is not in operation, *fear* is in operation. And *fear* is the entry point for Satan to enter your life and wreak all kinds of havoc and confusion. Don't ever forget, everything in the Kingdom of God operates by *faith*!

Once you start reading and meditating on God's Word repeatedly, the Word of God will *tune* your spirit. Your *spiritual ears* will become *tuned* to hearing *the truth* spoken by the voice of God. As your *faith* begins to grow in the Spirit, by reading God's Word, the spiritual *ear* of your *heart* will also begin to recognize God's voice. When you hear that little voice on the inside of you, *don't ignore it! Your conscience is the voice of the Holy Spirit!* So often, people dismiss the voice of their conscience as insignificant. People tend to think, "Oh, that's just *me* talking." Or, "Maybe I'm just being paranoid." Another common thing is that people tend to label that little voice as an "instinct." For example, they say, "My *instincts* told me not to go out with that guy." Or, "My *instincts* are telling me I shouldn't take this job."

You see, people who *act* on "good instincts" are people who recognize that the voice of their conscience is not to be ignored. They may not even be religious, by the world's standards. Similarly, they may not profess a belief in Jesus Christ. *But* they will attest to a belief that there is a "voice of reason" that speaks to them when there are decisions to be made.

Well, I'm here to tell you that the Word will *enlighten* you to the *whole truth*. The Spirit of God will speak to the *heart* in all kinds of situations. I've already given you a 5-factored checklist to consult when you have a notion that God may be speaking to your *heart*. At this point, that's not the issue. The issue, rather, is whether the *ear* of your *heart* is *conditioned* to *hear* him. That "conditioning" comes only with *obedience – perpetual obedience*.

### THE DIVIDING TRUTH

*"The Blessing"* is the empowerment for success. To receive *"the blessing"* means that you are empowered to succeed. Success comes from *hearing* and *obeying* God's Word. Now, I could say that 100 times, and you may still miss the importance of what I just said. Success is based on *hearing* and *obeying* God. In other words, success is tied to your *honor*. This is what it should resemble: (1) In all things, put *Him first; acknowledge* God in everything that you do; (2) *hearing ears* are the key (fine-tuned by time spent in fellowship with the Holy Spirit reading and meditating on how he tells us to live our lives; (3) *obey* (do what he tells you to do). It's an infallible formula for success. Of course, to enact the formula, everyday of your life, requires knowledge, understanding, discernment, sound judgment, and wisdom. All of these things are freely given to us if we seek God with our whole mind and our whole heart.

You see, the *truth* is a divider. *Truth* always divides. *Truth* always separates. When *truth* is revealed or made known, by default, what is *false* is also revealed or made known. As soon as you discover *truth*, falsehoods, lies, and deception are left uncovered, bare, and exposed. Well, the Word of God is *truth*. Jesus is *truth*. The Son of God said,

"I am the way and *the truth* and the life." (*See*, John 14:6, NIV) Emphasis added.

When Jesus prayed to God for his disciples, he also said,

"Your *word* is *truth*." (*See*, John 17:17, NIV) Emphasis added.

So, God's Word is *truth*. It is a divider; a separator. In Jesus' same prayer to God for his disciples, Jesus said the following:

"*Sanctify* them by the truth; your word is truth." (John 17:17, NIV) Emphasis added.

Look again at the word, "*sanctify*," and then reference its definition directly below.

**Sanctify** – to set apart for sacred use or sacred purpose; make holy.

I call your attention to the first three words of the meaning of "sanctify" (*i.e. to set apart*). The *truth*, which is the Word of God, has the power to *set apart, separate,* or *divide* for God's sacred use or sacred purpose. Do you understand what I am saying to you? *Hearing* and *obeying* God's Word (or, living by the *truth*), *sets you apart* from what is *false. Hearing* and *obeying* God's Word, *separates* you from the things of this life that have *no truth* in them. Contextual learning is learning at its finest, so let's add practical context for the sake of clarity and understanding.

As you should be well aware by now, when I refer to "the World," I am referring to a certain mentality that pervades so much of human society. I am *not* referring to the planet Earth. God created the Earth, but God is not of "the World." In Jesus' prayer to God for his disciples, this is what he says,

(14) "I have given them your word and *the world* has hated them, *for they are not of the world any more than I am of the World.*

(15) My prayer is not that you take them out of the world but that you protect them from the evil one.

(16) They are not of the world, even as *I am not of it.*

(17) *Sanctify* them by your *truth*; your *Word* is truth." (John 17:14–17, NIV) Emphasis added.

As Jesus conveyed in His prayer to God, the Father, the Word of God has the power to separate, set apart, and sanctify a person from "the World." The Word is separating *you* from the things of the World; those things that are not *truth*. The Bible even warns us:

(15) "Do not love the world or anything in the world. If anyone loves the world, the love of the Father is not in him.

(16) For everything in the world – the cravings of sinful man, the lust of his eyes and the boasting of what he has and does – comes not from the Father but from the world.

(17) The world and its desires pass away, but the man who does the will of God lives forever." (1 John 2:15-17, NIV)

Don't you see what's going on here? For some people, it's difficult, if not impossible, for them to *spiritually hear* God's *truth*. It doesn't truly resonate with a lasting effect for some people who merely hear the Word with their natural ears. That's why the Word is designed to speak to the *ear* of the *heart*. It takes more than just listening. It takes labor, on your part, to seek God with all of your *heart*.

In this life, if you're not aware of God's *truth*, then you're standing in the contradiction. If you're not making a concerted effort to live your life according to God's Word, then by default, you're living your life in darkness. Think of all of the times that you've felt as if there was "no way out." Some of you have felt as if the roads that you've been traveling have only led to "dead-ends." How many of you feel "trapped" or "bound" by a job situation, a relationship, an addiction, emotional feelings, or ungodly activities? Are you living your life with no flashlight and no lamp? Are you simply proceeding forward in life with no real light to guide you? By default, if you are not under God's spiritual authority, which is the Word of God, then you are susceptible, and most likely, caught up in the deception that is "the World."

There is nothing in "the World" but the cravings of sinful man, the lust of his eyes and the boasting of what he has and does. Think about it and don't be *offended* by the *truth*. Take time and really think about it. People *suffer* in this life. People feel absolutely empty inside going through the days of their lives. They may not say it outwardly. Some people may not show it. But, if *you* are one of these people, then you can relate to what I am saying. *truth* is the *antithesis of deception*. It's the complete opposite. *Truth is God's word. Deception starts as soon as you take one step away from God's word. Self-deception* is the worst kind of deception because the basis for how you are living your life is what *you* feel and what *you* think, as opposed to the Word of God and what God says. God is the spiritual authority and the Word is the final authority for our lives. However, this is how most people operate: "Yeah, I believe in God...*but*...I don't want to do that." Or, "Sure, I believe that God exists...*but*...that has nothing to do with my life."

You see, when you enter into that place of "*yeah...but*," then, you've stepped out of the spiritual authority for your life, which is the *first step into deception*. The World does not operate by the Word of God. They are contrary to one another. The Bible says,

"Do not love the world or anything in the world. If anyone loves the world, the love of the Father is not in him. (1 John 2:15, NIV)

Clearly, there is a *division* in operation. There is a line of *separation* that has been drawn. Something is being *set apart* from something else. And the instrument, the tool, the divider, the separator, the sanctifier, *the sword*, that divides *is the word of God*. Read it for yourself!

"For the word of God is living and active. *Sharper than any doulbe-edged sword*, it penetrates even to *dividing* soul and spirit..." (*See*, Hebrews 4:12, NIV)

Which side of the line do *you* fall on? Are you standing with God in his Word, or are you operating within the World's mentality? You cannot serve two masters. You can't straddle the line. It's one or the other. Do you put God's Word first, or do you put *yourself* first? I'm speaking to believers and non-believers. Many people say that they are Christian, but the better question is, "What kind of Christian are you?" Are you *really* making every effort to *know* God's Word, and then *obey* it?

God's Word tells us,

"Therefore come out from them and *be separate,* says the Lord." (*See*, 2 Corinthians 6:17, NIV) Emphasis added.

What does the scripture mean by "be separate?" It means that you have to know who you are and start acting like it. You must now make a conscious effort in your daily life to think, act, and move, as *one who is set apart* for God's use. Come out from them and be separate.

So, we've established that God's *truth*, which is his Word, has the power *to separate*, sanctify, and set apart. We've also established that if you're not in God's *truth*, then you're most likely operating within the World's mentality. Put another way, if you're thinking isn't in line with the Word of God, by default, your mentality is in line with the World's way of thinking. There is no middle ground. Either you are in *truth*, or you are in *deception*. This is where the issue of *obedience* meets the issue of *self-deception*. People who merely *hear* God's Word, but don't *obey* what it says, *deceive themselves* in a variety of ways. It's not complicated. If you're not doing things God's way, then you're doing things *your way*, or *somebody else's way*. Deviation from the *truth* means that you have ventured out from under the final authority for your life (the Word of God) in what amounts to disobedience. Along this road of *self-deception* await the demons of darkness that influence you right along a path to destruction. (We'll talk about what happens to those who are living their lives in *deception*, rather than in *truth*, in the pages to come. For now, please stay with me as I continue to lay the foundation for the issue of *perpetual obedience*, as it pertains to conditioning your heart to *hear* God's Word.)

You must realize that all of your *success* and all of your *peace* is found in God's will for your life, not in what *you* want! You must be willing to *hear* from God, and you must be willing to *obey* God. Your success depends upon your willingness to *submit your will* to God's will. I want you to write this down and remember it.

*Submission brings freedom*

*rebellion brings bondage*

It's a simple rule that is counterintuitive by the standard of human wisdom, but lines up perfectly with the wisdom of God.

When you open your Bible and begin to read, you'll inevitably come across *something* that could be compared to, or related, to a situation in your life. (If you open directly to the New Testament, the connection will be more obvious than the Old Testament). If you take that Word on whatever issue you come across that relates to your life, *and obey it*, you will discover a *freedom* that came out of your *obedience* to God's Word. The feeling is that you are *submitting your will*, your actions, your words, and your decisions, to God's commands, laws, and decrees, as the *final* authority for your life. In doing so, you will be *freed* from the binding thing that is the object of the decision.

For example, imagine the guy who has fallen into a *pattern* of *angry behavior* towards his wife and finds himself using verbally and emotionally abusive speech towards her on occasion. Then, he locates in God's Word, and submits, to where it says,

(25) "Husbands love your wives, just as Christ loved the church...

(28) In this same way, husbands ought to love their wives as their own bodies. He who loves his wife loves himself. (*See*, Ephesians 5:25,28, NIV)

You see, *submission to God's Word* (*i.e. obedience*) as the *final authority* in his life on this issue has the result of *freeing him* from the pattern of regrettable words said in anger.

Or, take drinking wine or other mixed "party" drinks for example. Maybe you don't think that you have a problem with drinking. Maybe you only drink "socially." After all, isn't that what most people are concerned about - the socially-acceptable behavioral norm? They are "social" drinkers, which means that they imbibe only when they're with friends, or out dancing, or when they need to "unwind." This mentality, of course, is predicated on "worldly wisdom" as the *final authority* for a person's life. According to the world, drinking "socially" is just fine. You're not hurting anyone. You're not an alcoholic. Besides, lots of people drink "socially." It's the norm.

Now, use your spiritual eyes and your spiritual ears and tell me what you see and hear. I pray that you can see what's going on. The Word is truth, and it is also *light*.

When you use "worldly wisdom" as your barometer of *authority* for your life, you begin to *reason* why certain actions and decisions are the "right" actions and decisions. When you don't use God's Word as the *final authority* for your life, you begin to engage in a process of *reasoning* which path is the best path to take. And a few, if not all, of the choices which are set out before you *seem right!* The Bible says,

"The way of a *fool seems right* to him, but a wise man listens to counsel. (See, Proverbs 12:15, NIV) Emphasis added.

Now, because the *final authority* for your life is *not* based on what God has said, but rather it's based on your *emotions* (*i.e.* what you *feel* is right), you are now traveling down a road of *self-deception* – a road which leads to destruction. In the case of our example of the guy who continues to *reason* why "social drinking" is justified, the Word says,

(17) Therefore do not be *foolish*, but understand what the Lord's will is.

(18) *Do not get drunk on wine*, which leads to debauchery. Instead be filled with the Spirit.

(Ephesians 5:17–18, NIV) Emphasis added.

By submitting to God's Word on this issue, it's the guy who *now* decides, "Ok, even though I may not see anything wrong with drinking socially, I'm going to base what I do on God's Word as the *final authority* for my life." As a result, he is now *set free* from the unseen, dark spiritual "law" that was in operation causing him to be in bondage to the world's socially-acceptable norm. Remember, *self-deception* begins as soon as you take that first step outside of God's will. A person will *reason* his way into a *course* of action (or down a *seemingly right* path) based on how they feel rather than on the basis of what God's Word says. And since God's Word is <u>not</u> the final authority for their life, the person proceeds down a path of deception headed toward destruction. Because that person stepped out from under God's authority, they are subjected to the influence of the demons of darkness of this world. At this point, negative manifestations start to appear in the person's life. Not only is there an inability to attain the desired measure of success, but things may also begin to go *noticeably* wrong. Generally speaking, the person doesn't even realize that they are on a path of deception *until* they walk right into the destruction. And let's be clear about something. Unfortunately, there are many people who have *never* recognized the Word of God as any kind of authority in their life. I submit to you that a closer look into the lives of many of these individuals would render a showing of *lack* of some kind. It could be a lack of peace, a lack of wealth, a lack of mental or emotional health, or even a lack of hope.

At the point of despair or destruction, people turn to God. Whether they were believers beforehand, or non-believers, people start to pray, and they ask God why would *HE* allow such a destructive thing to happen? That's when you start to hear people disparage God saying things like, "Well, if there was a God, how could *HE* let this happen to me?" In reality, the person speaking these words has completely overlooked the issue of *obedience* to God's Word as the *final authority* for their life.

*Submission brings freedom*

*rebellion brings bondage*

How many of *you* want and need some kind of *change* in *your* life? Yet, you remain powerless to do so. The reason is because all of your success lies in God's will for your life! It's what *He* wants, not what *you* want. When you begin to understand how God wants you to live your life, then you become empowered for success. That's *the blessing* – empowerment for success. You live according to his Word, not your wants and wishes. You begin to realize the difference between a "good idea" and a "God idea." You *submit yourself* to God, and in doing so, you break *free* of the very things that you want to change!

People tend to get caught up with the associations that come along with "religion." People also make all kinds of excuses. In doing so, they are simply fulfilling what the Bible has spoken of. There is a division. Some are enlightened, some remain in thick darkness. Just listen to what the prophet Isaiah said:

"Arise, *shine*, for your *light* has come, and the glory of the Lord rises upon you. See, *darkness covers the earth* and *thick darkness is over the peoples,* but the Lord rises upon you and his glory appears on you. (Isaiah 60: 1-2, NIV) Emphasis added.

You see, when you know God's Word, there are no surprises. There are only things that you should've recognized ahead of time because God's Word warned you of the very thing that just occurred in or around your life. You view things from a *spiritual perspective* and you have a *spiritual understanding* of what your eyes see in the natural sense. You see "the World" for what it is. You have *truth*, which gives you the ability to *spiritually discern deception. Spiritual discernment* is rooted in knowing the Word of God.

So, if we're talking about success in our lives, then we must discuss the issue of *obedience* (*i.e.* obeying God's Word as the *final authority* for our lives). Clearly, we must *first acknowledge Him* in our daily decisions and thought processes. Then, we must locate in the Word of God what God has to say about that particular issue that we are facing in our lives. Once we have *heard* what it is that God has to say about that issue, we must now *obey* what he said. This is the *right path! Acknowledge, hear, and obey.* This is what it means to operate under the right authority for our lives. Read what Jesus has to say about the guy who actually *does* what God tells him to do, as opposed to merely *hearing* it, and deciding to go his own way:

(24) Therefore everyone who hears these words of mine and *puts them into practice* is like a wise man who *built his house on the rock.*

(25) The rain came down, the streams rose, and the winds blew and beat against that house; yet it did not fall, because it had its foundation on *the rock.*

(26) *But* everyone who hears these words of mine and does *not put them into practice* is like a foolish man who built his house on sand.

(27) The rain came down, the streams rose, and the winds blew and beat against that house, *and it fell with a great crash.* (Matthew 7:24-27, NIV) Emphasis added.

It's the person who *hears and obeys* that is likened to a man who built his *house* on a *rock* that did not fall when the rains came, the streams rose, and winds blew. But, the person who *hears, but does not obey* is likened to a *foolish* person who built his *house* on *sand*. And when the rains came, the streams rose, and winds blew, the house built on *sand*, fell with a great crash.

I want you to recall the fundamental principle that I illustrated to you in the *Second pillar: depart from sin.* "You are the temple. *You are the house!*" The person that *hears and obeys* God's Word will not be shaken when the rest of the world is facing an "economic crisis." The person that *hears and obeys* God's Word will not be destroyed when their spouse or partner gets up and leaves them after 20 years of marriage. The person that *hears and obeys* God's Word is like a HOUSE that won't be rattled when the rest of the world *fears* issues of the day such as global warming or swine flu.

Let me assure you of something that is of value to your spiritual and natural well-being. There is a place that you want to get to. That place is having the ability to *hear* from God. It can only be achieved through reading and meditating on his Word and seeking him with all your heart, mind, soul, and strength. Hearing ears are the key. But, when you get to that place where the *spiritual ear* of your *heart hears* what God has to say to you, *obey* it. Don't "try" to obey it. *obey* him. And the result will be an *honor* that comes from God that will lead you to a place of success, peace, and joy. It is the *knowledge* that you receive directly from God to the ear of your *heart* that is *revelation knowledge*. The *rock* that is referred to in the scripture above is *revelation knowledge*. Build your house on the knowledge of God, *revealed* to you by God's Holy Spirit.

### You are the house

When your *foundation* is built on what God told *you* to do, *now*, you become a candidate for *exploits*. *Now*, you become a candidate for *change*. *Now*, you become a candidate to receive an *honor* that can only come from God, and not from men. *Now*, you become a candidate for *the blessing*, which is, empowerment for success. *Now*, you put yourself in a position to start a new business; get a higher educational degree; get a promotion; attain financial wealth; travel around the world if you desire. *Now*, you take action based on what your *spiritual authority* told you to do, as opposed to what *you felt* like doing. *Now*, you are operating *by faith*, rather than being motivated by *fear*. *Now*, you are being led by the *Spirit* of God. In him, you have *authority* over all things. All things are possible with God.

There is *peace* attached to *truth*. Think about situations in your own life. If anyone has ever lied to you, deceived you, or misled you, there was absolutely *no peace* surrounding the situation. Where there is an absence of the *truth*, there is disorder, chaos, stress, and worry. In many cases, where *truth* is absent, there will also be *fear*. When *fear* is in operation, *faith* is paralyzed. *Fear* is the antithesis of *faith*. Where *fear* is present, *faith* is absent. *Fear* tolerated, is *faith* contaminated. Well, *deception* and *fear* go hand-in-hand, in the spiritual *and* in the natural.

Let's first take a look at *deception* and *fear* in the natural sense. Remember, *deception* begins as soon as you take that first step away from God's Word. Well, picture the person who, for whatever reason, is in the midst of deceiving someone through a web of lies. (The interesting thing here is that I started to use the example of a child who tells a lie to illustrate the relationship between *deception* and *fear*, but I don't anticipate children reading this book. In other words, there are plenty of *adults* who lie and deceive on a consistent basis. So, let's focus on that reality).

We all know that *relationships* can be a breeding ground for *deception*. Whenever one partner is operating deceitfully through the telling of lies, there is also an element of *fear* that attaches itself to that relationship, on *both* sides! The proponent of the lie *fears* that their lies will be *exposed*, and the recipient of the lie *fears* that something is just not right (*i.e.* something is *"off"*). The *fear* may extend to the children, if there are children involved. Kids may *fear* that their parents will divorce, hurt each other, separate, or all of the above. In other words, *deception* can cause the *fear* of not knowing what your future holds. Living in *fear* is a terrible way to live.

Let's take another example in the natural sense. I've known women who have been sexually abused and/or raped in their past and who have maintained a sense of normalcy, on the outside, but who were tormented by *fear* on the inside. Unresolved *fear* can be so emotionally heavy that it can cause a person to literally *choose* a life of *self-deception* because facing the *fear* attached to the reality of the situation is too difficult and too great. Abuse is a prime example. Many women and children that suffer serious abuse (sexual, physical, and/or emotional) at the hands of men embark upon a life that is relegated to an *emotional survival* rather than a life of free will. It's not uncommon for that person to create a "split-reality" as a response to the *fear* that is attached to the harmful situation. This *self-deception* can be a survival tactic that is ultimately rooted in an unresolved *fear. Living in fear is captivity. It's bondage.* Satan would have you think that there is "no way out." He wants you to believe that you don't have the *authority* to do anything about your situation. He wants you to operate as if you have no choice, you have no say, and you have no power. But, as the saying goes…

*Nothing is further from the truth!*

This is why it is incumbent upon me and upon *you*, to spread God's *truth*! When you operate in the Word of God, you are operating in *love.* The scriptures say, "God is love." (*See*, 1 John 4:16, NIV). In *love*, you have compassion for people. You want people to *live*, not perish. You want people to have *peace*, not turmoil. You want people to have *faith*, not *fear*.

Well, we know that *deception* begins when you take that first step away from the *spiritual authority* for your life, which is the Word of God. Essentially, you are taking a step *away* from the *truth*. Recall Jesus' prayer to God for his disciples. Jesus said, "…*your word is truth.*" (*See*, John 17:17, NIV). Well, God's Word, which is *truth* according to Jesus, also tells us that *obeying God's Word will free you from anything that binds you, such as fear.* Jesus said,

"If you *hold to my teaching*, then you will know *the truth*, and *the truth will set your free. (See*, John 8:31, NIV) Emphasis added.

*Obedience* is the issue. To "hold to [his] teaching" means to *obey*. Stated another way, whether you hear God's Word, *and put it into*

*practice*, is how God qualifies a person as *wise* or *foolish*. Look at that carefully. The line of demarcation for *wisdom* and *folly* that God has drawn is the line of *obedience*. It's not enough to simply *hear* God's Word. It's not enough to simply go to church or read the Bible at home, and *passively agree* with the words on the page, or nod your head in agreement when the pastor or priest is delivering the message. There is a big difference between knowing right, and doing right. But the place where people falter is where they fail to account for the importance of *knowing <u>how</u> to do right*. But, the Word of God doesn't just tell you that you *should* live right. The Word also provides instruction on *how* to accomplish *right living*. I'll show you what I mean.

When we submit to God's Word as the *final authority* for our lives, we do what the Word says. In other words, we **obey**. Certain godly commands are very direct and straightforward and the destructive element that would come from disobedience is evident. In other words, God tells us to do something specific; then, he tells us what will happen if we don't do it. For example, God's Word tells us the following:

"*You shall not misuse the name of the Lord* your God, for the Lord will not hold anyone guiltless who misuses his name. (Deuteronomy 5:11, NIV) Emphasis added.

(3) "But among you *there must not be even a hint of sexual immorality, or any kind of impurity, or of greed,* because these are improper for God's holy people.

(4) *Nor should there be obscenity, foolish talk or coarse joking,* which are out of place, but rather thanksgiving.

(5) For of this you can be sure: *No immoral, impure or greedy person — such a man is an idolater — has any inheritance in the kingdom of Christ and of God.*

(6) *Let no one deceive you* with empty words, for because of such things God's wrath comes on those who are *disobedient.*

(7) Therefore *do not be partners with them.* (Ephesians 4:3-7, NIV) Emphasis added.

Here, we have received God's instruction for what we *should* do. In short, these scriptures are essentially telling us that we *should* live right. But, there is no limit to God's goodness. The Word also provides the blueprint for *how* to accomplish *right living!* In other words, it's a great thing to know and quote these scriptures. But, it's an even better thing to know *how* to accomplish what the scriptures are telling you to do! The basic message found in the above-referenced scriptures is straightforward. I'll make them even plainer for you.

Don't walk around saying "God," "Jesus," "Jesus Christ," or "Christ" in an irreverent, disrespectful, casual manner. (Anyone who watches television programming originating from the USA has surely heard such speech).

Don't have anything to do with sexual immorality, impurity, or greed

No coarse, obscene "humor"

*Don't be deceived,* God will punish those who partake in this behavior

Don't be in association with such people

Take special note of God's words, *"Don't be deceived."* That's a clear warning. He's giving us his TRUTH and telling us *exactly* what is unacceptable in his sight. There's no dispute as to whether the forbearance of the things on this list equate to *living right*, by God's standard. That's not the issue. The issue, rather, is *how* do we accomplish *right living*? *How* do we accomplish the things on this list, especially, living in a world that doesn't recognize God's Word as the final authority for our lives? Well, God doesn't leave us hanging. He gives us the answer in his Word. The Word says,

(33) "Do not be misled: *'Bad company corrupts, good character.'*

(34) Come back to your senses as you ought, and stop sinning: for there are some who are ignorant of God – I say this to your shame." (1 Corinthians 15:33, NIV) Emphasis added.

Did you see that? *"Bad company corrupts good character."* To me, that is truth beyond truth. Whoever you "hang out" with has a major *influence* on you. They *influence* the way you talk, the words you use, the thoughts that you have, your feelings, emotions, your decisions, and your actions. If you're spending time in the presence of "bad company," sooner or later, that *influence* will manifest itself in *your* life.

Somebody might say, "Well, what *is* bad company?" "What does that *really* mean?" Here's the simple answer. "Bad company" is any influence that opposes God's Word. Or, stated another way, any influence that doesn't line up with God's way of thinking. People complicate things by making excuses. There is no excuse and it's not complicated. Either you're with God, or you're against him. There's no middle ground. So, my question to you is, "Who are you hanging with?" "Who are you spending time with?" "Who is influencing you?"

*The company you keep determines how you live; right company for right living.* Considering our list above of things we *should not do*, God clearly tells us *how* we may accomplish what he has commanded. He says, *"Come back to your senses."* Stop hanging around *"bad company!"* People that are consistently misusing God's name, using obscenities in their everyday vernacular, and sleeping around outside of marriage, are not living a life that lines up with God's Word. Conversely, they are living a life that *opposes* God's way of thinking. I don't care if the "bad influence" is your uncle, your best friend, your cousin, or your co-worker – you've got to take some time and think about *you* and whether *you* are living the way God wants *you* to live. The Bible is full of scriptures that tell of how man will be judged according to the deeds he has done in the body, here on Earth. It doesn't say anything about excuses. Stop being *afraid* to take a stand on something because of what *somebody else* might think about the stand that you're taking. You must understand this principle: *You can't serve God in people-bondage.* It doesn't work. This is the very reason why we are talking about *honor.* *Whose word in your life holds the most weight?* If your *actions* show that God's Word holds the most weight, well, you're *honor* is in the right place. If your actions reflect *anything but* obedience to God's Word, you're operating outside of God's will. As we've seen above, *deception* begins as soon as you take that first step away from God's Word as the *final authority* for your life. And what is it that God's Word says to us in the scriptures above? It says,

*"Don't be deceived!"* (*See*, Ephesians 4:6, NIV)

*"Dont't be misled!"* (*See*, 1 Corinthians 15:33, NIV)

*Obedience is the issue!* When we *put into practice* what we *hear* from God, then we are structuring our lives on knowledge from the Lord. You are like that man who built his house upon a rock that could not be shaken when the rains came, and the streams rose, and the winds blew. You *separate* yourself from those who *don't* obey God's Word. And the *obedience* that you have displayed concerning God's Word will be *richly rewarded*.

(35) "So do not throw away your confidence; it will be *richly rewarded*.

(36) You need to persevere so that when you have done the will of God, you will receive what he has promised." (Hebrews 10:35-36, NIV)

Not only will we receive God's promises in the time that is to come, but *obedience* to God's Word helps us to achieve *wholeness* in *this* life. Life is tough. I don't need to tell you that. It's full of ups and downs. But, the attainment of *wholeness*, *peace*, and *joy* is the goal, and it's attainable.

So, let's recap. Whether we are talking about *hearing* God's *written* Word through reading the Bible, or *hearing* God's *spoken* Word revealed to you through *time spent* in the Word, *in fellowship* with the Holy Spirit (*i.e. revelation knowledge*), there is one constant that must take place if you want to see the *power* of God manifested (*i.e. the ability to get results*) in your life. You must *obey* his Word.

In the area of *revelation knowledge*, the Spirit of God acts as *"the revealer,"* or *"the enlightener."* Your goal is to cultivate a personal relationship with the Holy Spirit, which God has freely given to you, by spending time in his presence. The way to do that is by spending time in the Word and by *acknowledging* the Spirit in everything that you do. Talk to him. Go to him in prayer. He is your friend and your guide. Time spent in fellowship with him will result in the tuning of the spiritual ear of your *heart*. And when you listen to that voice, and *do what he says*, you are making decisions based on *revelation knowledge*. It is knowledge that has been *revealed* to you by God's Spirit. And according to the Word, God's Spirit knows *the mind* of God. God's Spirit knows God's thoughts concerning you and your life! And he's given his Spirit *to you*!

(9) "It is written: No eye has seen, no ear has heard, no mind has conceived what God has prepared for those who love him,

(10) but God has *revealed* it to us *by his Spirit*. The Spirit searches all things, even the deep things of God.

(11) For who among men knows the thoughts of a man except the man's spirit within him?" In the same way, *no one knows the thoughts of God except the Spirit of God*. (*See*, 1 Corinthians 2:9) Emphasis added.

You see, the Holy Spirit knows the thoughts of God. He knows God's plans for your life. And when you begin to cultivate a personal relationship with the Spirit of God through *time spent* in the Word, *in fellowship* with him, then you begin to know and recognize his voice. When you repent of your past sinful behavior and truly make Christ the head of your life, the Holy Spirit moves in just as a person would move into a new house. Well, essentially, *you are a new house*. When you develop *hearing ears* you should rejoice because the Spirit of God is *revealing* to you the *right path* for your life!

Here is the process. Study and meditate on the Word. Ask the

Holy Spirit what to do concerning decisions in your life. Hear the voice of the Spirit and *obey*. You will know if the Spirit of God is speaking to your *heart* because his spoken Word will *always* line up with his *written Word*. *Obey* what he tells you to do. Remember: *partial* obedience is disobedience; just as, *delayed* obedience is disobedience. Do what his Word says. This is all done by *faith*.

"*Do not merely listen* to the word, and so *deceive* yourselves. *Do what it says*. (James 1:22, NIV) Emphasis added.

Again, we see the line of demarcation for what's considered "wise," and what's considered "foolish." The line of demarcation is *obedience*.

When you *don't* do what God says...

When you are living life on your own...

When you think that everything is fine just the way it is...

When you say, "Yeah, I know...*but*...

When you hear the Spirit trying to speak to your heart and you ignore him...

You are walking in *self-deception*

It's a *path* that is lacking all of the good things that God intended for you to have! God loves you. It's not a *fear* tactic. That's how so many people receive the *truth*. They immediately get *offended* as if someone is judging them. That's why the *humble person,* who accepts instruction, is considered wise.

"The wise in heart accept commands, but a chattering fool comes to ruin." (Proverbs 10:8, NIV)

There is a *path* for your life that God has already prepared for you. It's a path to the good life. To find that *path*, and *stay on it,* you've got to *honor God* by *obeying* what he tells you to do. Success comes from *hearing* and *obeying*. If you *don't* obey, it *hardens* your hearing. It's no different than the average dynamic between a parent and a child. When a parent consistently tells a child to do something, or not do something, and the child *disobeys*, there comes a point when the parent just stops talking. Just think about your own life. If there is a *friend* or *acquaintance* who you have repeatedly tried to counsel, but they refuse to listen, there comes a point where you simply stop trying to give helpful advice to that person. Well, the same principle applies when we, as God's children, don't obey what he wants us to do in our everyday lives. *Disobedience hardens your hearing.* It's more difficult to discern the voice of the Holy Spirit when you simply won't obey the *last* thing he put in your heart to do.

If you can't hear, well, there's nothing to obey. This is a bad place to be because that means you're likely making decisions outside of your *spiritual authority.* At that point, you're making decisions based on what *feels* right to you. The Word is not your final authority any longer. Your *emotions* have become your final authority. And you are now traveling down a road of *self-deception,* thinking everything is under control, but you're really on a path that ultimately leads to destruction (*i.e. lack of peace, lack of joy, worry, hurt, sickness, etc.*). Are you beginning to see how this works?

So, if success comes by *hearing* and *obeying* God's Word, but *hearing* is "driven by" *obedience,* then it reasonably follows that *perpetual obedience* is the real issue. *Hearing* and *obeying* God's Word *consistently* allows the manifestations of *God's blessings* to take hold, and be seen, in our lives. And what is *the blessing? The blessing is the empowerment for success.* But, don't look for money to just drop out of the sky. This is not a magic act. Things don't magically appear. The empowerment for success may come in the form of the following:

Wisdom and Insight

Concepts

Witty Inventions

Anointed Ideas

God has already given you unique abilities that will produce wealth. The success lies in the process of *discovering* these abilities and putting them to use for God's intended purpose, rather than for the selfish motivation of acquiring personal wealth. *perpetual obedience* allows you to *continue* to *hear*, and gives you the opportunity to *continue* to *obey*, which is what releases the *power* of God. What have I told you from the start of this book? There is *power* tied to God's voice, if you (1) can engage the Word *of* God long enough to get a Word *from* God, and (2) *obey* what he told *you* to do.

But, it all begins with *acknowledging God* at the start of every decision, both large and small. *Acknowledge* the Holy Spirit in all things so that He will direct your path. (*See,* Proverbs 3: 6, NIV). If you go to the Holy Spirit *first* (*i.e. put Him first*), then that means that you are *honoring God.* To *honor God* means that you have given him the right to speak into your life, and that his words hold more weight than anything else in your life. Then, through *time spent* in the Word, in fellowship, with the Holy Spirit (who knows the mind of God), he will *speak* to the ear of your *heart* (*i.e.* revelation knowledge) telling you *exactly* what you should do concerning decisions in your life. When you *obey* what he told you to do, you are now operating under God's *spiritual authority* and his Word is your *final authority*. When the difficult times come (remember, the "rains," "streams," and "wind"), you will *stand firm* and not be shaken because you are a house that is built on the *rock of revelation knowledge*. You will be operating in *truth*, as opposed to *deception*. You will also be operating in *wisdom*, as opposed to *folly*. And finally, rather than traveling down a road leading to destruction, *you'll be on the path to success, peace*, and *joy*. It's the path to the *good life*.

It's time that we *honor God* with our lives!

It's your life. You own the choice. But remember:

Once you choose, your choice owns you.

So, choose *wisely*!

# FIFTH PILLAR:
## *Love*

There are two systems in operation. There is God's way of thinking, and there is the world's way of thinking. The Kingdom of God's way of thinking is based in *faith* and has its power rooted in *love*. The world's way of thinking is based in *fear*. It has its roots in *selfishness* and its power is *money*. *Love* is the strongest force in existence. This cannot be overstated. There is no limit that can be put on *love*. The issue, here, is the power of *God's* unconditional *love*.

There is an *earthly* love that is based in *human* emotion. Emotional love that comes from man is conditional. It is not perfect love. As Christians, our objective is *not* to love based on our emotion. Instead, we should strive to *love* based on God's commandment to *love*. To "walk in *love*," or "operate in *love*," means to "walk in him," or "operate in him". The Bible says,

"God is love. Whoever lives in love lives in God, and God in him." (*See,* 1 John 4:16, NIV)

"And this is love: that we *walk in obedience to his commands.* As you have heard from the beginning, his command is that you *walk in love.* (2 John 1:6, NIV) Emphasis added.

The thing that I want you, the reader, to begin to focus on is that *love* is a way of *being*. Put aside your notions of love as a human emotion. You must begin to think of *love* as a *mindset*. It is a *way of living* that is exemplified by the person who decides to *"walk in obedience"* to God's commands. The decision to walk in *love*, (or walk in God, since God is love), is tantamount to the decision to *obey his commands*. In this way, we begin to see that *love* encompasses much more than a emotional connection between two human beings. Instead, we begin to uncover a more profound interrelation between God, Jesus, and man in our attempt to truly understand *love*.

The Bible says, "We love because he first loved us." (1 John 4:19, NIV)

(9) "This is how God showed his love among us: He sent his one and only *Son* into the world that we might live through him.

(10) This is love: not that we loved God, but that he loved us and sent his *Son* as an atoning sacrifice for our sins. (1 John 4:9–10, NIV) Emphasis added.

According to these scriptures, we know that God loved us first by sending his only Son, *Jesus Christ*, to die on the cross for the atonement of sins in the world. In other words, God displayed his *love* for us *through* Jesus. Well, Jesus is also the conduit by which human beings display our *love* for God. If we *obey God's commands*, given to us through words spoken by Christ Jesus, we display our *love* for the Father, and the Son.

Jesus said,

(21) "Whoever has my commands and *obeys* them, he is the one who *loves* me." (*See*, John 14:21, NIV) Emphasis added.

(23) "If anyone *loves* me, he will *obey* my teaching." (*See*, John 14:23, NIV) Emphasis added.

(9) "As the Father has loved me, so have I loved you. Now remain in my love.

(10) If you *obey* my commands, you will remain in my *love*, just as I have *obeyed* my Father's commands and remain in his *love*. (John 15:9-10, NIV) Emphasis added.

So, what do we see using our spiritual eyes and spiritual ears? We see that...

*love* = *obedience*

Jesus instructs us that he has remained in God's *love* by *obeying* God's commands. He tells *us* to remain in *his* love by obeying *his* commands. So, what we're seeing is the interrelation between God, Jesus, and mankind as it pertains to *love*. Jesus affirms that the *greatest* and *most important commandment is to...*

"Love the Lord your God with all your heart and with all your soul and with all your mind and with all your strength." (Mark 12:30, NIV)

And the way that we show our *love* for God is by *obeying* his Word!

Now, there is only one piece of the equation that is missing: man's relation to man. Or, plainly stated, *how people treat each other!* This is what Jesus deemed to be the *second most important commandment*. In regard to the "greatest commandments," Jesus said,

"The second is this: 'Love your neighbor as yourself. There is no commandment greater than these.'" (Mark 12:31, NIV)

In other words, we should *love* others, as we *love* ourselves, simply because God commanded us to do so.

Therefore, our *love* for the Lord is shown through our *obedience* to God's Word, as taught through his Son, Jesus Christ. If we follow Jesus' teachings, we remain in Jesus' love and his love remains in us. Additionally, if we *love* our fellow man, on this Earth, as we *love* ourselves, then we are effectively *obeying* God's Word, as taught by Jesus, and we remain in *Jesus' love* and his *love* remains in us. So, *obedience* has everything to do with *love*, whether the relationship is vertical (*i.e.* God, Jesus, and man), or horizontal (*i.e.* man-to-man).

Once again, do you see the importance of knowing the Word of God for yourself? If you aren't making an earnest effort to *know* and *understand* God's Word for yourself, then you are at a serious disadvantage in more ways than one. *Everything in the Kingdom of God operates within the circle of love.* Let me say that again. *Everything in the Kingdom of God operates within the circle of love.* So, if that's the case, how would any person who is operating *outside* of the circle of *love* (*i.e. disobedience*) receive a manifestation of *God's blessing* in their life? The answer is simple; they wouldn't! And that's important if we're talking about achieving success, wholeness, peace, soundness, and security in our everyday lives. You must *know your spiritual weapons.*

Allow me to turn your attention to something that I told you earlier in the model.

Hearing God's voice is by *faith*. Obeying God's voice is *love*. You can't talk about *hearing* without mentioning *obeying* because they go hand-in-hand. Similarly, you can't talk about *faith* without mentioning *love* because they also go hand-in-hand. Hearing is to Obedience, as Faith is to Love. The *power* of God is released in your life when you *obey* what you heard from God. And that *obedience* is a reflection of your *love* for God. Jesus said, "If you obey my commands, you will remain in my love, just as I have obeyed my Father's commands and remain in his love." (John 15:10, NIV). That is why *faith* and *love* are "power twins" in the life of a Christian. Your love drives your faith. Your love for God is exhibited by your *obedience* to his Word, and his spoken Word is heard by *faith*.

*Love* is the Kingdom of God's source of *power*. It is the most powerful force that any person can exercise.

Now, allow me to provide you with an example illustrating how *love* can be utilized as a powerful *spiritual weapon* in times of trouble. Contextual learning is learning at its finest, so follow me closely as I take you through a set of real-life circumstances that involved using *love* as a *spiritual weapon* to get the victory in a very difficult situation.

After accepting God into my life, my perspective as to certain things in life changed. Specifically, I began living under a self-imposed responsibility to become a champion of the *truth*. Once I became enlightened to the *truth* that is found in God's Word, it was that *truth* that began to help me through a difficult situation that I was facing. In the First Pillar, *faith*, I gave an in-depth account of a past personal battle that I encountered involving helping a friend cope with an unfortunate instance involving rape, sexual abuse, and the emotional results that commonly flow therefrom. In my humble opinion, *compassion* played a pivotal role in my decision to help the person through a difficult time. But, *compassion* and *love* is not the same thing.

In *compassion,* there is often a level of sympathy. If you've ever helped anyone through a difficult trial in their life, perhaps, you also felt a measure of sympathy for what that person was facing. I want to be clear in pinpointing the real issue. There is a power in *love* that comes from *obeying* God that is separate and distinct from any power that could come from a *compassionate love* exhibited between people. In helping a friend uncover the *truth* of an ugly abusive past, and thus, start to recover from that past, the power of compassionate love was on display. Here is the point. It's not a far stretch to help those in our lives who are already near and dear to us. But, when you exhibit *Godly love* in a situation where you are confronted by the adversary, *this* is where the *real power* is displayed.

There came a point when I stood face to face with an alleged rapist. Now, there may be numerous images that a person conjures up as to the physical appearance or the personality traits of a rapist. Unfortunately, it would be impossible to put one common face to a person that commits such atrocities. Evil comes in all forms, shapes, and sizes. And that was never more apparent to me than in this case.

Here's the deal. Put yourself in a situation where you have the opportunity to confront a person who has caused an immeasurable amount of pain and suffering to someone that you hold dear to you. These are the situations where lots of men have lost all control and committed acts of revenge that, frankly, can be judged only by God himself. Think about it. It's not uncommon in modern society for person "A" to exact revenge on person "B" because person "B" initially hurt someone that person "A" loved or cared about. To the human emotion, it's totally understandable and arguably justifiable. By nature, we want to protect those whom we love. Even in ancient biblical society, this principle held true. Read it below for yourself.

## TAMAR

There is a powerful biblical story in the ancient times of David, King of Israel, where a man named Amnon, son of David, raped his half-sister, Tamar. In the story, Tamar's brother, Absalom (also a son of David), was so angry at Amnon that Absalom killed Amnon for raping his sister, Tamar. Here are a few short excerpts of the story:

(1) In the course of time, Amnon son of David fell in love with Tamar, the beautiful sister of Absalom, son of David.

(2) Amnon became frustrated to the point of illness on account of his sister Tamar, for she was a virgin, and it seemed impossible for him to do anything with her.

(6) So Amnon lay down and pretended to be ill. When the king came to see him, Amnon said to him, 'I would like my sister Tamar to come and make some special bread in my sight, so I may eat from her hand.

(11) But when she took it to him to eat, he grabbed her and said, "Come to bed with me, my sister.

(12) 'Don't, my brother!' she said to him. 'Don't force me. Such a thing should not be done in Israel! Don't do this wicked thing...'

(14) But he refused to listen to her, and since he was stronger than she, he raped her.

(22) Absalom never said a word to Amnon, either good or bad; *he hated Amnon* because he had disgraced his sister Tamar.

(28) [Two years later] Absalom ordered his men, 'Listen! When Amnon is in high spirits from drinking wine and I say to you, "Strike Amnon down," then kill him.

(29) So Absalom's men did to Amnon what Absalom had ordered. (*See*, 2 Samuel 13:1-29, NIV)

Take note that Absalom's action of killing Amnon was done out of *anger*. Whether you think his actions were understandable or justifiable is not really the issue. What I want you to see is that he acted in ANGER, rather than in *love*.

Let's look at another example from the Bible that illustrates this same point, but that occurred hundreds of years *earlier* than the time of King David as seen in the example above.

### DINAH

Jacob (later known as "Israel") had a daughter named Dinah. Dinah was raped by a man named Shechem, who was not of the lineage of the descendants of Abraham. Dinah's brothers (Jacob's sons) were so furious at what happened to their sister, they exacted revenge by killing Shechem and *every male* in the city of the Hivite people. Here are few key excerpts:

(1) "Now Dinah, the daughter Leah had borne to Jacob, went out to visit the women of the land.

(2) When Shechem, son of Hamor, the Hivite, the ruler of that area, saw her, he took her and *violated her.*

(7) Now Jacob's sons had come in from the fields as soon as they heard what had happened. *They were filled with grief and fury,* because Shechem had done a disgraceful thing in Israel by lying with Jacob's daughter – a thing that should not be done.

(25)...two of Jacob's sons, Simeon and Levi, Dinah's brothers, took their swords and attacked the unsuspecting city, killing every male.

(26) They put Hamor and his son Shechem to the sword and took Dinah from Shechem's house and left. (*See*, Genesis 34:1-26, NIV)

Again, here we see an action of revenge exacted out of *"grief and fury."* Another way of stating "grief and fury" is *hurt* and *anger*. So, from days of old, we see the dynamic that is at play involving a very specific situation. A man rapes or abuses a woman. People who care for, or love, the woman that was raped or abused, respond with action that is based in *hurt* and *anger*. Now, here's what I want you to see.

Problems, complications, and destructive outcomes arise when action (or revenge) is exacted out of *hurt* or *anger*. You see, *hurt turns* to *anger*. Or, put another way, *anger* is just another form of *hurt*. When someone you love has been *hurt*, or is *hurting*, it hurts *you*. Unresolved *hurt* turns to *anger* and that's where things can really unravel, quickly. How many times have you tried to *hurt* someone because they *hurt* you first? Well, it's the same concept except the initial *hurt* is inflicted upon someone you care for rather than on you directly.

So, imagine a situation where you discover someone you care for, or love, has been raped, or sexually abused. In all likelihood, the fact that they have been hurt (or, that they are still hurting), is going to hurt *you*. If you have knowledge of *who* allegedly committed the rape, now the *hurt* that resides in you can quickly escalate or transform itself into *anger*. And that is a dangerous place to be for certain people who consider themselves "protectors," because a person acting in *anger* is being led by *emotion*. (Remember, *emotions* are Satan's way into your life. Since Satan doesn't have a body, he's always trying to get *some*-body. The way he does that is by seducing your *emotions,* your thoughts, and your feelings.)

Unfortunately, this was the situation that I was facing. Knowing the acts of atrocity that this person had allegedly committed in times past against an individual that was near and dear to me, I sat directly across from him for the purpose of communicating pertinent information. Knowing the indescribable pain that he had caused the victim, the victim's family, and other unsuspecting people, I sat directly across from him to express what needed to be said. I want to be clear. This was not a physical fight. This was not a hand-to-hand combat situation. This was a *spiritual* battle. It was a spiritual battle against a force of evil that was exposed and uncovered. I want you to truly understand what I'm saying to you, so please give me a little latitude in my explanation so I can break this down carefully.

If I hadn't been studying and meditating on the Word of God, like I was at the time, I would have surely been led by my *emotions*. As soon as I was within the spatial proximity of the person who allegedly committed these acts of rape and sexual abuse against someone that I knew and cared for, I would have been operating in *anger* (in the same order of Absalom, Simeon, and Levi from the stories above). If I was operating in *anger*, then by default, I could not be operating within the circle of *love*. And I told you before, *Everything in the Kingdom of God operates within the circle of love*. Once you allow someone or something to get you to operate *outside* of the circle of *love*, you paralyze the power that comes from God. Hear what I'm saying to you because this is one of the most valuable jewels of wisdom that anyone can acquire.

The Kingdom of God's system of thinking is based in *faith*, but its power is rooted in *love*. *Love* is your power. If the enemy can seduce you to operate *outside* of your power (*i.e.* outside of the circle of *love*), that's his entry point into your life. *Love* drives *faith*. If *love* is not in operation, then *faith* is not in *operation*. And if your *faith* is not in operation, then *fear* is in operation. *Hurt* and *anger* are nothing more than expressions of *fear*. They are manifestations of a sense of *powerlessness*. Once you're outside of your power, which is *love*, then Satan can wreak all kinds of havoc, disorder, and chaos in whatever situation you're facing. This is why people who are in *fear*, who are *hurt*, or who are *angry*, don't make good decisions. They are operating *outside* of the circle of *love* and *faith*. They are operating *outside* of their power.

There would have been no way for me to sit directly across from an alleged rapist in complete self-control, composure, and confidence without the *spiritual understanding* of my greatest *spiritual weapon, love*. Stay with me on this. You cannot let situations in life change your decision to walk in *love*. If Satan can get you out of walking in *love*, then he can now take over in your life. When you are there, in the heart of the situation, it won't feel

286 *Change Your Mind, Change Your Life*

good to you. But, if you handle the situation by walking in *love*, you will *honor* God and you will feel good about it afterwards. So, what am I saying to you?

*When you can be seduced out of love, You're seduced out of your power!*

I saw firsthand the pure, unmitigated evil that surrounds the act of rape. It goes beyond the person who is committing the act. It's deeper than that. If there was ever a question of whether evil forces exist that are unseen to the natural eye, let me put your inquiry to rest. There are unseen spiritual forces of evil, just as there are unseen spiritual forces of good. Don't be deceived in your manner of thinking. There are unseen demons of darkness and evil dark forces that prey upon *fear*. This is why you cannot tolerate *fear* in your life, not for one second. *Fear* is Satan's entryway into your life. When people are *afraid*, they are susceptible to be manipulated, tormented, abused, taken advantage of, walked on, hurt, and even terrorized.

Threats are simply words that evoke *fear*. Acts of terrorism throughout the world are designed to evoke *fear*. *Fear* can keep you stuck in one place for years. Satan wants you to be in a place of *fear* in your life: *Fear* of being poor; *fear* of losing your health; *fear* of being alone; *fear* of being a failure; *fear* of retaliation; *fear* of the unknown. Some people allow *fear* to absolutely rule their life and it's a miserable way to live. *You must confront the fears in your life, or they will manifest themselves in your life one day and confront you. You cannot live your life in fear!* This is such a true statement. I hope you are receiving these truths in the context of your own life because they will help you in whatever situations that you may be going through.

The alleged rapist (who was also committing alleged illegal acts of fraud, scamming innocent people out of their monetary savings) that sat in front of me derived all of his power from instilling *fear* in people. Remember, when you have the Word of God, you possess the power of *spiritual discernment*, which means that you have the ability to recognize the contradiction (or, the lie) from the truth. Put a simpler way, you have the ability to discern truth from falsehood. This man's entire arsenal of power was based on instilling *fear* in people. (This *fear* is what kept the rape victim from speaking out and revealing the truth to the proper authorities for quite some time.) But it didn't stop there. It quickly became evident to me that his "business" of defrauding innocent people out of their money was all predicated on *fear*. Listen carefully. In general, this is the reason why, in the midst of any economic crisis, fraudulent behavior surrounding real estate and residential property investment, skyrockets! It's because there is a rise in the climate of *fear*. People are *afraid*. And dishonest people who lack integrity prey upon this *fear*. They seize upon it, take advantage it, and swindle innocent people out of money. But, you have to know what's going on. You must be able to view circumstances that occur in the natural with your spiritual eyes and spiritual ears, and express situations using spiritual language, because then you will know how to fight the *right* fight using the *right spiritual weapons!*

It would have done me absolutely no good to confront a man who is allegedly capable of rape, using anger, yelling, and threats. That would only empower the enemy. But, *love*, you see. *love* is a force of God. *Love is God*, and *God is love*. It confuses the enemy and leaves evil powerless to do anything to you. This is why you must do your best to *never* become *offended*. "Offense" is the quickest way that the devil can seduce you out of *love*. Think about it. When you get *offended,* what happens? You get mad. You get hurt. You get upset. You get angry. People who get *offended* easily have the least amount of control over their emotions. More importantly, they put themselves *at risk* to respond to things *emotionally* rather than through wisdom.

I want to be clear. Walking in *love* is not always easy. By no means have I reached a place of proficiency in every area that I am teaching to you. In reality, these are not principles that can be fully attained. They can only be practiced with some measure of consistency. But, one thing is for certain. You can't do better until you know better. And there are people in this world that can benefit greatly from the *spiritual understanding* of how to better live their lives.

*Faith speaks!* Don't ever forget that. *Fear* is the opposite of *faith,* and it has the effect of silencing a person or stilling a person. For example, take the bully at school who continues to instill *fear* in his smaller classmate. What usually happens? The smaller child is *afraid* to tell anyone because he is in a place of *fear*. *Fear* silences the smaller child. Well, life doesn't change, people just get older. *You must never allow someone to take away your voice! Love speaks! Faith speaks!* And they both speak according to the Word of God. You *cannot* allow *anyone* or *anything* in this life to put you, and keep you, in a place of *fear*. Think about it carefully. It's very difficult to harm a person, stop a person, or do anything to a person who isn't afraid of anything. Without the element of *fear*, the bully has no power. A person who has no *fear* can accomplish anything they set their mind to do. But, without the *insight* that comes from the Word of God, some people are fighting the *wrong* fight using the *wrong weapons*. *Anger* is not a spiritual weapon. *Anger* is just another face of *fear*. *Love is* a spiritual weapon. And *love* starts from the inside, not the outside. It begins with the spiritual, not the natural. What you don't see controls what you see.

The *power* of God is in the *love* of God. The Word says,

"God is love." (*See*, 1 John 4:16, NIV)

"There is no fear in love. But perfect love drives out all fear" (*See*, 1 John 4:18, NIV)

Where there is God's *love, fear cannot* stand. And what is the gift that God has given to us?

"For God *did not* give us a spirit of *fear*, but a spirit or *power, love,* and of *sound mind*." (2 Timothy 1:7, NIV) Emphasis added.

God has given *you* a spirit of power, *love*, and of sound mind. In the center of your power and your sound thinking is *love*. There is no *fear* in *love*. *Love drives out all fear.*

So, let's review exactly what we've discussed to this point. Let's say that you're a person who makes the *decision* to walk in *love*. This *decision* exhibits *sound thinking* in line with the *sound mind* that God has freely given you. Your *power* lies in your ability to operate in *love*. If you are operating in *love, fear* cannot and will not stand in the presence of *love*. It can't because perfect *love* drives out all *fear*. *Love* that is perfected means *obedience* to the Word of God. It's a cycle that is designed to empower us, but only works *if* we are willing to submit our own will to the will of God's Word.

As for me, and the confirmation that came with my willingness to *obey* God's Word regarding staying in *love*, even in the face of the pure evil that is rape and abuse, I became a witness that day as to the *power of God's love*. Now, you can appreciate the difference and distinction between God's *love*, which is from above, and earthly emotional love, which is from below. This book was written for the sole purpose of *enlightenment* and *empowerment*. If you've been through sexual abuse in your life, *love* (which is *obedience* to God's Word) is where your *power* lies. If something has happened in your life that has caused *hurt* and/or *anger*, *love* (which is *obedience* to God's Word) is where your *power* lies. If you've been subjected to an element of *fear* in your life by someone *or* something, *love* (which is *obedience* to God's Word) is where your *power* lies.

*Love* eradicates *fear*. *Love* subdues *anger*. *Love* overcomes *hurt*. *Love* is the strongest force in existence. *God* is *love*. You will never be able to *forgive* someone without a commitment to operate in *love*. Remember, *godly love* is higher than human emotional love. It's on a higher plain. You'll find all kinds of things outside of the circle of *love*. Some people are mean. Some people are bitter. Some are angry. Some are hurt. Some are cynical. Some are selfish. And some are unforgiving. Yet, these same people say things like, "I want to be a better person." (Or, a better wife, a better husband, a better son, daughter, sister, brother, grandmother, grandfather, boyfriend, girlfriend, boss, employee, or friend). You can't do so until there is a commitment to operate in *love*. It has less to do with the other person, and has everything to do with *you*. You'll *never* be able to *forgive* someone who *hurt* you operating in *human emotional love.* Why? Because you'll be *afraid* that you'll be *hurt again*! And that leaves you operating in a place of *fear*, which is the devil's access point into your life to wreak havoc, disorder, and confusion. You've got to go *deeper.* The Bible says,

"For the word of God is living and active. Sharper than any double-edged sword, it *penetrates* even to dividing soul and spirit…" (*See*, Hebrews 4:12, NIV)

The Word of God, (or, the Word of *love*, since God *is love*) *penetrates* even to dividing soul and spirit. You see, the soul meets the spirit at the *heart.* The Word of God (or, the Word of *love*, since God *is love*) goes *deeper* than emotional love. The Word of *love* is the only thing that can get *deep* enough to reach the very root of the pain, or the heartache, or the deception, or the addiction, or the abuse, or the *fear*, and yank it out completely! That's why *forgiveness* is not meant for the person who committed the act that needs to be forgiven. *Forgiveness* is for the person who *has been hurt* because it allows them to *root out* the anguish, suffering, anger, anxiety, and despair that they are carrying around in their heart, soul, and spirit. Admittedly, people face some unimaginable scenarios in this life. I may have stated it best at the beginning of the book. *Never take for granted what somebody else might be going through or has already been through in life.* With that said, we must do everything that we know to do to keep our spiritual, emotional, psychological and physical health in right standing. *Everything in the Kingdom of God operates within the circle of love.* This includes *forgiveness.*

### LOVE FOR GOD IS TO OBEY HIS COMMANDS

This was the basis of God's *old covenant promise* with the people of Israel in the Old Testament. To those who *obeyed* and kept all of his commands, God set *life, blessings* and *prosperity* before them. (*See*, Deuteronomy chapters 28, 29, and 30). *The blessing was the empowerment to succeed.* To those who allowed their hearts to be turned away from God, who were *disobedient*, and who allowed other things to take priority in their hearts over him, God set *death, curses*, and *destruction* before them (*See also*, Deuteronomy chapters 28, 29, and 30). This was the *old covenant.* As you read the Bible, you will discover that the people of Israel were *disobedient*. True to his Word, God allowed the Israelites to be overtaken by armies of other nations and destroyed in great numbers. As a result, they forfeited their inheritance (*i.e.* the land of Canaan "flowing with milk and honey," given to them after 400 years of captivity in Egypt). This was the *old covenant.*

Generations later, God made a *new covenant* with the house of Israel. The *new covenant* that God made with Israel was this:

(10) This is the new covenant I will make with the house of Israel after that time, declares the Lord. *I will put my laws in their minds and write them on their hearts. I will be their God, and they will be my people.*

(11) No longer will a man teach his neighbor, or a man his brother, saying, 'Know the Lord,' because they will *all* know me, from the least of them to the greatest.

(12) For I will forgive their wickedness and will remember their sins no more. (Hebrews 8:10-12, NIV) (Emphasis added)

When *Jesus* died on the cross to take away our sins, the *new covenant* was sealed.[17] Jesus, essentially, became the centerpiece of the *new covenant*. The Bible says,

"For this reason Christ is the mediator of a *new covenant, that* those who are *called* may receive the *promised eternal inheritance* – now that he has died as a ransom to set them free from the sins committed under the first covenant. (Hebrews 9:15, NIV) Emphasis added.

Here is the point. A *covenant* is an agreement between God and his people in which God makes certain promises and requires certain behavior from his people in return.[18] This is an important point. Whether we are referring to the *old covenant* or the *new covenant*, God has set forth *promises* in return for *obedience*.

Now, jump to modern day. According to the Bible, if *you,* the reader, are of the *faith* of Abraham, then you are also a descendant of Abraham and *you too* are *heirs* to God's *covenant promises*. Read it very carefully:

(16) Therefore, *the promise comes by faith,* so that it may be by grace and may be guaranteed to *all Abraham's offspring* – not only to those who are of the law, *but also to those who are of the faith of Abraham*. He is the father of us all." (Romans 4:16, NIV) Emphasis added.

So, what am I really saying? If you operate in *faith* as Abraham operated in *faith*, then you are considered Abraham's *seed*, which

---

17      "In the case of a will [or, covenant], it is necessary to prove the death of the one who made it, because a will is in force only when somebody has died; it never takes effect while the one who made it is living." (Hebrews 9:16-17).

18      *See, Wikipedia.org* – Covenant *defined*.

makes you an heir to the *inheritance* that God has *promised*. What does it say in the scripture directly above? It says, *"…the promise comes by faith."* Therefore, if your *belief* (or, *faith*) in Christ Jesus is in the same form or fashion as Abraham's *belief* (or, *faith*) in God, then **you** are included in God's *covenant promises.* The Bible tells us

(26) You are *all* sons of God through *faith* in Christ Jesus…

(29) If you belong to Christ, then you are Abraham's *seed*, and *heirs* according to the *promise*. (*See*, Galations 3:26-29, NIV) Emphasis added.

Through Christ Jesus, all who were not heirs to the promise, by law, have become heirs by *faith*. In other words, if it wasn't for Jesus Christ, people all over the world that are not of Israel descent (also known as "Gentiles"), would not be included in God's *covenant promises.* But, to God's glory, through *faith* in Christ Jesus, *all* mankind may be considered as the *seed* of Abraham, and have an *inheritance* that comes through God's *promise.* The Word says it clearly:

(11) Therefore, remember that formerly you who are *Gentiles* by birth and called "uncircumcised" by those who call themselves "the circumcision" (that done in the body by the hands of men)

(12) remember that at that time you were separate from Christ, *excluded from citizenship in Israel and foreigners to the covenants of promise, without hope and without God in the world.*

(13) But now in Christ Jesus you who once were far away have been brought near through the blood of Christ. (Ephesians 2:11-13, NIV) Emphasis added.

Do you see it? This is why you must know *who* you are in Christ Jesus? You must be knowledgeable on what you are *entitled to* as the *seed* of Abraham, and a son or daughter of God. Formerly, "Gentiles" (*i.e.* everyone who is not of Jewish descent by law) were "foreigners to the covenants of promise, *without hope, and without God in the world.*" "But now," according to the Word of God, "in Christ Jesus you who once were far away have been brought near through the blood of Christ." Praise God! I implore you to see the significance of this *truth* in the greater context of *love*.

Through *faith* in Jesus Christ, you have a blood-bought right to God's covenants of promise in this life. You don't have to be "without hope and without God" in this world, according to God's Word. He has *promised* through a covenant, which was sealed by the blood of Jesus Christ, that he will be your God, and you will be his people. "We have this *hope* as *an anchor* for the soul, firm, and secure." (*See,* Hebrews 6:19, NIV). And "it is impossible for God to lie." (*See,* Hebrews 6:18, NIV). And it's the *hope* in God's promises that is filled by our *faith*. Remember, *faith* fills *hope*.

But, *obedience* to the Word of God is what he demands of us. In the Old Testament, God's commands were delivered to God's people through the words of Moses and were written on stone tablets for people to see and hear. In the New Testament, God's commands were delivered to God's people through the words of Jesus Christ and were written on the tablets of man's heart for the spiritual eye and the spiritual ear to see and hear. We must *hear*, and we must *obey, if* we are to receive the *inheritance* of the *promise* which comes by *faith*.

Just knowing who you are in Christ Jesus is of great importance and a big step in the right direction. It is a key step in acquiring *spiritual knowledge* and *spiritual understanding.* A "born-again" Christian is the *seed* of Abraham; an *heir* to a certain inheritance entrenched in a covenant *promise. The empowerment to succeed* in this life (*i.e. the blessing*), has been *promised* to those who *obey his commands.*

*This* is what you stand on. *This* is what you meditate on. *This* is what you dwell on when challenges and tough times arise in your life. You have been given a choice: *obedience* or *disobedience.* What you choose determines whether you receive the blessings or the curses of his promise. In other words, the empowerment to succeed, or the empowerment to fail, is merely the by-product of the choice of obedience or disobedience. Think about it. If any person had before them the choice of success or failure, they would choose success. That's obvious. Similarly, if any person had set before them the choice of blessings or curses, they would choose blessings. That's obvious too. But, the answer that is *not* so obvious is when you set before a person the choice of obeying God's Word or disobeying God's Word. Many people, even though they are told that the result of disobedience will be destruction, will still choose to go their own way. Why? Because their hearts have been hardened to the *truth*, they are operating in *selfishness* and *pride*, and often times they *fear* the *truth.*

My sole purpose is to convey the *spiritual truth* as the Holy Spirit has *revealed* it to me. My intent is not to frighten. The words of this book are words of LOVE, which means they are God-inspired, and they apply to me, the author, just as they apply to you, the reader. I don't get a "free-pass" because I've written the book. I, too, must *obey* God's *truth.* If the *truth scares* you, then that is a good assessment, an indicator, of where you are in your life because the Word tells us,

"...*fear* has to do with punishment. The one who fears is not made perfect in love." (*See*, 1 John 4: 18, NIV) Emphasis added.

So, the guy that *fears* hearing the *truth* is most likely in *fear* of punishment. This makes sense. If you are "made perfect in love" through your *obedience* to God's Word, then you have no reason to *fear* punishment...because you've been *obedient*. Although the *truth* is sometimes difficult to hear, it's the people who *humble* themselves to *accept* the *truth* that are deemed wise.

Walking in *love* translates to *obeying* God's Word. The scriptures are a blueprint for living! If you genuinely put forth the effort to read and understand God's Word, the Holy Spirit will enlighten you. Remember, this is the voice behind the written Word. This is the point where you begin to establish a personal relationship with the Holy Spirit as a result of *time spent* in fellowship reading God's Word. The *power of love* stems from *obeying* God's Word. *love* is a way of being. It's a mindset. It's a way of existing that is higher than human emotional love. It's a commitment to live your life according to God's direction. *Love* will empower you to *forgive*. *Love* will empower you to *persevere* in the midst of trouble. *Love* focuses your attention on what God's Word says as opposed to what you *feel*, because your primary concern is *obedience*.

If more people in the world understood *love* from God, we might see an increase in an *unconditional* generosity and compassion for others. Divorces and separations might decrease. Murderous and homicidal acts committed in jealously, rage, and revenge, cloaked under the guise of "heat-of-passion" homicide (or, involuntary manslaughter) may subside. The resultant self-control that comes from *obeying* God's Word would save a lot of people from doing regrettable things because God's Word is their *final authority* and <u>not</u> their *human emotion*. *Love* is the most powerful force known to mankind. God is *love*. And everything in the Kingdom of God operates within the circle of *love*.

SIXTH PILLAR:

_The path of confidence_

### NEVER STOP DREAMING

A man is not old until he allows regret to replace his dreams. When you start regretting, you've lost vision. And without vision (*i.e.* hope), you're not going to be able to make it. I've seen it time and time again. People who are without a vision, a hope or a dream, are those who a drifting aimlessly, unhappily, and unfulfilled. They sometimes look to latch onto someone or something else thinking that their fulfillment lies in the very thing or person that they want to latch onto. The truth of the matter is that if you allow circumstances in your life to stop you from dreaming because you've failed once, twice, or even three times, you've allowed the enemy to steal the image, the vision, the picture, the blueprint that God was going to use to make the dream become a reality.

*Never stop dreaming.* If you don't have a dream, get one. If you've lost your dream, find it. The difficulties of life can trample on your hope. A person without hope is a person that is in trouble because they will tolerate, put up with, and accept less than they deserve. With no hope, you have no expectation. If you don't expect anything in life, you will be satisfied with your present-day status. Without hope, a person will endure the worst of situations with respect to jobs, relationships, finances, and abuse. And it all has to do with your "thinking." The way you think determines how you live. Dreams, aspirations, goals, and imagination are health to a man's soul. They are vitamins to the spirit. More importantly, the images in your head create the vehicle by which God can bring you to the place where he always destined for you to be.

Why are you here? *What is your purpose in life?* Who are you? These are questions that some of us can answer and some of us can't. There's a reason for that distinction. It's called *enlightenment.*

Let's get something straight right now. There is no such thing as luck. Luck is yet another man-made substitute designed to give *honor* to something *else* rather than to God. Luck is nothing more than a word to which men have assigned belief, dependence, and trust. It's an idol. An idol is something or someone that takes the place of God in a man's heart. The world's mentality would rather give credit to *luck* for health, happiness, and welfare, than give credit to God. There's no such thing as luck. Luck does not exist. There is only *light.* Success shows up in a person's life because *light* showed up, not luck. The Word of God is indeed a *light* for our *path* in life. Let's see what the scriptures tell us about *light.*

"When Jesus spoke again to the people, he said, *"I am the light of the world. Whoever follows me will never walk in darkness, but will have the light of life."* (John 8:12, NIV)

"Arise, shine, for your *light* has come, and the glory of the Lord rises upon you." (Isaiah 60:1, NIV) Emphasis added.

"I will also make you a *light* for the Gentiles, that you may bring my salvation to the ends of the earth." (*See,* Isaiah 49:6, NIV) Emphasis added.

"Your word is a *lamp* to my feet and a *light* for my *path*. (Isaiah 119:105, NIV) Emphasis added.

This is what we have in the Word of God. It's a *light* for our *path*. Without *light*, many of us have been traveling blindly down the *wrong path* for years; for example, relationships that never seemed to work out; a career that wasn't what you expected; and dreams that never panned out to what you planned years ago. Often times, *fear* finds a place in your "thinking" in regard to the *path* that you are traveling on in life. Some of us are simply going through life aimlessly and without true purpose. Please, don't be deceived! Going to any ol' job day-in and day-out, week-in and week-out, year-in and year-out doesn't give you purpose.

I'm reminded of a past acquaintance who once invited me to her housewarming party years ago after she purchased a spacious, lovely 4-bedroom home as a young, single woman, which at the time, I deemed to be quite impressive. But, it was something that she said in response to my acknowledgment that her house was a lovely home which still strikes a chord in me to this day. It was a response that had less to do with her accomplished purchase and everything to do with her *path* in life. In response to my compliments on her newly-purchased home, she simply replied, "The house is great, but what do I do now?"

The process of *spending time* in God's Word sheds *light* on the choices and decisions that we need to make in life. I can't put it any plainer than that. In the Bible, there are answers to every question that life presents. Significantly, it's imperative that you don't automatically assume that what I am saying is tied to "religion." "Religion" turns people off and in my opinion, understandably so. "Religion" has earned itself a bad name in many respects around the world due to the fallacies and shortcomings of human beings. You have to look *past* "religion" to the personal connection with God that can only be developed and cultivated through *time spent* reading and pondering his Word. All excuses aside, if answers to life's questions are what you're seeking, who better to shed *light* on the subject than the creator of life himself? Sometimes, it takes a *crisis* to bring people to Christ. The Word says it best:

"When you are in distress and all these things have happened to you, then in later days you will return to the Lord your God and obey him." (Deuteronomy 4:30, NIV)

Some people may not consider that to be an ideal way to discover God's goodness. But frankly, for some, there won't be an ideal way to come to the *truth*. It doesn't matter how you get there. Just get there.

Goal-oriented plans, creative ideas, bold imagination, witty inventions, and genuine innovation are within *everyone's* capability. If you can see it, you can be it. But, you will never win the gold medal if you are running in the *wrong* race! Some people are born to lead. Some are born to sing. Some are born with a mind for numbers. Some are naturally great with foreign languages. Some have legal or medical minds. Some are entrepreneurs with a great business mind. Some have a natural talent for communicating and connecting with people. Some are good with their hands. Some are great homemakers. Some are great caretakers. Others are musically-inclined. Here is my point. God has given us all individual talents and abilities. I'm sure you knew that. But, what you may *not* have known is for what *purpose* God gave each person their ability. The answer is in God's Word directly below. Brace yourself. You may be pleasantly surprised at what you see!

"But remember the Lord your God, for *it is he who gives you the ability to produce wealth,* and so confirms his covenant, which he swore to your forefathers, as it is today." (Deuteronomy 8:18, NIV) Emphasis added.

Now, this scripture must be read in context. It wouldn't be prudent to twist the words of scripture for argument's sake. In other words, don't misunderstand what I'm telling you. God does not want for his people to be in lack. It is not the Lord's will that his people should lack anything. The Word tells of God's promise, made in covenant, to his people:

"Observe the commands of the Lord your God, walking in his ways and revering him. For the Lord your God will bring you into a good land…a land where bread will not be scarce *and you will lack nothing.*" (*See,* Deuteronomy 8:6-9, NIV) Emphasis added.

*God's people* are given talents and abilities so that they may produce wealth, to his glory, in fulfillment of God's covenant promise. Whether you are one of *God's chosen people* is likely to be reflected in the choices that you make in life. Jesus said,

*"My sheep listen to my voice; I know them, and they follow me."* (John 10:27)

What did Jesus mean by *"sheep?"* It's simple. Any idea, "way of thinking," or attitude that is not in line with God's Word is in line with "the world." The world's images are constantly in your face on television, the internet, billboards, everywhere. If you spend more time in-taking and meditating on worldly images, notions, and topics, you will conform to the ways of the world. It is God's will that you be molded in the image of Christ. That only happens through the Word of God. God's people submit and obey to God's Word as sheep submit and obey to their Shepherd. *Goats,* on the other hand, are stubborn. Goats, unlike sheep, resist being told what to do. That's why Jesus said,

(31) "When the Son of Man comes in his glory, and all the angels with him, he will sit on his throne in heavenly glory.

(32) All the nations will be gathered before him, and he will *separate* the people from one another as a *shepherd separates* the *sheep from the goats.* He will put the *sheeps* on his right and the GOATS on his left. (Matthew 25:31-33, NIV) Emphasis added.

Here's a visual which is a great way of seeing the distinction:

| GOATS | SHEEP |
|---|---|
| *People who are molded & shaped by the world and who conform to the world's standards of living are...* | *Those who shape their thoughts according to God's Word and whose actions are in line with God's Word are...* |

Now, you understand that *God's obedient followers* are likened to his sheep. *God's people* are given talents and abilities so that they may produce wealth in this life and glorify God in the process. To think that you are given a certain position in life that is rooted in *lack* is nothing short of the devil doing his best to deceive you. Don't let the enemy deceive you. Indeed, the Word says that "godliness with contentment is great gain," but that is in reference to people who simply want to get rich and who possess an idolatrous *love* of money. Wealth, riches, health, abundance, and prosperity are in line with God's *plan* for his people and God has bestowed talents, abilities, imagination, and his Spirit of *power* on us in order that we may attain *the good life* while here on Earth. The Sixth Pillar, *the path of confidence*, is intended to show you how to find your *path* to the good life and how to utilize the power of *confidence* that comes with being *assured of God's presence* in your life.

---

God knew you *before* you were birthed into this world. Understand what I just said. God knew you *before* you were in your mother's womb. The Lord himself said,

"Before I formed you in the womb I knew you, before you were born I set you apart..." (*See*, Jeremiah 1:5, NIV)

"This is what the Lord says – he who made you, who formed you in the womb, and will help you..." (*See*, Isaiah 44:2, NIV)

"For you have been my hope, O Sovereign Lord, my confidence since my youth. From birth I have relied on you; you brought me forth from my mother's womb. I will ever praise you. (Psalms 71:5-6, NIV)

You see. The Lord knew you *before* you entered this world. That equates to three things in particular: (1) God knew the *purpose* that He had for your life; (2) God knew the *plan* that he had for your life; (3) God knew the *path* that he had for your life.

Purpose, Plan, Path

### PURPOSE

Hear me accurately. God knew the purpose that *HE* designed for your life. Please note, I didn't say the purpose that *YOU* designed. We've talked about this before. What *God* wants for your life, and what *YOU* want for your life, may be two totally different things. Your job is to discover your purpose in life. Know your purpose. God spoke through the prophet Isaiah and said:

(8) Remember this, fix it in mind, take it to heart, you rebels.

(9) Remember the former things, those of long ago; I am God, and there is no other; I am God, and there is none like me.

(10) I make known the end from the beginning, from ancient times what is still to come. I say: *my purpose will stand*, and I will do all that I please.

(11) From the east I summon a bird of prey; from a far-off land, a man *to fulfill my purpose*. (*See*, Isaiah 46:8-11, NIV) Emphasis added.

You see, God knew you from the start *before* he formed you in the womb. He knew when you would enter this life. He knew and chose a purpose for your life. Before you were born, you were separated and appointed, consecrated and set aside. And the only way you're going to arrive at the destination in which God called you to be is if you follow his instructions, which is in the Word of God. Then, you can get to the place of appointment, the place of the consecration, the place of the calling. But, you have to follow the instructions! If you let pride, arrogance, or sin stand in the way – those things will deceive you and lead you down a path that *seems right*, but is not right. What is *your* purpose in life?

That's all Satan wants to do. His whole job is to keep you out of the place in which God called you to be. The enemy labors to keep you out of your calling. He absolutely must keep you from reaching your destination of divine appointment. Once you know your purpose, you can make the necessary changes in your life accordingly that will put you on the path to God's intended destination for your life.

### Plan *and* path

I have often heard people cite Jeremiah 29:11 as their favorite Bible scripture. For those who may not be familiar with this passage, it reads in pertinent part,

"'For I know the *plans* I have for you,' declares the Lord, "*Plans* to prosper you and not to harm you, *plans* to give you hope and a future.'" (Jeremiah 29:11, NIV) Emphasis added.

For many people, there is a reassurance in knowing that God has a *plan* for their life. However, it is of no benefit to believe that God's *plan* for our lives will somehow be magically revealed to us without any effort on our part to find out what pleases God by reading the Bible, and *doing* what God has commanded us to do. God's *plan* for your life has already been set. It was set when God created you. Recall what the Lord said,

"I make known the end from the beginning..." (*See*, Isaiah 46:10, NIV)

God has already set a course, or a race, for you to run. You don't choose your own race. It's your job to discover the race that he chose for you. The Word tells us,

"...let us throw off everything that hinders and the sin that so easily entangles, and let us run with perseverance *the race marked out for us.*" (*See*, Hebrews 12:1, NIV) Emphasis added.

Frustration and struggle often come because you're running the wrong race rather than humbling yourself to the course that has already been appointed by God. This is what happens when a person seeks the *honor* that comes from the world as a higher priority than the *honor* that comes from God. All of your talents, gifts, and equipment have been designated for a set, certain place. The race has been set for you. And there is a *power* that shows up when you're absolutely certain you're in the perfect place for your life.

Once you give your life to Jesus and start reading the Bible consistently, and doing what it says, the Holy Spirit will speak to the ear of your heart. God's *plans* for your life are *revealed* through *time spent* reading and pondering God's Word. It's a measure of *faith*, and it works! Power is defined as the ability to get results. It's difficult to deny, rebut, or resist an asserted truth when there are *results* perceivable by the human senses. For example, the 7 Pillars of the Model for Daily Living which I have set before you on the pages of this book were revealed to me through my decision to read the Bible and seek God with my whole heart and soul. To some, it may sound ridiculous. To others, it may seem questionable. But, it is very difficult for anybody to argue or dispute the physical manifestation or evidence that sits before you. You're holding the book in your hands! This book, in conjunction with the grace of God, is the *result* of the *power* that comes from adhering to the 7 Pillars of the Model for Daily Living.

God's *plan* for my life (as it pertained to writing a book) had already been set for me before I was even formed in my mother's womb. The race was set. But, if I kept on partying, kept on entertaining all kinds of distractions, kept on refusing to pick up the Bible and read it on a *consistent* basis, and kept on putting *my* wants and desires ahead of what God wanted me to do, I would not have been "available" for God's Spirit to work through me. In other words, there would be no *manifestation* of the 7 Pillars of the Model for Daily Living. There would be no book. Consequently, the talents, gifts, and equipment that God bestowed upon me before I was even born would have been wasted as it pertains to this particular project. Certainly, these talents, gifts, and equipment would not have been utilized to affect *someone else's* life.

Now, always remember that nobody is perfect. People make mistakes. Christians make mistakes. No one is without sin. People make mistakes before and *after* they decide to walk with God. You may be in the process of serving God and for whatever reason make a mistake, or a series of mistakes. It happens. The key is to remember that we are not Christians because we are perfect. We are Christians because we are *forgiven*. Your job is to seek God with all of your heart and all of your soul. If you are doing your part, the rest is up to him.

You *must* discover God's *plan* for your life! Otherwise, you are at risk of running the wrong race, without purpose. The Bible says,

(24) "Run in such a way as to get the prize.

(26) Therefore, I do not run like a man running aimlessly; I do not fight like a man beating the air." (*See*, 1 Cor. 9:24,26, NIV)

You want to be *certain* of the race you're running. This is the *path of confidence!* Read the following scripture and think about how reassuring it is to know that you're on the right *path*.

(23) "If the Lord delights in a man's way,

he makes his steps firm;

(24) though he stumble, he will not fall,

for the Lord upholds him with his hand.

(Psalms 37:23-24, NIV)

God has established your steps. And though your steps have been established, we've all taken detours. Yet, God faithfully brings us out of the hurtful and destructive situations that we find ourselves in and he puts us back on course. He allows us to once again enter into his presence when we correct our behavior and begin to seek him earnestly and diligently. God is *love* and his *love* surrounds you.

Everyone has steps already made for them. Find *your* steps. It can be a dangerous thing trying to follow in the footsteps of somebody else, *if* that's not what God intended for you. Again, it doesn't mean you won't stumble, but if you're in Christ, you will not fall. The Word commands us,

"Acknowledge him in all thy ways and he will direct your paths." (Proverbs 3:6, NIV)

That's why you must condition your hearing as a sheep that knows his voice. The only way to do that is to cultivate a personal relationship with the Holy Spirit. God's Spirit will give you counsel and will tell you what to do when you don't know what to do. *Find your path in Him!*

"Your word is a lamp to my feet and a light for my *path*." (Proverbs 119:105, NIV) Emphasis added.

"As for the deeds of men – by the word of your lips I have kept myself from the ways of the violent. *My steps have held to your paths; my feet have not slipped.*" (Psalm 17:4-5, NIV) Emphasis added.

"Show me your ways, O Lord, *teach me your paths;* guide me in your truth and teach me. (*See*, Psalm 25:4-5, NIV) Emphasis added.

In other words, the Word is your lamp which provides light for your path. Think of it this way:

No Word, No Lamp

No Lamp, No Light

No Light, you can't find the *right* path for your life!

Of course, a person may pose the reasonable question, "How will I know if I've discovered the *right path* that God has set in place for me? Well, the Bible provides an answer to every question in life. Along *God's path* for you, there is *joy*, and there are *eternal pleasures* at his right hand. Read it for yourself:

"You have made known to me *the path of life;* you will fill me with **joy** in your presence, with *eternal pleasures* at your right hand." (Psalm 16:11, NIV) Emphasis added.

Put in a more *practical* way, when you get into God's Word and consistently begin to seek and submit to his Word, you are effectively *in God's presence.* As you begin to shape your way of thinking according to his commands for your life, there is an unmistakable *joy* and *peace* that come from being in his presence and being on the path that he has already set out for you. When you get into God's Word, he opens your mind. He gives you ideas. He shows you how to utilize your talents and your gifts. And perhaps the most important aspect of being in God's presence is the *confidence* to put action behind what you believe. *That is true faith!* Reading God's written Word allows you to cultivate a relationship with the Holy Spirit and subsequently become a candidate to hear **the voice** behind the written Word. The voice of God (*i.e.* the Holy Spirit speaking to the ear of your heart) *reveals* the mysteries of God as they pertain to your life. Remember what the Bible tells us:

"No eye has seen, no ear has heard, no mind has conceived what God has *prepared* for those who love him, but God has *revealed* it to us by his Spirit." (*See,* 1 Cor. 2:9-10, NIV) Emphasis added.

These things that are revealed to us by the Spirit are the *plans* (*i.e.* secrets, mysteries) of God, and once revealed, they are ours! The Word tells us,

"The secret things belong to the Lord our God, but the things revealed belong to us and to our children forever…" (*See,* Deuteronomy 29:29, NIV)

God's *plan* for *your* life was established before you were born. His plan for you is in him and God's Spirit knows the mind of God. The Holy Spirit knows God's secret plans for your life. So, unless you spend time in the Word cultivating a personal relationship with the Holy Spirit, you won't have access to God's plans for your life. You won't have access to the **joy** and the *eternal pleasures* that are at God's right hand. Essentially, you will continue to stumble through life without a lamp and without a light. Hopelessness is the result of traveling through life on the wrong path. With no hope, this life is a very difficult life to live.

Take the apostle Paul for example. Prior to coming to Christ, the apostle Paul fervently persecuted and imprisoned Christians. After giving his life to Christ, he referred to *himself* as "the prisoner of Christ Jesus." (*See,* Ephesians 3:1, NIV). More importantly, once the apostle Paul became a follower of Jesus, the Holy Spirit *revealed* to him God's plan for *his life!* Paul stated it best when he said,

(1) For this reason I, Paul, the prisoner of Christ Jesus for the sake of you Gentiles –

(2) Surely you have heard about the administration of God's grace that was given to me for you,

(3) that is, the *mystery* made known to me *by revelation,* as I have already written briefly.

(4) In reading this, then, you will be able to understand my insight into the *mystery* of Christ,

(5) which was not made known to men in other generations as it has *now been revealed by the Spirit* to God's holy apostles and prophets.

(6) This mystery is that through the gospel the Gentiles are heirs together with Israel, members together of one body, and share together in the promise of Christ Jesus.

(7) I became a servant of this gospel by the gift of God's grace given me through the working of his power.

(8) Although I am less than the least of all God's people, this grace was given me: *to preach to the Gentiles the unsearchable riches of Christ,*

(9) *and to make plain to everyone the administration of this mystery,* which for ages past was kept hidden in God, who created all things. (Ephesians 3:1-9, NIV) Emphasis added.

So, we see in this example that as soon as Paul gave his life to Christ, he became a candidate to receive God's *plans* for *his* life, as *revealed by the Holy Spirit*. True to form, since God is a God of LOVE, Paul's natural talents and gifts were used to spread the gospel of Jesus Christ throughout the world. You see, God's Spirit, which is poured out on the inside of you when you make him the Lord of your life – when joined with your God-given natural, earthly physical talents and gifts - results in a supernatural ability to get results. This is *power!* Think about it carefully. In the Bible, there were great men and women who came from very humble beginnings, but did great things once the power of God was on them. David was a shepherd boy, but as a servant of God, he became one of the greatest kings over all of Israel. Moses fled to Midian in fear after killing an Egyptian, but as a servant of God, led thousands of Israelites out of captivity. We've already seen that the apostle Paul was a persecutor of followers of Christ, but as a servant of God, spread the gospel to Gentiles throughout the world in the face of opposition and resistance. My question to you is simple. What are the *mysteries* and *plans* that God prepared for *your* life which have gone undiscovered because you're not in Christ Jesus? What godly *plans, secrets,* and *mysteries* for *your* life have yet to be *revealed* by the Holy Spirit? What great things would *you* accomplish if God's Spirit combined with your natural talents and gifts to result in a supernatural ability to effect change? Here is my point: You've got to be *in the Spirit* for God's *plans* and mysteries to be *revealed* to you concerning your life. Take with you the wisdom found in the scripture below:

"For we are God's masterpiece. He has created us anew in Christ Jesus, so we can do the good things he planned for us long ago." (Ephesians 2:10, NIV)

Your path has already been set. Your race is already marked out for you. God's plan for your life is in Christ Jesus. When the Holy Spirit reveals *God's plan for your life,* this is the *right path for your life.* This is the Path of Confidence and it's the path to success, prosperity, and wholeness in every area of life.

So, let's review quickly because finding the Path of Confidence cannot be overstated. Open the Bible and humble yourself to God's Word. The Holy Spirit, which is on the inside of you, given to you the day you gave your life to Christ, will help you understand the Word. In regard to the specifics of *your* life, when the Holy Spirit reveals things to you, *these things* were already planned by God at the beginning, long ago. The plans already existed. This is why we must be in tune with the Holy Spirit. The Spirit knows the mind and thoughts of God. The Spirit knows where God's plans for you are kept. Indeed, God gave us *His Spirit* so that *we* may know and understand what he planned for us from the beginning. But, here's the deal. You have to get in constant fellowship with the Holy Spirit. The only way to do that is to open your Bible, read God's Word, meditate on it, talk to the Holy Spirit, and of course, depart from sin.

Stay on it until you hear the voice of the Holy Spirit speak to the ear your heart about whatever situation is currently before you. The knowledge that the Holy Spirit reveals to you is *revelation knowledge;* knowledge that comes from God, revealed to you on the inside, regarding the plans, mysteries, secrets, and wisdom of the Lord. The *power* of the Lord comes when you *obey* whatever instructions were revealed to you.

Of course, any person who hears these words, if they are *not* reading God's Word or have *not* given their life to Christ, will likely be critical. But as you have learned thus far throughout the 7 Pillars of the Model of Daily Living, there are two systems in existence. There are two ways of thinking. There is the Kingdom of God's way of thinking, and there is the world's way of thinking.

The Kingdom of God's way of thinking is *faith-based* and the Kingdom's power is rooted in *love.*

The World's way of thinking is *fear-based* and the World's power is rooted in *selfishness.* The Kingdom of God's power is love and faith. The World's power is money.

Christians operate by faith. The World has a difficult time comprehending faith because it is not tangible, nor can it be seen. The World's authority is scholastic knowledge. The World's reasoning comes out of textbooks, universities, and classrooms. In reference to the World's way of thinking, the Bible says,

"The god of this age has blinded the minds of unbelievers, so that they cannot see the light of the gospel of the glory of Christ, who is the image of God." (2 Corinthians 4:4, NIV)

Spirituality, however, or Kingdom knowledge, derives its understanding and reasoning from the Word of God. In regard to the Kingdom's way of thinking, the Bible tells us,

"For God, who said, 'Let light shine out of darkness,' made his light shine in our hearts to give us the glory of God in the face of Christ." (2 Corinthians 4:6, NIV)

To be more like Christ is the ultimate goal of a Christian. The manual of how to achieve that is the Bible and the Bible is our final authority.

To the person whose life has become without purpose and lacks hope, you may be traveling down the wrong path for your life. The Spirit of God can enlighten you to ideas that you've never thought of which may, in turn, enable you to add to your existing stream of revenue. The Spirit of God can enlighten you to unique concepts that could become the foundation for a new business. It's not by magic, it's by *faith*.

There are 3 levels to *faith*:

(1) Belief

(2) Confidence

(3) Action

Often times, Christian people define *faith* as believing in the unseen. After all, Hebrews 11:1 (NIV) says, "Faith is being sure of what we hope for and certain of what we do not see." Well, allow me to enlighten you. Defining *faith* as believing in what you cannot see is not incorrect, but it is incomplete. In James 2:17 (NIV), the Word provides that "…faith by itself, if not accompanied by action, is dead." So, if our goal is to get results in life using our *faith* as a tool, it is clear that there are at least two levels that need to be addressed: *Belief and Action.* The woman who merely believes that God has given her the dynamic gift of voice to sing, but never takes steps to develop that gift, or never actually opens her mouth to sing, will see no results (*i.e. no power*). The man who merely believes that God gave him the desire to travel the world, but never makes an effort to sit and plan *how* he can bring his desire to fruition, will never see any results. *Faith* is *belief* in God and his Word, supported by *action.*

But, I submit to you that there is a middle tier that is of great importance: *Confidence.* You see, confidence is everything in this life. A man who is confident in himself, or confident in an idea, or confident in his *faith* can accomplish anything. The reason is because *confidence trumps fear.* Confidence tramples doubt. They are opposite sides of the same coin. The person who takes strides to start a new business is operating under a measure of *faith.* In contrast, the individual who has the same idea to begin a new business, but remains paralyzed in their efforts to actually start the business has allowed doubt, fear, anxiety, or worry to paralyze their action.

So, we see that *true faith*, in regard to revelation knowledge, requires *belief, confidence, and action*, if we are to see the *power* of God manifested in our lives (*i.e.* the ability to get *results*). *Faith* has legs, it's not dormant. *Faith* is forward-moving, not stationary. *Faith acts! Faith does! Faith speaks!* When you get to the place where the Spirit begins to reveal God's plans for your life, the question becomes, "now, what am I going to do?" Think about it. The Spirit has revealed to you an idea for a new business, for example. Of course, in that moment, you can't see it with your natural eyes *yet*. Essentially, the new business is still in the spirit realm, rather than the natural realm. You have the idea birthed on the inside of you given to you by the Holy Spirit as a result of time spent in his presence reading, meditating, and obeying God's Word; however, you don't know how to bring the idea from the spirit realm into the natural. What do you do?

*Faith speaks!* The first thing you must do is to *speak it into existence*. As Christians, we must get into the habit of "*Calling things that are not as though they were.*" I love how the Bible characterizes the God that we serve as,

"…the God who gives life to the dead and *calls things that are not as though they were.*" (*See*, Romans 4:17, NIV)

When the Spirit of God reveals to you the purpose, plan, and path for your life, this is the time to declare the thing, *vocally*, by faith. In the beginning, when God created the heavens, the Earth, and everything therein, he did so by *speaking them into existence*.

(3) *"And God said,* 'Let there be light,' and there was light."

(6) *"And God said,* 'Let there be an expanse between the waters to separate water from water.' And it was so. God called the expanse "sky."

(9) *"And God said,* 'Let the water under the sky be gathered to one place, and let dry ground appear.' And it was so. God called the dry ground "land." (*See,* Genesis 1:1-9, NIV)

*Things that exist in the spirit realm have to be called forth.* God spoke these things into existence. *He called things that were not as though they were.* Well, this is the goal that we are striving for as Christians. Through our *faith* in Jesus Christ, and the covenant promises of our Lord and Savior, we too have the power to speak things into existence. By *faith,* we have the authority to call things that are not as though they were. Speaking things from the spirit realm into the natural realm can only be achieved if it is done with *confidence.* And confidence is simply a level of *faith,* literally! Remember, there are 3 levels to *faith:* (1) Belief (2) *Confidence,* and (3) Action.

Among other reasons, why do you think God tells us to *depart from sin?* Sin makes you feel guilty. Sin makes you feel separated from God. The result of sin is that it strips you of your *confidence* to approach God in whatever situation you're facing. The attack from Satan comes to try to get you to waver in your *confidence* and not be *confident* in your *faith.* This is why the 7 Pillars of the Model for Daily Living must be viewed in its totality. The 7 Pillars of the Model are *not* mutually-exclusive. They go hand-in-hand.

Therefore, the *path of confidence* is action taken on your part based on knowledge revealed to you by the Holy Spirit regarding the purpose, plan, and path for your life. By *faith,* we speak into existence what we believe was revealed to us by the Spirit of God. Just look to the Word. It clearly says,

"It is written: *'I believed; therefore I have spoken.' With that same spirit of faith we also believe and therefore speak...*" (*See*, 2 Corinthians 4:13, NIV) Emphasis added.

Life can be difficult. Perhaps you've been searching for answers to many of life's questions but haven't found the solutions. What I lay before you in this book doesn't require that you suddenly become a perfect human being. That's not going to happen. You have made mistakes in the past and you will make mistakes in the future. As stated above, Christians are not Christians because they are perfect, but because they are *forgiven*. But, the Word of God is light. It is a lamp that will light your pathway in life. Until you *humble yourself* to the point of opening the Bible and reading and understanding God's Word, *none* of the content of the 7 Pillars of the Model for Daily Living can take hold in your life. It's not magic. I can't do it for you. Spirituality is a personal walk that can only be achieved through an individual's decision-making process. But what I can tell you is that it's good to know that there is a God who will forgive you, love you, and care for you, no matter who you are or what you've done in the past. There is a God who promises to give you *perfect peace* in exchange for your decision to give your mind and your heart to him. (*See*, Isaiah 26:3, NIV). There is a God who will keep you and sustain you in the midst of turmoil, stress, anxiety, hurt, and difficult times. The Bible is not just an instruction manual on how to find eternal life, but also it is a manual for how to live life while here on this Earth.

In Christ Jesus, waiting for you, God has already set a *purpose,* a *plan,* and a *path* for your life. Your job is to discover what was ordained for you from the very beginning; to find the race that God intended for you to run. Your course has been set. The only way to find it is to spend time with the one who knows the mind of God. Get in the Word and cultivate a personal relationship with the Holy Spirit and allow him to reveal the secret plans of God for your life. By *faith,* you can then speak into existence, with confidence, the things that God has put into your spirit. You may then call the things that are not as though they were and have the confidence to put action behind your belief in the knowledge that has been revealed to you by the Spirit of the Lord.

This is the *path of confidence.* Praise God!

# SEVENTH PILLAR:
# *Tithing*

The Bible tells us,

"For where your treasure is, there your heart will be also."
(Matthew 6:21)

This scripture needs little explanation. You would be hard-pressed to find someone in the world that hasn't been introduced to the role that money plays in their respective culture and society. Some people might even say that "money makes the world go around." Money buys food. Money buys clothes. Money plays a part in determining your social status in life. Money *is* the World's power. And I *thank God* that I *don't* operate within *this* system of thinking. Money can ruin lives. Issues with money can cause people to willingly *end* their lives. It can cause dissension amongst brothers and spouses. It can cause people to commit criminal acts with no regard for another's welfare.

Of course, there's a flip side to this argument. Money can be used to accomplish great charitable acts. It can feed and clothe the homeless. The acquisition of money can alleviate financial-induced worry and it can afford a level of peace. Money can supply the seed investment for great ideas, businesses, projects, and philanthropic visions. It can get you the best medical care and education. Simply stated, money allows you to do things that you otherwise would not be able to do if you didn't have it.

There is nothing inherently wrong with money. Truth be told, when you have money, it makes life easier in several regards. But where people get themselves into trouble is when they attach a value to money that is above all else. The Bible says,

"For the *love* of money is a root of all kinds of evil." (1 Timothy 6:10, NIV) Emphasis added.

At this moment, I want you to accept the premise that *giving*, without expecting something in return, is viewed favorably in the eyes of the Lord. Jesus said, "

"It is more blessed to give than to receive." (Acts 20:35)

The bottom line is that different people have different attachments to money. Some people release money easier than others, for what could be any of a variety of reasons. But *honoring God with your money* involves much more than the act of *giving*. At this point, those who *humble themselves* are about to learn something that is of *great value* to their success in life.

*Tithing is not a part of your giving program; It's a part of your blessing program!*

Some people become wary when it comes to giving their money to the church for a variety of reasons. One reason may be that there is distrust as to where the money is actually going. A common question or concern is whether their money is going directly to the pastor or priest? Other people may feel that they work too hard for their money to simply surrender their hard-earned cash to a basket being passed around during a Sunday service or mass. But here's what I ask of you right now. Forget all of the various "religious" connotations surrounding the subject of monetary giving that exist in the world. They're completely irrelevant. It doesn't matter if you consider yourself to be Christian, Catholic, or any other denomination; what you are about to read applies to *everybody*.

Offerings and tithes are different. A monetary *offering* to the Lord, in church, may be of any amount, paid on no particular basis of consistency. Whether a person goes to church three times in one year or thirty times in one year, that person may bring a monetary *offering* to the Lord whenever he or she has the notion to do so. Offerings are *not* the focus of this discussion.

*Tithes,* however, are *a systematic release of 10% of all your increase.* In other words, if your wealth has been increased by $100, then $10 goes to the Lord as a *tithe.* The concept is biblically-based and is found throughout the Bible. But, like anything else in life, a lack of *exact* knowledge hinders our understanding and can keep us out of the place of promotion that God has made readily available to us.

Throughout the 7 Pillars of the Model for Daily Living, we have defined "the *blessing*" as *the empowerment for success.* The converse is also true. A "*curse*" is *the empowerment for failure.* In the Bible, God's *blessing* fell upon the patriarchs that systematically released their *tithe* to the High Priest out of *honor.* Specifically, Abraham (the father of our *faith*) didn't get *established* in the *blessing* until he released his *tithe* to the Most High Priest, Melchizedek.

(18) "Then Melchizedek king of Salem brought out bread and wine. He was priest of God Most High,

(19) *and he blessed Abram*, saying, 'Blessed be Abram by God Most High, Creator of heaven and earth.

(20) And blessed be God Most High, who delivered your enemies into your hand.' *Then Abram gave him a tenth of everything.* (Genesis 14:18-20, NIV) Emphasis added.

Do you see what happened between Abraham (formerly Abram), and the Most High Priest, Melchizedek? Do you see the *exchange* that took place?

The most important thing to understand in the Seventh Pillar is that *tithing* is *not* synonymous with "giving." According to God's Word, 10% of all your increase *already* belongs to God. *Tithing* involves *returning* to God what already belongs to Him. Therefore, you must disabuse yourself of the notion that *tithing* is synonymous with *giving*. It's not. But rather, *tithing* is part of an *exchange*. The exchange that takes place between you and God is the release of the tithe *in exchange* for the blessing! In other words,

*Tithing is not a part of your giving program; It's a part of your blessing program!*

Or, put another away,

*Tithing activates the blessing*

### JESUS: OUR MELCHIZEDEK

In the example above, we see Abraham (the father of our FAITH) receive the blessing from Melchizedek, the Most High Priest, *in exchange for* the release of the tithe (*i.e.* one-tenth of Abraham's increase). Well, this principle still applies today. The New Testament tells us that *Jesus is our Melchizedek!* Specifically, the Word tells us in relation to Jesus,

"For it is declared: 'You are a priest forever, in the order of Mechizedek." (Hebrews 7:17, NIV)

This is relevant because those who are of the *faith* of Abraham are considered to be "the seed of Abraham" (*See*, Romans 4:16, NIV). Therefore, just as Abraham brought his tithe to Melchizedek and received the blessing, so likewise are the seed of Abraham to bring their tithe to Jesus and receive the blessing.

### THE CHEERFUL GIVER

But, the key element that must not be overlooked is that *tithing* is an act of *love*, not obligation. This is important because the law in biblical times *required* the descendants of the tribe of *Levi* to collect tithes from the people (*See*, Hebrews 7:5, NIV). In other words, the people were *obligated* to give one-tenth of their increase to the Levitical priests, *by law*.

Well, Jesus says in Matthew 5:17 (NIV), "Do not think that I have come to abolish the Law…I have not come to abolish them but to fulfill them." (*See*, Matt. 5:17, NIV). Jesus goes on to say that "Love is the fulfillment of the law." (*See*, Romans 13:10, NIV). Here is my point.

If *tithing* was the law, and Jesus declared that *love* was the fulfillment of the law, it reasonably follows that tithing is fulfilled through *love* (as opposed to obligation)! You see, Jesus was *not* a descendant of Levi, but rather a descendant of the tribe of Judah (*See*, Hebrews 7:14, NIV). This begs the question, why wasn't Jesus declared a High Priest in the order of Aaron (a Levite descendant), as opposed to *Melchizedek*?" (*See*, Hebrews 7:17, NIV). The answer, in short, is that *love* took precedence over the letter of the law. Jesus was declared a High Priest "not on the basis of a regulation as to his ancestry, but on the basis of the power of an indestructible life." (*See*, Hebrews 7:16, NIV).

Therefore, we are to bring our *tithes* to our Most High Priest, Jesus Christ, out of the law of *love*, not out of the law of obligation. As Abraham released one-tenth of his increase out of *honor* to the greater man, Melchizedek, so too are we to display our *honor* for Jesus in the systematic release of our tithes.

Remember, there are two systems in operation that are in stark contrast to one another. There is the Kingdom of God's system (or, way of thinking) and there is the World's system (or, way of thinking). They are not to be reconciled. They do not line up with each other. They are not in agreement with each other. You cannot operate in both systems simultaneously. They are as different as day is from night. The World's system of thinking is built on earthly knowledge and wisdom that come from men. The Kingdom of God's system of thinking is built on spiritual knowledge and wisdom that come from God. The World's way of thinking does not support the Kingdom of God's way of thinking because the World operates under a different *system*. God has a system that is not like the World's system and you're going to have to choose which side of the line you come down on.

The Kingdom of God's way of thinking is based in *faith* and the Kingdom's power is rooted in *love*.

The World's way of thinking is based in *fear* and the World's power is rooted in *selfishness*

The Kingdom of God's power is *love* and *faith*

The World's power is *money*

Think about it carefully. Paying your *tithe* is the systematic release of 10% of all your increase. This involves the physical act of releasing money to God. To believe that *one-tenth* of all your increase already belongs to God, and that you are *returning* it to him, undoubtedly requires *faith*. Well, we know that...

The Kingdom of God's way of thinking is based in *faith*.

To believe that the release of the *tithe* is done *in exchange* for the *blessing (i.e. the empowerment for success)* requires *faith*.

The Kingdom of God's way of thinking is based in *faith*.

*Believing* that God's *blessing will actually manifest itself in your life* upon the release of the *tithe* is a measure of *faith*.

The Kingdom of God's way of thinking is based in *faith*.

The guy who is *afraid* to systematically release 10% of his increase attaches a higher priority to the *worry* of not having enough money to pay his bills, or get through the month, than to operating in *faith*. What do you think this represents in our understanding of the two systems?

The World's way of thinking is based in *fear*.

Some people, who say to themselves, "I *could* give 10% of my increase after every paycheck, but frankly, I need my money." This could very well fall on the side of...

the World's power is rooted in *selfishness*

Of course, not everyone has a lot of money. But if you have allowed such a notion to become the premise for your understanding of *tithing*, then you have completely missed the point. Obviously, you can't give what you don't have. *Honoring God with your money* should not be done out of *obligation* or *fear.* You see, some people are "put off" by the fact that someone expects them to give a certain amount. Some people feel bad or embarrassed because they simply don't have money to give, or they don't have an amount that they *wish* they could give. But, the important thing to remember is that God looks at the *heart.* The Bible says,

"Each man should give what he has decided in his *heart* to give, *not reluctantly or under compulsion, for God loves a cheerful giver.* (2 Corinthians 9: 7, NIV) Emphasis added.

If some people find it "uncomfortable" to release a small amount of money to a homeless person that they *see* on the street, most likely it will be a "painful experience" for them to systematically release 10% of all their increase to a God that they *cannot see.* This lends support to the premise that *nothing* works in the Kingdom of God outside of *faith.* Remember, the Bible tells us,

"For where your treasure is, there your heart will be also." (Matthew 6:21, NIV)

If your heart is in your money, then you will likely find it difficult to release it and you won't be a "cheerful giver," which pleases God.

God wants us to *trust* in *him.* It's a very interesting dynamic when you take the principle of *honor,* and the *Him first* mentality, and you set it beside the World's perspective of *money.* If you put *Him first,* then by default, you must put *self* second. That entails *acknowledging* God's Word which commands that we pay our tithes and offerings out of *love* for him. To *honor God with your money* means that your money cannot have a first-place position in your heart! It's as simple as that. I want you to be cognizant that God's promise of the *blessing* is attached to the release of the *tithe*.

If you don't believe me, read it below. For the Lord God, himself, says,

"Test me in this, and see if I will not throw open the floodgates of heaven and pour out so much *blessing* that you will not have room enough for it." (*See*, Malachi 3:10, NIV) Emphasis added.

The Word also says,

(9) *"Honor the Lord with your wealth,* with the *firstfruits* of all your crops; then your barns will be filled to *overflowing*, and your vats will *brim over* with new wine."* (Proverbs 3: 9-10, NIV) Emphasis added.

*Tithing is not a part of your giving program; It's a part of your blessing program!*

*Tithing activates the blessing*

It's time that we *honor God with our money!*

# Conclusion

You are to be commended. You have made it through the 7 Pillars of the Model for Daily Living which is not an easy thing to do. Not everyone has the courage to receive truth. It is my hope that the words of this book have served, and will continue to serve, as a source of inspiration, support, and guidance for those of you who are in need. You are never alone. God is with you always.

I have spoken candidly about many of life's difficult challenges including, but not limited to, sexual abuse, rape, and addiction. Essentially, the 7 Pillars of the Model for Daily Living were written for those who have been plagued and paralyzed by negative emotions such as hurt, fear, and anger. Peace, prosperity, and fulfillment are achieved when you locate the will of God for your life. And it all begins through hearing the Word of God.

I respectfully urge you to use the 7 Pillars of the Model for Daily Living as a resource in your everyday lives. Draw strength from the knowledge that is found in each Pillar. Forgive yourself and forget the past. We all have to start somewhere. Understand that God loves you and it doesn't matter who you are, where you live, where you come from or what language you speak, nothing is impossible once we accept Jesus Christ into our lives and lean on him in difficult times. The 7 Pillars of the Model for Daily Living are:

Faith

Depart from sin

Getting past hurt

Honor

Love

The path of confidence

Tithing

Everyone wants to live the good life. The real issue, however, is how *the good life* is defined? Being able to do *what* you want to do, *when* you want to do it, and *how* you want to do it is true prosperity. But the time has come for you to recognize that there may be changes and adjustments to your manner of thinking that need to be made. *Change your mind, change your life.* Renew your mind, renew your life. Knowledge and understanding from God's Word will enlighten you to see the importance of exchanging your thoughts for God's thoughts. Exchange your words for God's Word. Keeping your mind on things that are unseen and that are above will bring greater returns than a mindset that is focused on the afflictions, the drama, the troubles, and the dreary situations which are seen and that are below.

To the women of this world who have suffered the grave injustice of abuse, you have now been equipped with *the right spiritual weapons to fight the right fight.* To any reader who questions whether a substance addiction can be broken, you now have the knowledge that nothing in all of creation is more powerful than the Word of God. Don't doubt Jesus. Don't doubt his love for you and the authority that he has given to you. Be strong in the Spirit and don't take the process of renewing your mind with God's Word lightly. Rather, fortify your mind with God's truth as much as possible. Keep the Word in front of your eyes, in your mind, in your mouth, and in your heart. That's the only way to everlasting life, peace, and happiness.

Life is nothing but a series of decisions. What decisions will you make? What actions will you take? In other words, what will you do? Every decision in life is yours. If you are hurt, you decide if you will remain in a hurtful state or go forward. If you are afraid, you decide if you will remain in fear or go forward. If you are angry or depressed, you decide if you will forgive, heal, and go forward. Every choice is yours. You own the choice. But in every decision, choose wisely, because once your decision has been made, your choice owns you for all eternity.

Live well, prosper, be happy, forgive, love, operate in faith, honor the Lord, pay your tithe, and make every decision confidently in full knowledge that you are being led by the Spirit of God.

Make your breaking point your turning point and live life to the fullest.

# ABOUT THE AUTHOR

David E. James is the founder and director of Team Spirit International Ltd., a subsidiary of Landmark Ministries Church of God, located in northern California. Team Spirit International Ltd., a web-based language solutions company, has provided English language instruction to adults, youth, small businesses, and corporations in countries around the world, including, but not limited to, Brazil and China.

James has earned a Bachelor of Arts degree in Sociology from the University of California, Los Angeles, in addition to a Juris Doctorate degree from the John F. Kennedy School of Law. He has served as a judicial clerk for two consecutive terms in the United States District Court, Northern District of California. Additionally, James has worked for the Alternative Dispute Resolution Center in Rome, Italy, as well as the Chilean Ministry of Education in Santiago, Chile.

At the age of 33, James wrote *Change Your Mind, Change Your Life* with an eye towards equipping women, on a global scale, with the spiritual tools to address the unfortunate realities of sexual and emotional abuse. In specific, James' "7 Pillars of the Model for Daily Living" were derived from a traumatic real-life experience involving helping a loved one cope with the aftermath of rape.

A native of Oakland, California and a former collegiate athlete, James speaks four languages and resides in both northern California and Salvador-Bahia, Brazil.